The Pinocchio Effect

On (De)Coloniality: Curriculum Within and Beyond the West

Series Editor

João M. Paraskeva (*School of Education, University of Massachusetts Dartmouth, USA*)

On (De)Coloniality: Curriculum Within and Beyond the West is a beacon in the struggle against epistemicide and the colonialities of being, power, and knowledge. It attempts to bring to the fore an analysis that focuses on non-Western/non-Eurocentric epistemological frameworks. In a world that still struggles to see its own overt epistemological diversity, *On (De)Coloniality* is an open space in which to challenge epistemological fascism. It encourages curriculum scholars to engage in dialogues about non-Western/non-Eurocentric epistemologies within and beyond the Western Eurocentric platform. We invite 'complicated conversations' that dig into new avenues such as those of Itinerant Curriculum Theory (ICT), and, in so doing, introduce a new language that will take us to alternative levels of articulation and re-articulation of meanings, through endless and spaceless processes of coding, decoding, recoding, and 'encoding.'

VOLUME 3

The titles published in this series are listed at *brill.com/cwbw*

The Pinocchio Effect

Decolonialities, Spiritualities, and Identities

By

Elizabeth Janson

BRILL
SENSE

LEIDEN | BOSTON

All chapters in this book have undergone peer review.

Library of Congress Cataloging-in-Publication Data

Names: Janson, Elizabeth, author.
Title: The Pinocchio effect : decolonialities, spiritualities, and identities / by Elizabeth Janson.
Description: Leiden ; Boston : Brill Sense, 2020. | Series: On (de)coloniality : curriculum within & beyond the West, 2666-3775 ; volume 3 | Includes bibliographical references and index.
Identifiers: LCCN 2019037950 (print) | LCCN 2019037951 (ebook) | ISBN 9789004416031 (paperback) | ISBN 9789004376151 (hardback) | ISBN 9789004416048 (ebook)
Subjects: LCSH: Critical pedagogy--United States. | Education and state--United States. | Children with social disabilities--Education--United States. | Youth with social disabilities--Education--United States.
Classification: LCC LC196.5.U6 J36 2019 (print) | LCC LC196.5.U6 (ebook) | DDC 370.11/5--dc23
LC record available at https://lccn.loc.gov/2019037950
LC ebook record available at https://lccn.loc.gov/2019037951

Typeface for the Latin, Greek, and Cyrillic scripts: "Brill". See and download: brill.com/brill-typeface.

ISSN 2666-3775
ISBN 978-90-04-41603-1 (paperback)
ISBN 978-90-04-37615-1 (hardback)
ISBN 978-90-04-41604-8 (e-book)

This book is printed on acid-free paper and produced in a sustainable manner.

Contents

Foreword

Elizabeth Janson's *The Pinocchio Effect: Decolonialities, Spiritualities, and Identities* provides an intellectually insightful, most timely, politically, educationally, and academically qualified interdisciplinary contribution to what it means to be a teacher today. This book is creatively crossing over myriad of 'studies' or disciplines: curriculum studies, decolonial studies, political studies, education policy studies, teacher education studies, teachers' lives studies, gender studies, youth study, globalization studies, literary and art studies, and subaltern studies.

Janson's study is an awesome composition of erudite, touching, moving, humorous, playful, artistic, tragic, in sum a heroic tribute to the teacher and teaching profession in our neoliberal times. The worth of Janson's oeuvre is particularly accentuated that it is created in the country that, despite its propagandist fame as flagship of democracy, has seldom, if ever, in its official education policy practice fully recognized the dignity, significance, and importance of the teacher profession for imaginable and real spheres of human life: arts, economy, ethics, politics, science, and, after all, the quality and meaning of life for all its citizens. Actually, the watchdog of liberalism, *The Economist* magazine, ranks the US in the 2018 *Democracy Index* as a *flawed democracy* at position 25 after Estonia and Chile.

From an outsider point of view, there is a glaringly unparalleled gap between advancing curriculum theories in the US and the practices of US education policies, its latest instances of which are represented by subsequent education policy programs of presidents George W. Bush's NCLB, Obama's RTTT, Trump's sporadic and unnamed one that nevertheless seems to make no qualitative difference with the previous ones. As William Pinar (2013) has perceptively observed the Democrats and Republicans can disagree in foreign policy, fiscal policy, military policy, etc., but, regardless of the regime in power, education policy remains the same outside the otherwise political divides and disagreements.

Against that tentative observation of the US practices of education policy and in the spirit of *Itinerant Curriculum Theory* (e.g. Paraskeva, 2016, 2017), I will briefly let my mind itinerate in some intellectual and geographical locales inspired by Janson's aesthetic-pedagogic-political collage of teaching. She is thinking with a rich itinerant mosaic of decolonial theories and exposes their composition as convincing experiences and counterarguments for the mainstream US education and curriculum policy backed up by bureaucratic and anti-intellectual variants of mechanistic behaviorist and cognitive theories that appear entirely helpless in face of real theoretical, political, and practical complexities of teaching. Those intellectually torso accounts may serve, as they have done and do, the academic career of their advocates, "learning" scientists and educational psychologists of that mechanist and technological ambience. If you are a practicing teacher—as I too doubted already in the beginning of my teaching career amidst the "quite normal chaos" (cf. Beck & Beck-Gernsheim, 2004) of teaching—it is hard to see those mechanistic, linguistically limited, and clumsy psychological accounts much more than deeply harmful to teaching and education worth of its name and mission. Those a matter of fact a-psychological, life-alienated and self-alienated, quasi-scientific control instances of education mean a huge 'waste of experiences' (Santos, 2014), of talents, intellectual resources, money, time and (professional and academic) life.

One of the most potent mechanism for effecting knowledge in positive and negative senses, such as instances of *epistemicide*, will be made available in the educational system, with the curriculum and teacher as its very core. Education policy studies more often than not omit or neglect the decisive intellectual, organizational, and practical role of the teacher for the epistemic and moral qualities the teacher is able to create and provide within the system. For education policy studies, the teacher often seems a less important, marginal residue, an impersonal cog-in-the-machine factor in the education system.

Janson's unique study specifies how the teacher is positioned within the education system as one of the most significant instances of and for the existing *epistemicide*. Drawing on Giroux's (2012) rationale she concretely discloses the huge, chaotic, and unjust weight put on the shoulders of teachers by the supposedly rational yet suppressing, misinformed, and misguided chorus of education policies, politicians, business elite, education stakeholders, and bureaucrats:

> we are told—not surprisingly by the hedge fund reformers and billionaire gurus—that schooling is about the production of trained workers; memorization is more important than critical thinking; standardized testing is better than teaching students to be self-reflective; and learning how to read texts critically is not as important as memorizing discrete bodies of allegedly factual knowledge. Having their desires and skills shaped in such a way, students and teachers are reduce to permanent underclass, denied the opportunities to develop the capacity and motivation to challenge the power and authority of a rich elite. Pedagogical practice in this neoliberal framework is cleansed of any emancipatory possibilities, stripped clean of its ability to teach students how to engage in thoughtful

> dialogue and use their imagination in the service of understanding lies and experiences of individuals and groups different from themselves. (pp. 21–22)

Janson's sensitive and perceptive intellectuality, theoretical curiosity and erudition intertwined with her other personal-professional qualities: pedagogic giftedness, resilience, and mission, frank openness and empathy related to cognitive, aesthetic, political, and moral issues with her maturing and often plagued students makes her study a unique contribution to education policy and leadership studies, curriculum and teachers' lives studies, to say the least.

Simultaneously, her study is redefining, intensifying and creatively mingling the borders of an internationalization of curriculum studies beyond geographical map toward a novel intellectual itinerant curriculum theory cartography (see Paraskeva, 2016, 2017) by introducing the elements of Curriculum of the South at the heart of neoliberal education and curriculum practices, in the United States. Janson's explication of neoliberal measures at the level of teaching practice essentially sharpens what is pedagogically at stake when the scientific-commercial-political alliance of psychometric educational psychology and neoliberal policy rules. The structural congruence between test scores in education and the 'bottom line' in business render the neoliberal ideological core of concerted efforts to standardizing the world under one capitalist maxim, a maxim that after the collapse of the Soviet Union long hold the US in a kind of moral hostage about the superiority of the social and economic model particularly after the 1957 Sputnik shock.

> The economic and managerial stress on education, as part of an ongoing globalization process, draws on political demands for uniformity as former U.S. foreign minister Colin Powell put it: "a major challenge for the millenium is to install freely elected democracies all over the world, under one standard for the world which is the free market system … *practiced correctly*." The big political picture infusing such maxims is a vision of the world united by standardized, normative, even coercive notions of One Subjectivity, One History, One Humankind, One Politics—and, consequently, One Curriculum. Globalization in these terms would denote the pressures toward increasing uniformity, toward colonization and standardization of all spheres of human action, education as no exception. (Autio, 2009, p. 69)

The political euphoria caused by the collapse of the Soviet evidenced in the too-hasty claims in 1992 by Francis Fukuyama of the "*End of History*" where "liberal market democracy" assumedly has reached the apex of cultural evolution. The tone of the voice has already changed from euphoria to explicit authoritarian neoliberal dictation ten years later in 2003 by the US Secretary of Foreign Affairs Colin Powell: "free market system *practiced correctly.*"

The seeds for the turn of liberalism to neoliberalism preceding the Soviet collapse were sown in the 1980's UK when Prime Minister Margaret Thatcher ideologically reconceptualized capitalism as the reinvention of biblical values. In Thatcher's reading, "It is not material goods but all the great virtues exhibited by individuals working together that constitute what we call the market place" (Autio, 2012, p. 153). In fact, Thatcher, herself a Protestant believer, laid the seedbed of commercialized conception of secular morality, detached and cut off from any religious or philosophical commitments. That shift towards thoroughly secular and marketplace source of morality extends and legitimizes the neoliberal *Zeitgeist*: "economic thought is coterminous with rationality" (Couldry, 2012); "neoliberalism as a theory of everything" (Goodson, 2014).

Soon after the Soviet collapse in 1991, *"the spirit of capitalism"* (Weber, 2005) violently burst out of the bottle transforming, shaping, and colonizing all public institutions and organizations—and the sense of public good—assimilating into the organization model, discourses and vocabularies of American *business corporate.* As a rule, with any world political upheavals, the provision of education is among the first to be colonized by new orders. Today all the education institutions worldwide from kindergarten to universities are colonized under the simplistic economic rule in the name of educational effectiveness: 'high outputs at lowest costs.' Janson's elegant summary is exhaustive:

> neoliberalism values market exchange as an "ethic in itself, capable of acting as a guide to all human action, and substituting for all previously held ethical beliefs," it emphasizes the significance of contractual relations in the marketplace. It holds that the social good will be maximized by maximizing the reach and frequency of market transactions, and it seeks to bring all human action into the domain of the market. This requires technologies of information creation and capacities to accumulate, store, transfer, analyze, and use massive databases to guide decisions in the global marketplace. (Chapter 3)

The heaviest burden of reception and translation of education reforms, "implementation" in neoliberal rhetoric, is always on the teacher, the touchstone and cornerstone of any educational system. Elizabeth Janson's study render sensible and perceivable through all registers of human senses this Sisyphean labor of teaching in the current austerity of neoliberalism.

I have elsewhere (Autio, 2017, pp. 44–45) claimed how neoliberalism discards the concept of knowledge altogether and redefines the basic curriculum question: *What knowledge is of most worth?* to *What skills and competences are of most worth?* General education is atrophied and 'vocationalized' as conveniently measurable skills and competences. The primitive simplification of education is an outcome of education policies purposefully informed by obsolete methodologies of learning theories in tandem with political intentions of neoliberalism. The existential original *Quest for Certainty* (Dewey, 1930) has been vulgarized into standardization, accountability and control, the political consequence of which we may be witnessing in the decay of democracy. Pinar (2011) emphasizes the historical succession of the US mainstream educational policy logic by a comment that critically underlines the current political connection between behaviorist-cognitive psychology and neoliberal education policy:

> Since *No Child Left Behind*, "behavior" itself has been reduced to test-taking. It is in this sense that I have asserted that accountability in the United States is a form of neo-fascism. (p. 185)

I feel a temptation—in the spirit of Walter Mignolo's (2000) *I Think Where I Am*—to briefly expose the North European *Bildung/Didaktik* positioning of the teacher as contrastive to the American Curriculum, summarized on the basis of Ian Westbury's (2000, pp. 15–39) instructive juxtaposition of those two 'superdiscourses' of curriculum theory, and their respective reflections on the image of the teacher as a North European autonomous professional or the image of the American teacher, driven by neoliberal accountability, standardization and controlling measures.

The view of the teacher and curriculum in the Anglo-American context:
- Teacher's role as the intellectually passive "agent of the system" (Westbury, 2000).
- Teacher-proof curricula: "existing teachers are a (if not *the*) major brake on the innovation, change and reform that the schools always seem to require" (Westbury, 2000).
- Curriculum-as-manual; a very limited space for professional autonomy, freedom, creativity, and judgment.
- Teaching essentially means teaching to the test.

The view of the teacher and curriculum in the Bildung/Didaktik tradition:
- Curriculum is an organizational *and intellectual* centerpiece of education

- "An autonomous professional teacher ... has complete freedom within the framework of the *Lehrplan* (*curriculum*) to develop her or his own approaches to teaching" (Westbury, 2000).
- The relationship between the curriculum and the teacher; the teacher as the curriculum theorist is implicitly internalized and respected in Finland
- Teaching ideally is a combination of academic knowledge and personality: external testing and efforts of standardizing teachers' work render a foolproof failure
- High trust in highly educated teachers
- Tests are not externally mandated but teacher-driven
- Task-oriented, not test-oriented, atmosphere in the classroom

On this idealized charting, there is present a dramatic non-democratic structural preference of the system to the individual: in the American education policy view of the teacher, living teachers bring into the system a factor of human error; "existing teachers are a (if not the) major brake on the innovations, change, and reform that the schools always seem to require" (p. 21). It is perfectly feasible to think of a succession of the long instrumentalist continuum of American education that the effect of human error factor by existing teachers, could be diminished by automatization, robotization, and digitization of teaching and curriculum in accordance with other production models. This neoliberal ideal image of curriculum, teaching, and the teacher is undoubtedly in strict contrast with aspirations to promote cosmopolitan democracy, decoloniality, epistemic, social as well as educational justice and equality.

Due the neoliberal pressure on education, the above charting is in the process of transformation also in Germany and Sweden, formerly strong advocates of education and curriculum in terms of rationality as egalitarian practice, now favoring the US kind of technical and instrumental rationality as effectiveness and efficacy, supported by the ally of evidence-based scientism and neoliberal austerity, where the intellectual and political resources for education policy are anemically and detrimentally drawn mainly from the measures of external audit and assessment.

In the early 1990's, the collapse of the Soviet Union released the spirit from a capitalist bottle with far reaching consequences particularly in education and in countries, which previously appreciated professional autonomy of teachers to apply the national framework curriculum. Sweden adopted the US style education policy drivers in their basic schooling, *standardization* and *privatization* (*"fri skolor"* as equivalent to US charter schools) with the result that the touch and cornerstone of any education system—the teacher—is literally disappearing. Since the early 1990's, the Swedish right-wing politics (now social democrats are in power again) has led to the situation where there is according to the Teachers' Union the dramatic lack of competent teachers, 60,000 in a relatively small country of about ten million inhabitants.[1] The phenomenon can be related to teachers' own assessment of how they think their work is appreciated by the public. According to the TALIS survey from 2013, 5% of Swedish teachers think their work is valued and respected; post-Soviet Estonia, who soon after new independence in 1991 adopted the US education and curriculum models, also suffers from the lack of competent teachers and low professional appeal among the youth: 14% of the Estonian teachers think their work is appreciated in public. The closest neighbor, Finland makes a dramatic difference: 57% of Finnish teachers think their work is appreciated by their people.[2]

Finnish basic education system lacks altogether externally mandated tests and exams; in fact, tests is a rarity in Finish basic education on the global scene: no inspecting, no testing, and no ranking. All tests are teacher-driven. There is a silent and consensual antipathy among teachers, their unions, and education administration to issues, which particularly in English speaking countries, are "implemented" as 'quality assurance and evaluation' (QAE) measures.

> Finnish hostility towards ranking, combined with bureaucratic tradition and a developmental approach to QAE strengthened by radical municipal autonomy have resulted in the construction of nationally and locally embedded policies that have been rather effective in resisting a transnational policy of testing and ranking. It is significant, however, that those policies represent a combination of conscious, unintended and contingent factors. (Simola, 2015, p. xv)

The design of successful education and curriculum policies may seem to require "conscious" efforts but the space and resources should be preserved, like in Finnish case, for "unintended and contingent factors" as well. These unintended and contingent factors are engendered through the daily work of academically educated, competent teachers who enjoy professional freedom, public trust and minimum of external intervention for the good of the system. The moral dimension of the curriculum is a key when teachers can combine personal, free judgment with academic knowledge and other relevant knowledge and experiences: "Scratch a good teacher and you will find a moral purpose" (Fullan, in Autio, 2012, p. 157). In Goodson's (2014) terms,

> *New research findings in education reform patently show that personal and professional commitment must exist at the heart of any new changes or reforms ... Good teacherhood is a personal quality ...* The countries that have pursued neo-liberal reforms in the fastest and deepest manner, such

> as England, perform very poorly in educational standards. Meanwhile, those that have defended a social democratic vision and have explicitly valued professional autonomy, such as Finland, have produced top-rate educational standards. It would seem time to seriously scrutinise the neo-liberal orthodoxy in the field of education. (pp. 42–44)

Elizabeth Janson's book is a vivid and moving, intellectually inspiring, honest and deep commitment to the most worthwhile educational and political mission she considers and feels dear and personal: "Revealing to youth different layers of the world and analyzing *with* them is part of decolonizing." Her curious, receptive and resilient teacher's bodymind convincingly discloses the role of *Itinerant Curriculum Theory* at work as providing intellectual and moral vision, strength and wisdom; her curriculum travels through times and places with theories and sensitively registers cultural, social, and individual differences, disclosing a cosmopolitan resources that critically evaluates, corrects, and complements Western cultural, social, and political discourse to her students. In her teaching context, education and the curriculum are defined as a social, political and economic complex that recognizes and recognizes variation rather than standardization. Yet, all the time her touch to teaching as personal is preserved.

> The problem arises when a young person is ignored. When he is treated as an object or when he is left to his own fortune. Too many young people have to live without safe adults in their neighborhood. Children enter institutions and become aware that they are problematic. Many of them begin to behave accordingly. This is the most recurring story when I talk to young people with criminal backgrounds. They report that they were plunged into deeper problems because they became cases in the authorities books. They were diary files on computers and notes in folders. They stopped being ordinary children. (Aleksis Salusjärvi[3])

Notes

1 https://www.lararforbundet.se/artiklar/lararbrist-sverige-behover-fler-larare

2 https://www.hm.ee/en/activities/statistics-and-analysis/talis, http://www.oecd.org/sweden/TALIS-2013-country-note-Sweden.pdf

3 Aleksis Salusjärvi is a literary and visual critic, cultural journalist living in Helsinki. He teaches arts at all levels.

References

Autio, T. (2009). From gnosticism to globalization: Rationality, Trans-Atlantic curriculum discourse, and the problem of instrumentalism. In B. Baker (Ed.), *New curriculum history* (pp. 69–96). Rotterdam, The Netherlands: Sense Publishers.

Autio, T. (2012). *Subjectivity, curriculum, and society: Between and beyond the German Didaktik and Anglo-American curriculum studies.* New York, NY: Routledge.

Autio, T. (2017). Education as liberating experience: Bill Doll's scholarship and contested legacies of Euro-American curriculum theories from Descartes onwards. In M. Quinn (Ed.), *From the echo of God's laughter: Essays on the generative and generous gifts of William E. Doll Jr.* (pp. 38–47). New York, NY: Routledge.

Beck, U., & Beck-Gernsheim, E. (2004). *Normal chaos of love.* Cambridge: Polity Press. (Original 1990: *Das ganz normale Chaos der Liebe.* Frankfurt am Main: Suhrkamp)

Couldry, N. (2012). *Why voice matters: Culture and politics after neoliberalism.* London: Sage.

Dewey, J. (1930). *The quest for certainty.* London: George Allen & Unwin.

Goodson, I. (2014). *Curriculum, personal narrative and the social future.* New York, NY: Routledge.

Giroux, H. (2012). *Education and the crisis of public values: Challenging the assault on teachers, students, & public education.* New York, NY: Peter Lang.

Jacques, M. (2016). The death of neoliberalism and the crisis in western politics. *The Guardian/Opinion.*

Mignolo, W. (2000). *Local Histories/Global designs: Coloniality, Subaltern knowledges, and border thinking.* Princeton, NJ: Princeton University Press.

Paraskeva, J. (2016). *Curriculum epistemicide: Towards an itinerant curriculum theory.* New York, NY: Routledge.

Paraskeva, J. (2017). *Towards a just curriculum theory. The epistemicide.* New York, NY: Routledge.

Pinar, W. (2011). *The character of curriculum studies: Bildung, Currere, and the Recurring question of the subject.* New York, NY: Palgrave Macmillan.

Pinar, W. (2013). *Curriculum studies in the United States. Present circumstances, intellectual histories.* New York, NY: Palgrave Macmillan.

Santos, B. (2014). *Epistemologies from the South.* Boulder, CO: Paradigm.

Simola, H. (2015). *The Finnish education mystery: Historical and sociological essays on schooling in Finland.* New York, NY: Routledge.

Weber, M. (2005). *The protestant ethic and the spirit of capitalism.* New York, NY: Routledge.

Westbury, I. (2000). Teaching as a reflective practice: What might Didaktik teach curriculum? In S. Hopmann & K. Riquarts (Eds.), *Teaching as a reflective practice: The German Didaktik tradition* (pp. 15–39). New York, NY: Routledge.

Tero Autio
Tallinn University, Estonia

SERIES INTRODUCTION

On (De)Coloniality: Curriculum Within and Beyond the West

João M. Paraskeva

The field of curriculum studies is theoretically shattered and profoundly disputed to such an extent that disputes have become an endemic part of the field's DNA. Such quarrels, on some occasions, have been intellectually sanguinary. Sometimes the field appears to be an estuary of ideological debris upon which new cultural battles will be fought. What/whose knowledge is of most worth, for whom, as well as the way such knowledge has been produced, packaged, legitimized, taught, and evaluated have all always been sites of open ideological carnage among different groups—dominant and counter-dominant—aiming to conceptualize and perpetuate a specific power matrix. The struggle for curriculum in the United States was always a struggle for the ideological foundation of its society. As a social construct, curriculum was always both a starting and arrival point of acute political battles, imposing itself as one of the most refined mechanisms of economic, cultural, and political segregation of capitalist societies. The nexus, or the lack thereof, of curriculum and society colonizes the field's theory and development.

The curriculum field, as we know it, is a eugenic 'agora' perpetrated by a Western Eurocentric power matrix that takes no prisoners. Blinded by the cult of positivism as the 'only' pedagogical scientific power, curriculum was always a beacon of epistemological cleansing and witnessed countless crucial critical transformative projects championed by counter-dominant groups and individuals, only to succumb, despite certain noteworthy achievements, in the face of the ever-demanding challenges of a threatening capitalist society. As such, curriculum is epistemicide. An epistemological field of blindness supported by a specific growth pattern of knowledge and science that simultaneously fertilizes noisy silences and shameful absences framed by traditional power and interest groups. Such groups have been facing severe challenges from a myriad of counter-dominant movements and intellectuals fighting for a more just, equal, relevant curriculum, one that could promote a more democratic society. However, while counter-dominant groups—especially those working from and within radical and critical platforms—were able to score some major victories by challenging some conservative curriculum reforms, the truth of the matter is that such counterhegemonic perspectives ended up being as functionalist as the functionalism they criticized, and thus attempted to smash the hegemonic curriculum from traditional dominant positions. To be more precise, counter-hegemonic traditions with radical and critical impulses fail to understand the need to expand their epistemological latitude within and beyond the Western Eurocentric epistemological terrain. The results of such distraction were and are devastating: 'conscientized' epistemicide and the production of more and more invisibilities in the richness and diversity of knowledges.

On (De)Coloniality: Curriculum Within and Beyond the West is a beacon in the struggle against epistemicide and the colonialities of being, power, and knowledge. It attempts to bring to the fore an analysis that focuses on non-Western/non-Eurocentric epistemological frameworks. In a world that still struggles to see its own overt epistemological diversity, *On (De)Coloniality Curriculum Within and Beyond the West* is an open space in which to challenge epistemological fascism. It encourages curriculum scholars to engage in dialogues about non-Western/-Eurocentric epistemologies within and beyond the Western Eurocentric platform. We invite 'complicated conversations' that dig into new avenues such as those of Itinerant Curriculum Theory (ICT), and, in so doing, introduce a new language that will take us to alternative levels of articulation and re-articulation of meanings, through endless and spaceless processes of coding, decoding, recoding, and 'encoding.'

As I have explained elsewhere (Paraskeva, 2011, 2014, 2016a, 2016b), ICT did and does try to say something to the field. It posits new terrains and theoretical situations. ICT participates in a complicated conversation (see Trueit, 2000; Pinar, 2000)—one that cannot bend under the yoke of Western academicism—challenging Western curriculum epistemicides (Paraskeva, 2017) and alerting us to the need to respect and incorporate non-Western epistemes. William Pinar (2012, 2013) acknowledges the influential synopticality of ICT in his recent *Curriculum Studies in the United States.* He states:

> There are other discourses influential now, sustainability perhaps primary among them. Arts-based research is hardly peripheral .... One sign is the synoptic text composed by João M. Paraskeva. Hybridity is the order of the day. Pertinent to the discussion is that even Paraskeva's determination to contain in one 'critical river' the multiple currents of understanding curriculum politically floods its banks; he endorses an 'itinerant curriculum theory' that asserts a 'deliberate disrespect of the canon' (2011, p. 184). In Paraskeva's proclamation, this 'river' has gone 'south' (2011, p. 186). That South is Latin America, where we can avoid 'any kind of Eurocentrism' (2011, p. 186) while not 'romanticizing indigenous knowledge' (2011, p. 187). Addressing issues [such as hegemony, ideology,

> power, social emancipation, class, race, and gender] implies a new thinking, a new theory ... an itinerant curriculum theory. (Pinar, 2013, p. 64)

Although Pinar's reading of ICT is crucial, I would clarify (maybe complexify) that "the" South is not just Latin America. Again, Santos (2009) is vital here:

> The South is metaphorically conceived as a field of epistemic challenges, which try to address and repair the damages and negative impacts historically created by capitalism in its colonial relation with the world. Such conception of South overlaps the geographical South, the group of nations and regions in the world that were subjugated to European colonialism and that, with the exception of Australia and New Zealand, never achieved levels of economic development similar to the Global North (i.e. Europe and the United States of America). (pp. 12–13)

Thus, we "designate the epistemological diversity of the world by South epistemologies" (Santos, 2009, p. 12). In this way, ICT addresses Santos' (2006) claim about the need for a new critical theory, a new emancipatory praxis (p. xi). As he states, "contrary to their predecessors, [such] theory and practices must start from the premise that the epistemological diversity of the world is immense, as immense as its cultural diversity and that the recognition of such diversity must be at the core of global resistance against capitalism and of alternative forms of sociability" (Santos, 2006, p. xi).

ICT is an unblemished claim against dominant multiculturalist forms that are "Eurocentric, a prime expression of the cultural logic of national or global capitalism, descriptive, apolitical, suppressing power relations, exploitation, inequality and exclusion" (Santos, 2007a, pp. xxiii–xxiv), which have been legitimizing a monoculture of scientific knowledge that needs to be defeated and replaced by an ecology of knowledges (Santos, 2003). ICT challenges the coloniality of power and being (cf. Quijano, 2000; Mignolo, 2000; Grosfoguel, 2007); it is sentient that the "politics of cultural diversity and mutual intelligibility calls for a complex procure of reciprocal and horizontal translation rather than a general theory" (Santos, 2007a, p. xxvi). ICT, Süssekind (2016) reinforces, helps one to re-think one's own arrogant ignorance within the curriculum as lived experience toward social and cognitive justice. Formalizing ICT in my mind, through my writing, through dialogues with others, and through the wor(l)d has meant, and still does, considering the intricacies of its conceptions and assertions. Yet, its conceptualization and creation is a natural complex interaction with the wor(l)d, as was perhaps the case for Michelangelo and Picasso with their art.

When one day Michelangelo was asked how a certain frame was painted, i.e. where his idea came from, he answered, "I had no idea. The figure just stood there, looking at me. I just gave it life/birth." Picasso had a similar dialogue with a Gestapo officer. In occupied Paris during World War II, a Gestapo officer who had barged into Picasso's apartment pointed at a photo of the mural, *Guernica*, asking: "Did you do that?" "No," Picasso replied, "you did." Writing is, Gilles Deleuze (p. 141) argues, "bringing something to life, to free life from where it's trapped, to trace lines of flight" (p. 141).

These words of Michelangelo and Picasso also highlight the *theory of translation* that works through art. Similarly, ICT is a theory of translation that attempts to prevent the "reconstruction of emancipatory discourse and practices from falling into the trap of reproducing, in a wider form, Eurocentric concepts and contents" (Santos, 2007a, p. xxvi). Translation is crucial to the processes of coding and decoding between the diverse and specific intellectual and cognitive resources that are expressed through the various modes of producing knowledge about counter-hegemonic initiatives and experiences aimed at the redistribution and recognition and the construction of new configurations of knowledge anchored in local, situated forms of experience and struggle (Santos, 2007a, p. xxvi).

In such a context, examples such as Yacouba Sawadogo, an African farmer of Burkina Faso who has been restoring the soil damaged by centuries of drought (and desertification) through traditional farming techniques, cannot be arrogantly minimized or eugenically produced as non-existent or non-science, just because this work cannot be translated and framed within Western scientificity. Western intellectuals need to consciously acknowledge that the Western epistemological platform—both in its most sophisticated dominant and/ or radical critical counter-dominant perspectives—is insufficient and inadequate to explain and change its own effects (Seth, 2011). A new system cannot emerge from the ashes of the old. It is pointless to think about the future just with(in) the Cartesian modernity model. It is hopeless to frame the present within such a dated model.

Western counter-dominant perspectives are crucial in the struggle for social and cognitive justice, yet not enough. As Sandra Corazza (2002) courageously argues, "we need to start taking seriously the task of a real theory of curriculum thought" (p. 131), one that opens the Western canon of knowledge and is responsive to the need for a new epistemological configuration. Such a journey of belligerent struggles—against the dominant and within the counter-dominant Western epistemological platforms—aims to replace the so-called monoculture of scientific knowledge for an ecology of knowledges. Such ecology of knowledges is an invitation to the promotion of non-relativistic dialogues among knowledges, granting equality of opportunities to the different kinds of knowledge engaged in ever broader epistemological disputes aimed both at maximizing their perspective contributions to build a more democratic and just society and at decolonizing knowledge and power (Santos, 2007a, p. xx).

As with any other theoretical exercise intended to understand the educational world in order to transform it (see Pinar, 2004), ICT exhibits a certain latitude and longitude in borderless space to deepen certain claims. For example, among many issues, ICT highlights the linguistic imperialism framed by the English language and culture as an aspect of genocide. Conscious of this linguistic imperialism as a crucial part of genocide, ICT allows one to respectfully understand, for example, how 'camfrenglish'—"a language used in Cameroon's cities, created daily by Cameroon's urban youth"—deliberately violates the linguistic rules of French and English and, in so doing, desacralizes these imperial languages (Marc Ella, 2013, p. 24). In cities such as Yaounde, camfrenglish is the people's language.

Antonia Darder (2012), in her superb exegesis of the political economy of cultural theory and politics, brings language to the core of the battle against eugenics. As Darder claims, "the complexity of language and how the students produce knowledge and how language shapes their world represent a major pedagogical concern for all educational settings" (p. 105). Language, Darder argues, is more than a tool that epitomizes a specific learning theory or the cult of a flamboyant method. The language question intersects other social non-epiphenomena such as the question of authority, reframing equality as well as social and cognitive justice. *Any* critical theory that aims at cultural democracy cannot ignore the power of biculturalism as a *poesis* that determines culture and power relations in classrooms (Darder, 2012).

ICT also warns about the need to challenge any form of indigenitude, or the romanticization of indigenous cultures and knowledges, and it is not framed in any dichotic skeleton of West-Rest. In fact, it challenges such functionalist forms. Its itinerant dynamic pushes the theorist to a pluri-(or not-necessarily-) directional path. More importantly, ICT confronts the subject with a permanently unstable question: 'what it is to think?' Further, ICT pushes one to think in the light of the future, as well as to question how 'we' can actually claim to really know the things that 'we' claim to know, if 'we' are not ready specifically to think the unthinkable—and to go beyond the unthinkable and master its infinitude. ICT is to be (or not to be) radically unthinkable. ICT is a metamorphosis between what is thought, non-thought, and un-thought, but also fundamentally about the temerity of the colonization of the non/un/thought within the thought. ICT attempts to understand and to domesticate the infinity of thought and action. If one challenges infinity, and 'then it is chaos because one is in chaos;' that means that the question or questions (whatever they are)

are inaccurately deterritorialized and fundamentally sedentary. The focus is to grasp that ICT implies an understanding of chaos as domestic, as public, as a *punctum* within the pure luxury of immanence. In such multitude of turfs, ICT needs to be understood as *poesis*. It plays in the plane of immanence. Being as immanence is 'a life,' ICT is 'a life'. A life paced by a *poesis* or a revolution? 'Yes please,' in a full *Žižekian* way. ICT is a *poesis* that itinerantly throws the subject against the infinity of representation to grasp the omnitude of the real(ity) and the rational(ity), thus mastering the transcendent. Being more *poesis* than just theory (and not because it is less theory), its itinerant position *epitomizes* a transcendent nomadography.

ICT challenges book worship (Tse Tung, 2007, p. 45). In fact, ICT also encourages us to pay attention to the multiplicity of forms to read the wor(l)d. The verbalization of pain and oppression is quite visible in Africa, for example, in art forms such as dance and painting. Dance, Marc Ella (2013) argues, in a country financially and economically moribund, is not just a way to face inequality and oppression. It is, he states, "the very best way to face discouragement" (2013, p. 26). ICT is an attempt to help us to think in another form of being. Corazza's (2002) insightful framework is crucial here as well. As she claims, and I honestly think ICT addresses her claim, the challenge is to fight against what she coins as *assentado curriculum* towards a *vagamundo curriculum*; that is "to create [or co-create] a *vagamundo* curriculum one needs to question how can one think about the inaddressable, the unthinkable, the non-thinkable of the curriculum thought, the exteriorities, the self different, the self other, the other self" (Corazza, 2002, p. 140). Corazza adds that such curriculum thought is meaningless, a real vacuum, without the effective forces acting upon such thought, as well as without the effective indeterminations that force such thought [or forms of thought] to think otherwise, differently, through the creation of new concepts required by real experience and not just by possible experience, thus allowing new life experiences. [In fact] the strength of (an)other knowledge, as well as a new philosophy, will be measured by the concepts that it is capable of creating, or its capacity to renew meanings which impose a new framework on things and to *assentados* actions, shuffle their syntax, and organize their thought in a clumsy logic (2002, p. 140).

Corazza's (2002) sharp take equips intellectuals with the necessary extraordinary tools to understand why some African scholars, such as Axelle Kabou (2013), Jean Marc Ella (2013), and others justifiably counter the Western and non-Western hegemonic apparatuses with the following question: "What if Africa refuses development?" The definition of development must be seen through other lenses beyond its Western monocultural conceptualization as the development needed by the Global South. *Whose* purpose does this development serve? What is the cost to those beneath its grinding wheel of so-called progress? In such a context, ICT is really a matter of human rights as well, due to its commitment to social and cognitive justice. This is a commitment that challenges dominant multicultural forms, creating the conditions for an intercultural reconstruction of human rights and moving towards an intercultural post-imperial form of human rights that respects, among other issues: (a) the right to knowledge, (b) the right to bring historical capitalism to trial in a world tribunal, (c) the right to democratic self-determination, and, (d) the right to grant rights to entities incapable of bearing duties, namely nature and future generations (Santos, 2007a, 2007b). ICT is a clarion call to challenge curriculum epistemicides (Paraskeva, 2017) by engaging fully in the complex struggle for social and cognitive justice. It is also a call to decolonize the 'decolonized.' This is an intergenerational matter of justice as well.

The struggle against epistemicides and curriculum epistemicides (Santos, 2014, 2007b; Paraskeva, 2011, 2016a, 2016b, 2017) is difficult but necessary. That it is impossible is a fabricated fallacy. Bragança's 'walking and being' is a wake-up call to all of us really committed to the struggle against curriculum epistemicides (Paraskeva, 2017). It allows one to grasp ICT as a political yarn that works within and beyond the capitalist system or against 'world system theory.' ICT is also a human rights issue, a challenge to the dichotomy of ethics and chaos since it is an ethic of [needed] chaos. ICT praises the consistency of inconsistencies and fosters a reckless philosophy of praxis above and beyond the rumble of 'being-non-being'; it is a eulogy of 'being.' ICT is à *la Marti*, 'an infinite labor of love,' one that perceives that the act of thinking is not just theoretical. ICT works in a never-ending matrix determined by sensations, forces, fluxes, 'happenings,' all of which are linked and reacting against the modes and conditions of production of the capitalist system.

ICT is a curriculum turn. A 'pluri-versal' not 'uni-versal' turn. A decolonial turn. ICT needs to be seen within the cartography of a decolonial being. Mignolo (2011a, 2011b) is of great help here, arguing that the genealogy of decolonial thinking is pluri-versal (not uni-versal). As such, each knot on the web of this genealogy is a point of de-linking and opening that re-introduces languages, memories, economies, social organizations, and at least double subjectivities: the splendor and the miseries of the imperial legacy, and the indelible footprint of what existed that has been converted into the colonial wound; in the degradation of humanity, in the inferiority of the pagans, the primitives, the under-developed, the non-democratic (Mignolo, 2011b, p. 63).

Such inquiry implies, as Deleuze and Guattari felicitously unveil, that an itinerant theory is not just a war machine that judiciously collides with ossified truths and fossilized realities. Its itinerant existence is actually only possible in a permanent theater of war. Needless to say, ICT is not cavalier with history. Nor it is just a pale reaction against the way history has been *quasi* suffocated by hegemonic and particular counterhegemonic traditions. While a concept—arguably a geophilosophical one—it goes well beyond an aesthetic wrangle between sedentary theoretical hegemonic and particular counterhegemonic platforms, and toward nomad(ic) approaches free from walls, dams, and institutionally-backward bourgeois turfs. ICT implies a nomadic inquiry, but one in which the foci occupy the truly total itinerant capacity of space(less)ness, a permanent smooth itinerant position, a perpetual search that wholeheartedly aims at saturation. The nomadography of such theory is framed in the nonstop itinerant posture in which creators of *poesis* seem to be part of the history of thought but escape from it either in a specific aspect (or in specific aspects) or altogether. ICT attempts to turn curriculum theory against itself as well. It is a philosophy of liberation, which is sentient of the pitfalls of the internationalization of dynamics within the curriculum field. ICT helps us understand how to situate curriculum theory in the project of modernity/colonialism/decolonization.

ICT contends that it is no longer viable to carry on with and in the same epistemological framework. Relying on Habermas, Mignolo (2008) argues that

> It is no longer possible, or at least it is not unproblematic, to 'think' from the canon of Western philosophy, even when part of the canon is critical of modernity. To do so means to reproduce the blind epistemic ethnocentrism that makes difficult, if not impossible, any political philosophy of inclusion. The limit of Western philosophy is the border where the colonial difference emerges, making visible the variety of local histories that Western thought, from Right and Left, hid and suppressed. (p. 234)

(An)other science is not just really possible; it is real. ICT is a claim for a just theory; a claim for just science. It is possible for an itinerant curriculum theory—which we argue is the best path for critical progressive curriculum scholars—not only to grasp precious concepts and dynamics, such as hegemony, ideology, power, social emancipation, class, race, and gender in the complex age of globalization (Santos, 2008) or globalisms, but also to better (re)address the towering questions of curriculum, starting with the one asked by Counts in the last century: *Dare the schools build a new social order?* So long as poverty and inequality keep multiplying, this question remains central. The devastating impact of neoliberal policies forces the intemporality of certain challenges. Given these conditions, ICT challenges the critical curriculum project to go beyond its counter-dominant and dominant-within-the-counter-dominant positions, thus turning the struggle for curriculum relevance into a struggle for social and cognitive justice. As we will see later on in examining Chomsky's (1971) approach, while the transformation of society is crucial, understanding it accurately is no less important.

I am not claiming that ICT is a perfect theory; I've actually claimed that there is no such thing as a perfect theory (see Quantz, 2011). Obviously, there is room for critique; for instance, the clashes within the post-structural positions could be expanded. The ecological domain should not be so silent. ICT questions the linguistic imperialism of English and other Western imperial languages. It also challenges the way science has been defined and legitimized based on the cultural politics of academic writing, which are not only social formulas but also legitimize 'the modern epistemicidium,' and are thus real obstacles to social and cognitive justice. ICT also challenges the momentum of internationalization, as well as in whose language this epoch is occurring. ICT is alert to the fact that the very struggle to internationalize the field of curriculum studies is a relatively recent phenomenon for the United States' academic milieu.

ICT aims precisely at 'a general epistemology of the impossibility of a general epistemology.' It is an itinerant posture that is profoundly engaged in its commitment to a radical co-presence. It is non-abyssal since not only challenges the modern Western cult of abyssal thinking but also attempts to dilute such fictional vacuums between the lines. ICT is an act of resistance also at the metaphysical level. That is, the struggle against modern Western abyssal thinking is not merely a policy matter. It is also above and beyond that: It is an existential and spiritual question. The struggle against the Western Cartesian model cannot signify the substitution of one Cartesian model for another. Also, the task is not to dominate such a model or to wrap it in a more humanistic impulse. The task is to pronounce its last words, to prepare its remains for a respectful funeral. The task is not to change the language and concepts, although these are key elements. The task is to terminate a particular hegemonic geography of knowledge, one which promotes an epistemological euthanasia.

ICT denounces how internationalization has been, in so many ways, the new apparatus through which modern Western epistemologies have been expanding the very process and significance of 'what it is to think.' It has exposed even more the open wound created by "the archives of Western knowledge and the question of cultural domination exercised by countries of advanced capital over imperialized countries" (Ahmad, 2008, p. 2). ICT is undeniably a call for a new 'never stable gathering epistemological point.' While it is strongly evident that the struggle against epistemicide is a human rights issue, it is also clear that such a struggle cannot be won with old weapons (Latour, 2005).

(De)Coloniality: Curriculum Within and Beyond the West is about 'curriculum from the South in the Global South and curriculum from the South in the Global North,' as connected with the different metamorphoses of coloniality. It unpacks the Western, Eurocentric, Anglo-Saxon epistemological fascism subsumed in the true colors of policy and reform matters, as well as in daily life within classrooms. It intends to help establish a multifarious corpus of scholarship that will open the curriculum canon to foster social and cognitive justice

in itinerant theory and impel movement toward a non-abyssal curriculum; work that fosters such shifts is a crucial part of our collective commitment to the struggle against epistemicide.

The Pinocchio Effect: Decolonialities, Spiritualities, and Identities needs to be understood in this context. The volume represents the outcome—another one—of a political project that was designed to prepare critical, transformative leaders, policy makers, and analysts in the South Coast of Massachusetts. The volume analyzes the impact of colonialities (Quijano, 2000; Mignolo, 2010; Dussel, 2005) within U.S. public education by examining the learning experiences that influence teachers' and students' spiritualties, affecting the construction and oppression of their identities. In order to support this analysis, the volume (a) examines the complexities of the wrangle between colonialism and colonialities; (b) examines how colonialities of being function within U.S. schools to create coloniality as a hegemonic philosophy of praxis that is perceived as liberatory instead of another oppressive system; (c) analyzes the contested spaces in which spiritualties as connected with knowledges and languages intersect as a result of hidden, written, and performed curriculum; (d) uses decolonial processes, such as conscientização (Freire, 2009) and consciencism (Nkrumah, 1964) to understand her pedagogical role in colonizing and/or decolonizing the classroom, which functions as a political arena as well as a critical space of praxis in order to reveal how realities and knowledges are made nonexistent—an epistemic blindness and privilege.

By embarking without hesitation and any euphemisms into curriculum praxis and the devastating effects on the lives of the oppressed communities in the light of the most sophisticated theories of coloniality, *The Pinocchio Effect* helps us to better understand the tentacles of a dominant pedagogical octopus, an octopus that assumes chameleon metamorphoses, which assumes a quasi-permanent state of innovation and adaptability to the ever different needs of perpetuating a fallaciously democratic and openly inequitable society through the solidification and legitimation of one dimensional and abyssal thought. In so doing, the volume opens the veins of the abyssal thinking that helps unpack the way for an itinerant curriculum theory an abyssal curriculum theory and development.

1 From Abyssal to Non-Abyssal Thinking

In order to contextualize the *Pinocchio Effect* and the wrangles of curriculum and pedagogical theories it takes on with humility, I will unfold the complexities of abyssal and non-abyssal thinking. As I was able to unveil elsewhere

(Paraskeva, 2011, 2014, 2016a, 2017), Boaventura Sousa Santos (2007a, 2007b) denounces Western modern thinking as "an abyssal thinking," consisting

> of a system of visible and invisible distinctions, the invisible ones being the foundation of the visible ones. The invisible distinctions are established through radical lines that divide social reality into two realms, the realm of "this side of the line" and the realm of "the other side of the line." The division is such that "the other side of the line" vanishes as reality, becomes nonexistent, and is indeed produced as nonexistent. Nonexistent means not existing in any relevant or comprehensible way of being. (p. 45)

In a way, Santos goes well beyond the notion of 'incomplete other' (Todorova, 1997). That is there is no 'incomplete other' (and also 'incomplete self') since there is nothing beyond the abyssal line. Hence, "non-existence, invisibility and non-dialectical absence" (Santos, 2007b, p. 45) of the "one side" are the roots of visibility and existence of the "[an]other side." That is the "exclusionary character of this abyss is at the core of the modern epistemological disputes between scientific and nonscientific forms of truth" (Santos, 2007b, p. 47). Such monopoly has been able to confine the epistemological struggle within a particular framework regarding "certain kinds of objects under certain circumstances and established by certain methods" (Santos, 2007b, p. 47). A monopoly that by producing other forms of knowledge as non-existent—since unfitted with the scientific scientificity of the Western modern thinking (Giroux, 2011) ruled by "reason as philosophical truth or faith as religious truth" (Santos, 2007b, p. 47)—erases its own relativism and the relativism of "scientific" truth. In such context, not just knowledge, but the very question/answer "what is to think" is totally prostituted.

Chomsky (1971) argues that a "central problem on interpreting the world is determining how, in fact, human beings proceed to do so. It is the study of the interaction between a particular biologically given, complex system—the human mind—and the physical and social world" (p. 3). The irrefutability of such insightful claim throws the Western Cartesian model abyssal thinking to the pillory sentenced to death without a possibility for an appeal. Chomsky's sharp claim (1971) validates the impossibility of one single way through which human beings will try to grasp the world, as well as the relativism of the totalitarian impulses that have been secularly produced by the Western Cartesian modern model to produce, reproduce, and legitimate one-dimensional human beings (Marcuse, 1964)—a one dimensionality that it is based on production of the 'other dimensions as non-existent' (Santos, 2014).

The intricate and different ways human beings experience the world exhibits how flimsy is the very modern hegemonic learning theory that has been coined scientific and thus official. Echoing Russell's consulate, Chomsky (1971) argues that the very study of "human psychology has been diverted into side channels by an unwillingness to pose the problem of how experience is related to knowledge and belief, a problem which of course presupposes a logicality prior to investigation of the structure of systems of knowledge and belief" (p. 47).

An abyssal framework fuels such only-one dimensionality "to the extent that effectively eliminates whatever realities are on the other side of the line" (Santos, 2007b, p. 48). Curriculum is bloody tainted in such abyssal line. Curriculum as we know it, needs to be understood as part of the epistemicide (Santos, 2014).

Moreover, such radical denial of co-presence, Sousa Santos argues (2007b), "grounds the affirmation of the radical difference that, on this side of the line, separates true and false, legal and illegal. The other side of the line comprises a vast set of discarded experiences, made invisible both as agencies and as agents, and with no fixed territorial location" (p. 48). Welcome to the colonial zone, "*par excellence*, the realm of incomprehensible beliefs and behaviours which in no way can be considered knowledge, whether true or false. The other side of the line harbours only incomprehensible magical or idolatrous practices" (Santos, 2007b, p. 51).

One cannot delink the abyssal thinking from the political economy and culture of the material conditions underlying the emergence and development of capitalism. Capitalism and abyssal thinking are the two faces of the same coin; the cultural and economic politics of radical negation have been upgraded since its emergence. Such nexus imposes a pedagogy of domination and violence based on a cult of Western Eurocentric superior culture, fostering a fallacy of development that paves the way for the necessary violence as the price of development and naturally "victims are culpable for their own violent conquest and for their own victimization" (Dussel, 1995, p. 66).

Needless to say, the abyssal global lines that have been framing the modern Western thinking are not static or fixed constructions. Nor do they express a monolithic movement. There are contradictory impulses within the very core of the modern Western thinking within the turfs of philosophy and religion as well as between both. Also, the advent of globalization opened space for the emergence of a post-abyssal thinking produced by what Santos (2007b) calls "subaltern cosmopolitanisms" (p. 55).

Acknowledging the limitations of particular modern Western counter-hegemonic impulses, Fraser (2014) requests a new critical theory that adapts to the new reality of our times by incorporating the dimensions of the social crises a crisis that was unable to interrupt as well. What Fraser (2014) is demanding is the need to run away from the functionalist temptation to focus exclusively in the logic of the system and to grasp the logic of the social action. Every critical approach that wants to address current social problems, needs to excel economicism by being multidimensional and excel functionalism by paying attention to the structure and agency. That is, "today's crisis is multidimensional, encompassing not only economy and finance, but also ecology, society and politics" (Fraser, 2014, pp. 541–542). Critical theory addresses the three strands fuelled by such crises: the ecological, the financialization and the social reproduction strands of the crisis (Fraser, 2014, p. 542). However, as she argues, today "we lack such a critical theory" (Fraser, 2014, p. 542).

Fraser's (2014) claim, I argue, is crucial and reinforces the claim to engage and move the critical path into a decolonized process. Otherwise, it is inconsequential. It needs to show the temerity to be post-abyssal. That is to be non-abyssal. Post-abyssal thinking "starts from the recognition that social exclusion in its broadest sense takes very different forms according to whether it is determined by an abyssal or by a non-abyssal line, and that as long as abyssally defined exclusion persists, no really progressive post-capitalist alternative is possible" (Santos, 2007b, p. 65). By recognizing the abyssal thinking as a hegemonic epistemological cartel, critical thinking—to be worth of its name—needs to play a huge role in debunking such eugenicist platform. That is "without such recognition, critical thinking will remain a derivative thinking that will go on reproducing the abyssal lines, no matter how anti-abyssal it will proclaim itself" (Santos, 2007b, p. 65). Post-abyssal thinking "is a non-derivative thinking; it involves a radical break with modern Western ways of thinking and acting [it implies] to think from the perspective of the other side of the line, precisely because the other side of the line has been the realm of the unthinkable in Western modernity" (Santos, 2007b, p. 65).

It goes without saying that challenging post-abyssal thinking, requires "a global [collective] response by its victims" (Amin, 2008, p. 77). Post-abyssal thinking is an alternative way thinking of alternative, an ecology of knowledges beyond the autocratic cult of 'scientific' knowledge founded on the idea that knowledge is inter-knowledge, (Santos, 2007b, p. 66). It claims a general epistemology of the impossibility of a general epistemology" (Santos, 2007b, p. 67). It claims a radical co-presence.

Elizabeth Janson's *Pinocchio Effect* addresses how itinerant curriculum theory echoes the major issues affecting, not only education and curriculum policy and politics, but also teachers' and students' daily lives the classroom in the South Coast of Massachusetts.

Chapter 1—*Colonial Heart and Silenced Spiritualities*—introduces the book's exigence, discussing the current situation of US public schools and the human crises that exists as emotional and spiritual gaps multiply within and beyond school walls. "For the Children" policies permeate schools in which youth are subjected to school choice, Common Core, Zero Tolerance (ZTP), and English-only policies that are purported as being for their well-being but, in reality, harm them and colonize and/or oppress their beings. Neoliberalism fuels these colonialities which work to create youth who are subjects to the market as well as though who are disposable. Chapter 2—*The Need for Decolonial Autoethnography in Education*—unfolds the need for decolonial autoethnography as well as how educators can enact this methodology for the sake of resisting the gag on them. The precipice for this methodology is the colonial mechanism that have oppressed the voices of educators and youth. No Child Left Behind (NCLB) and Race to the Top (RTTT) have brought a wave of "innovative" and "research-based" practices that narrate the ways U.S. public education should run, but a critique of this research is needed—informed not only by views from the outside, but from those influenced most by these top-down policies. In the next chapter—*Colonialism, Colonialities, and Imperialism Within and Beyond U.S. Education*—Janson draws from critical, post-structural, anti-colonial, feminist, and decolonial approaches and lays out colonialities, spiritualities, and technicalization of language in relation to the neoliberal momentum within U.S. schools. The use of decolonial autoethnography to analyze the dialectics amongst teachers and students is not to compare this to the continuing struggles of those who are oppressed in abject poverty, have experienced and are experiencing linguicide, genocide, epistemicide, and other violent forms of oppression. Rather it extends Constantino's (1966) discussion of the Philippines and the U.S. decision to use the school as its intellectual oppressor, something that is stronger than a gun. Kill a man and he is of no use to you, the colonizer, but destroy his spirit and colonize his mind, and you just gained an intellectual slave. Furthermore, this chapter unveils how there needs to be more attention to the way capitalism needed and needs a coloniality of gender.

Chapter 4—*Canary in the Mind: Colonialities, Biopolitics, and Body-Politics*—is where the argument unfolds about the way the colonizer has been colonized and there's a need to decolonize both the colonizer and colonized. For the decolonial momentum cannot be restricted to the cartography of the South or the East but rather needs to be concerned with all beings in the age liquid modernity (Bauman, 2013) and biopolitics (Foucault, 2010). This can be understood through the analogy of the canary in the mine in which miners focused on the canary to warn them of danger when in reality there were more likely to die from disasters that the canary could not be predict, but it gave them a false sense of security particularly through living connection. Similarly, cell phones are now a non-living connection for humans that is constructed as vital to life, but at what cost. How does this technology in fact own its human?

Chapter 5—*The Pinocchio Effect: Biopolitics and Coloniality*—lays out the analysis of the Pinocchio Effect as a theoretical mechanism to understand the colonial function of US public education. An education that extends beyond the school walls into media production and consumption. Within the Pinocchio Effect, youth are the puppets who are made real through their schooling or resist and become the "jack asses" of U.S. society. During their schooling, youth function as puppets with strings that are visible through their surrounding constraints. These strings are pulled by neoliberal forces, which demand conformity through choice. However, some students pull on the strings and meet resistance from the taut hold, learning the length of their strings of "choice." Youth must conform to the hegemonic demands in order to become "real *boys*" or resist through violence and/or pleasure-seeking actions that are often committed without a critical consciousness of questioning and understanding the larger societal forces; market and consumerist ideology lures them into these behaviors. In this chapter as in the others, examples from the classroom are used to provide a critique of herself while also a critique of the system as reflected by curriculum and human language within and beyond dialogue. The following Chapter 6—*Colonialities and Spiritualities: Voices, Silences, and Experiences in the Classroom*—focuses on colonialities, spiritualities, and beings of youth and educators as part of the *imaginicide* that is occurring in US public education. The call is for language to be seen beyond the technicalization of words and as a form of expression that is intimately connected with spirituality, knowledges, and beings that are oppressed. The rationality of *science* denounces its spiritual core in the name of the reproducible, foisting technoscientific knowledge down the throats of youth and teachers in the name of STEM and "best practice." Schools bow to the religious zealousness toward STEM, which not only allows for epistemicides (Santos, 2007b, 2014; Paraskeva, 2011, 2016a, 2016b, 2017) but also limits science to the boundaries of the standards and test. From the pre-K curriculum that is engineered by the Common Core to its push for informational texts in English Language Arts, educational reform under RTTT points to the *imaginicide* that is occurring within schools, where imagination and the humanities are not just devalued but systematically killed.

The author ends her critical exegesis putting forward a *Decolonial Manifesto for Public Education*. This chapter deepens the previous analysis to ask, "In the moral development of youth, how do seductions and punishments impact how they view themselves and others?" Here personal accounts are used to demonstrate the way lives and media intersect within the classroom and the curriculum of the spirit that often goes unnoticed by the colonial eye. Decolonizing the mind is a process in which educators need to actively enact with their students and colleagues. The final pages of the chapter include a painted montage of what de/colonial education is like today. She draws our attention to the way spiritualities are not always silenced within schools and the ways to the colonial anesthetization that permeates. The book does not conclude but rather she calls for the questions and dialogues to continue within our thoughts and actions as we reflect on our experiences and engage in conscientização, resisting the imaginicide and the colonization of spirituality.

Acknowledgements

Educational processes are always collective. This book does not escape such unquestionable rule. It is my duty here to express my sincere gratitude to all those who have made possible the success of a critically transformative educational political project collectively built on the South Coast of Massachusetts and, among the many objectives achieved, this volume is a worthy example.

References

Ahmad, A. (2008). *In theory*. London: Verso.

Amin, S. (2008) *The world we wish to see. Revolutionary objectives in the twenty-first century*. New York, NY: Monthly Review Press.

Chomsky, N. (1971). *Problems of knowledge and freedom*. New York, NY: The New Press.

Corazza, S. M. (2002). Noologia do currículo: Vagamundo, o problemático, e assentado, o resolvido. *Educação e Realidade, 27*(2), 131–142.

Darder, A. (2012). *Culture and power in the classrooms. Educational foundations for the schooling of bicultural studies*. Boulder, CO: Paradigm Publishers.

DeLeuze, G. (1995). *Negotiations 1972–1990*. New York, NY: Columbia University Press.

Dussel, E. (1995). *The invention of the Americas. Eclipse of the "other" and the myth of modernity*. New York, NY: Continuum.

Fraser, N. (2014). Can society be commodities all way down? Post-Polanyian reflections on capitalist crisis. *Economy and Society, 43*(4), 541–558.

Giroux, H. (2011). *Education and the crisis of public values. Challenging the assault on teachers, students and public education*. New York, NY: Peter Lang.

Grosfoguel, R. (2007). The epistemic decolonial turn: Beyond political economy paradigms. *Cultural Studies, 21*(2–3), 211–223.

Kabou, A. (2013). *E se A Africa se recusar ao desensvolvimento?* Lisbon: Edicoes Pedago.

Latour, B. (2005). *O poder da critica discursos*. Lisbon: Edicoes Pedago.

Marc Ella, J. (2013). *Restituir a historia as sociedades Africanas*. Lisbon: Edicoes Pedago.

Marcuse, H. (1964). *One dimensional man*. Boston, MA: Beacon Press.

Mignolo, W. (2000). *Local histories/global designs: Coloniality, subaltern knowledges and border thinking.* Princeton, NJ: Princeton University Press.

Mignolo, W. (2008). The geopolitcs of knowledge and colonial difference. In M. Morana, E. Dussel, & C. Jauregui (Eds.), *Coloniality at large: Latin America and the postcolonial debate* (pp. 225–258). San Antonio, TX: Duke University Press.

Mignolo, W. (2011a). *The darker side of western modernity: Global futures, decolonial options.* Durham, NC: Duke University Press.

Mignolo, W. (2011b). Epistemic disobedience and the decolonial option: A manifesto. *Transmodernity: Journal of Peripheral Cultural Production of the Luso-Hispanic World, 1*(2), 44–66.

Paraskeva, J. (2011). *Conflicts in curriculum theory: Challenging hegemonic epistemologies.* New York, NY: Palgrave.

Paraskeva, J. (2014). *Conflicts in curriculum theory: Challenging hegemonic epistemologies* (Updated paperback edition). New York, NY: Palgrave.

Paraskeva, J. (2016a). *Curriculum epistemicide: Towards an itinerant curriculum theory.* New York, NY: Routledge.

Paraskeva, J. (2016b). *The curriculum: Whose internationalization?* New York, NY: Peter Lang.

Paraskeva, J. (2017). *Towards a just curriculum theory. The epistemicide.* New York, NY: Routledge.

Pinar, W. (2000). Introduction: Toward the internationalization of curriculum studies. In D. Trueit, Doll Jr., H. Wang, & W. Pinar (Eds.), *The internationalization of curriculum studies* (pp. 1–13). New York, NY: Peter Lang.

Pinar, W. (2004). *What is curriculum theory?* Mahwah, NJ: Lawrence Erlbaum Associates.

Pinar, W. (2013). *Curriculum studies in the United States: Present circumstances, intellectual histories.* New York, NY: Palgrave.

Quijano, A. (2000). Colonialidad del poder y classificacion social. *Journal of World Systems Research, 6*(2), 342–386.

Santos, B. (2004). Para uma sociologia das ausências e uma sociologia das emergências. In B. de Sousa Santos (Ed.), *Conhecimento prudente para uma vida decente: Um discurso sobre as ciencias revisitado* (pp. 735–775). São Paulo: Cortez.

Santos, B. (2006). *The rise of the global left: The world social forum and beyond.* London: Verso.

Santos, B. (2007a). *Another knowledge is possible: Beyond northern epistemologies.* New York, NY: Verso.

Santos, B. (2007b). Beyond abyssal thinking. From global lines to ecologies of knowledges. *Review, XXX*(1), 45–89.

Santos, B. (2008). Globalizations. *Theory, Culture and Society, 23*, 393–399.

Santos, B. (2009). *Epistemologias do sul.* Coimbra: Almedina.

Santos, B., Arriscado, N. J., & Meneses, M. P. (2007). Opening up the canon of knowledge and recognition of difference. In B. de Sousa Santos (Ed.), *Another knowledge is possible: Beyond northern epistemologies* (pp. xix–lxii). New York, NY: Verso.

Seth, S. (2011). Travelling theory: Western knowledge and its Indian object. *International Studies in Sociology of Education, 21*(4), 263–282.

Süssekind, M. L. (2016, September–October). Currículos-como-experiências-vividas: Um relato de embichamento nos cotidianos de uma escola na cidade do Rio de Janeiro. *Currículo Sem Fronteiras, 15*(3), 614–625.

Trueit, D. (2010). Democracy and conversation. In D. Trueit, W. Doll Jr., H. Wang, & W. Pinar (Eds.), *The internationalization of curriculum studies* (pp. ix–xvii). New York, NY: Peter Lang.

Todorova, M. (1997). *Imagining the Balkans.* Oxford: Oxford University Press.

Tse Tung, M. (2007). Oppose book worship. In S. Žižek (Ed.), *Slavoj Žižek presents Mao on practice and contradiction* (pp. 43–51). London: Verso.

João M. Paraskeva
Series Editor

Acknowledgements

Writing this book was an act of political and intellectual resistance but also of hope. It is a product of my education not only within school but beyond, which was supplied by the love of my family. My Gram has shown me how to live with a heart that listens and laughs, accepting others for who they are and always trying to see the *other* stories. My mother revealed the incredible responsibility and joy of being an educator, and my father taught me to stop and hear nature and animals. My sister who, as we grew up, I always admired for her gregariousness and leadership. Finally, to my nephews, Jack and Conor, who, as I watch them grow and discover, teach me how much I have forgotten to hear, see, and feel. We must never forget to color outside the lines or to think beyond words. Theirs and my educational experience helped me see the *imaginicide* occurring in education.

Freire quotes Antonio Machado, claiming, 'we make the way by walking,' but I would add through dialectical listening. For that, I would like to thank my colleagues in this struggle, especially April who helped me edit and Dom and Carmelia who dialogued with me. I am also thankful for my students whom I shared much of my dissertation topic with and who confirmed for me through their affirmation and questions that I was writing a dialogue that needed to be heard—that silence has been growing for too long.

I owe gratitude to Dr. João Paraskeva, whose intellectual passion confounded me as a master's student and whose determination has inspired and driven me to a never-ending conclusion of my studies. Your leadership in navigating the "river" of these ideological struggles has been appreciated. This piece is part of a political and intellectual struggle for envisioning another education in which we fight against the *Pinocchio Effect*.

Figures

CHAPTER 1

Colonial Heart and Silenced Spiritualities

> Our humanity as well as our particular interests and ideals require us to resist and to fight. Through all this experience, we face a conflict between two conditions of our humanity that are just as important as the conflicting demands we place on connection. We need to engage in a particular social and cultural world. Freedom comes from engagement as well as from connection. However, every such engagement threatens to become a surrender: to reduce us from authors to puppets. Thus, we seem forced to choose, at every turn, between an engagement that both frees and enslaves us and a holding back, by mental reservation if not by outward rebellion. This holding back preserves our independence only by wasting its substance. Engagement, wholehearted if not single-minded, without surrender, is what we need.
>
> UNGER (2007, p. 33)

∵

Rise. *Rise.*
Kneel. *Kneel.* *Kneel.* *Kneel....Kneel...kneel..kneel.kneel............*
Rise.
The rhythm continues a painful beat of human bodies and souls, replacing the biological reflex that had stopped.
Kneel.

There I was with her. Her lips painted a deep red. Her eyes clogged with black mascara. The tiny wings of her eyeliner, accenting her eyes. Her personality so clearly painted. Her tan skin lightened with pale powder, and her fake nails stretched out on cold hands. Hands that had frozen at sixteen years. Talia.[1] I crossed myself and stood up to face the world again. Father, mother, sister, brother, aunts, uncles, vovó .... Her mother had lost custody of this beautiful little girl her freshmen year, but it had been an intermittent heartbeat of custody anyway. Her aunt was there explaining to the mother who people were. The man in front of me her school counselor, Mr. X.

 | DOI: 10.1163/9789004416048_001

Rise.

I couldn't look back.

The girl who owned the room and had been full of such life was boxed up.

"She spent a good amount of time with him," said the aunt, smiling genteelly in reference to Mr. X.

The little sister smiled impishly. "Yeah, she always talked about Mr. X and having to go to your office ... A LOT." She wore a sun dress and seemed oblivious to the reality of her sister's body encased in a coffin behind me. I knew she wasn't, but, in her seven year old mind, she was dealing with the loss in her own way. We laughed—an off key note in this dirge of suffering. The sobs of family and friends added a refrain of pain.

"I'm so sorry for your loss. I was her freshmen English teacher at Clayton."

They shook my hand and thanked me. I wanted to say that I had failed Talia. I had tried to reach her, but I hadn't reached hard enough .... It was all I had at that time. But, you always know that you could have done more. Her kindhearted vovó with soft hands grasped mine twofold and blessed me. In her sagacity, she knew that I needed that because, as I turned from her, I was caught off guard by a loving assault. Arms wrapped around my body tightly, and I heard sobbing on my shoulder, Carlos. I rocked him as if he were a baby. His chest crushed against mine, and his head cocooned against me, the tears seeping into my jacket. My own eyes full of tears suppressed as I looked out at my children.

"She's safe now," I crooned to him. *Please shelter her, Father. Care for her. In the name of the Father, Son, and Holy Ghost.* I prayed.

I was thankful for my students' arms that quickly pulled me into another hug. I was feeling the weight of guilt for not fighting harder for Talia. *Three dollars a hit, less than a grande iced latte, less than a gallon of milk, less than a gallon of gas.* It is cheaper to leave your body than to experience life. Power surrounds this coloniality with modernity's productions and consumptions. She consumed and was consumed. She was marked as deviant, as a problem student. More arms encircled me and then a tap on my shoulder.

"Do you remember me?" asked a young African American man.

I looked at him unsure, but, then, the voice and the smile hit me. I grinned, "Of course I do! How are you? What have you been up to?" Ricky—expelled at 14 for doing drugs in my class. For three years, I have regretted being so naïve as to report him. I didn't think about the fact that he would be expelled. I unconsciously knew it, but my response was perfunctory; drugs were against school rules. I didn't think that they would expel a freshman. I didn't think .... I naively assumed that he would get help even though I knew .... I knew of Zero Tolerance, but he was my first sickening experience with it as a teacher.

Youth are excluded for social problems that schools fail to address and results in labeling them deviant and legitimizes their exclusion. The automatization and systematic exclusion is beyond commonsense; it's hegemonic. When I hear on my way to work that it's *new* to not throw somebody in jail when he or she goes to the police station for help with drugs,[2] then I wonder: when did U.S. society ever accept that it was okay to throw someone in jail for asking for help? When I read "drug free school zone," while the nurse hands out little white cups of Ritalin and kids come in on anxiety and other medications just to *be* in this safe and drug free environment, I have to wonder how and what hegemony has invisibilized through the legitimization of some drugs for the quieting of the body while criminalizing others ... youth who are forced out of school as the waste of society. Santos (2014) claims that "[t]he epistemology of trash cannot be discarded as easily as the trash to which it refers" (p. 149). He wasn't referring to youth, but his words speak to youth who are physically trashed from schools through suspensions and expulsions, and whose spiritualities and identities are trashed through oppressive curriculum and disciplined pedagogies. I always found it interesting that refuse the noun and refuse the verb are spelled the same way. Refuse to conform, and you become refuse. Popkewitz (2002) explains, "[t]he deviant child is the child who does not learn the alchemy, does not follow the conduct of the alchemic problem solving, and thus needs to be rescued through better management and self-management" (p. 265). His discussion of education as alchemy highlights the way that education reform and the treatment of knowledge as static coupled with child psychology transforms disciplinary knowledge into little jewels of knowledge for students to obtain. Students who fail to buy into this are marked as deviant. Failure to buy makes you an enemy to the market, and you are excluded in order to be marketed now as a deviant product of society.

One "deviant" was cold in her coffin. Another was standing before me. He was all grown up but still such a little boy, looking for someone to understand him beyond the drugs and give him space for self-actualization—a space of spirituality where others are there with him to listen and care.

"I'm still going to night school."

"Good. I'm glad. I was hoping you were back in school." His mother died in bed with him when he was in elementary school. His grandmother sees in him that memory. His father forgets to pick him up because he can't forget either. His friend's explanation, not mine; it's her understanding of the truth. However, I felt these conflicts within his being when he was my student. I still feel the same spirit from him as I did three years ago—that longing for love and the need for the numbness that comes from a hit. One of my students told me he posted on Facebook the night of the funeral, "About to do something really stupid." He was taken to the hospital not too long after that.

Three dollars a hit, less than a grande iced latte, less than a gallon of milk, less than a gallon of gas ... way less than the $25 copay to see a therapist, never mind the gas to get there.

I left that funeral and passed athletic fields on my way home, thinking of my evaluation comment that I should try to attend more sporting events as well as the disdain for when the kids call me "Mama J"—Yet, Coach is welcome. Patriarchy welcome.

I was thinking of the disrespect of their grief. As part of honoring April as poetry month, we had daily haikus. On the morning announcements, two haikus written by students for Talia were read, without even saying her name, just in "memorial of a former student who died." How about saying we've lost three students to heroin in two months, and this one was 16 years old while her 20-something boyfriend watched her die, taking her to the hospital an hour later DOA?

No. I wasn't basking in the sun of the baseball field like some of my colleagues this Sunday. I had to kneel before death. They were clapping for life, while ignoring the dead bodies that were invisiblized by their consumption of joy. There were many students on that field who they were clapping for that were experiencing realms of pain that were hidden by the roar of the game as well.

I say this out of anger and sorrow. I recognize the incredible power that athletics can have for my youth, as can drama and music. I have seen youth who were failing and headed down a path of self-destruction become part of the football team in their junior year, finally finding the connection, the spirituality, that they had been missing. When I see the football team huddle on the gym floor at pep rally in preparation for their Thanksgiving game, I see the connection with each other and self. While others engage in the ritual because it is expected, some are still anesthetized and disconnected. Everything has multiple layers, and, easy as it is to dichotomize, reality demands that we feel silence, not just listen. A youth passes out on the floor in the midst of passing time in the hallway, but students keep walking by. Some fixated on their phones, others just walking, and some with a sideways glance of curiosity. No one stops. Just walk on by. When a well-liked and involved youth can punch out another youth causing him to have seizures and walk over him to return to class, we have to wonder what has allowed detachment from violence, detachment from others?

Every day teaching feels like working in a pediatric cancer ward. You see youth with cancers growing in them—drugs, alcohol, sex, depression, apathy, abuse, anger, etc. But, in some ways, it seems more frustrating than working in a cancer ward because I can't excise or radiate the memory and pain of sexual abuse or neglect. I can't kill it. I can listen and soothe, but my heart is the only medication I can administer with my bleeding ears.

What do you do when they tell you that they found their father after he had killed himself? Or, that their father put his foot on their face and beat them? Or, that their mother abandoned them in a house without food, but the child asks for food for her pet before asking for food for her? We can report it and file under a 51A, but what does that do? Does it heal or just metastasize the pain? How much can we hear and see before we go mad from an inability to heal so many?

Giroux (2015) referred to guidance teachers, and, although he was referring to guidance counselors, it struck me because counselors are often barricaded in their offices due to bureaucratic structures that have conditioned them as paper pushers, while many teachers are guiding, leading, listening, fighting with students—although the new evaluation system is trying to mold us as paper pushers as well. Popkewitz (2015) said, "[t]he mission of the profession of teaching is calling for the teacher, 'like psychotherapists, social workers pastors, and organization developers' who work directly on other humans, is 'to transform minds, enrich, human capacities and change behavior'" (Cohen, 2005, p. 280). I was trained as a teacher in child and adolescent development in order to provide me with the scientific rationale for a child's learning and to help me better my teaching. Where's the humanitarian and pedagogical reflection? Where's conscientização and consciencism? Where are the dialectical engagements with spirits not numbers? Children are studied and produced through teaching as a means to an end. However, as Nkrumah (1964) explained, "[t]he cardinal ethical principle of philosophical consciencism is to treat each man as an end in himself and not merely as a means" (p. 95). Yet, educators are taught psychology to understand students' minds for learning objectives; we are taught methods. A scientific method to produce results. But, how can I teach a corpse? How can I teach a zombie? How I can teach someone who is crying? My words are drowned out by the pain of their lives. Guidance, as I have seen as a student and teacher, is often the Circumlocution Office[3] in a Dickensian manner that is very much the epitome of bureaucracy. Tons of papers go into guidance, leaving counselors and students drowning. Need a guidance counselor? Take a number, and we will call you down. Teachers though .... We have no secretary, and our doors are always open.

Teach your lessons, prepare your evaluation binders, take new courses to demonstrate academic growth, document evidence, document your SMART goals, monitor your DDMs, restrain students, monitor hallways, write curriculum, counsel students, attend their events, run after school tutoring for free, run professional development, call parents, email parents, memorize fifteen

IEPs, teach 30 students while others have 4, care for 600 students, run 150 senior thesis projects .... Run, care, document, run, care, document, run, care, document. There are more elements to a teacher's life, but really it feels as if our bureaucratic responsibility is to document and our ethical responsibility is to care, and thus we are first class marathon runners trying to meet all of the emotional and intellectual needs of our students. We hear the chant of rigor and college and career readiness but are rarely thrown a water bottle of aid. This is the state of public education in the U.S.

In the U.S. educational system, words of rigor, 21st century learning, college and career readiness as well as competition hide the underside of these words—the effects on youth and teachers, the underclass of U.S. education. The objectification and commodification of knowledge(s) works to deny students and teachers critical engagement with their consciousness and identities. This commodification of knowledge(s) is part of a market-driven mentality to ensure that youth are college and career ready as mandated by Common Core. The leaders of the Common Core, National Governors Association (NGO), the Council of Chief State School Officers (CCSSO), and Achieve Inc., claim, "[t]he race is on among nations to create knowledge fueled innovation economies" (Jerald, 2008, p. 5). Youth are commodities, human capital, ready to be molded and exploited, which are processes of colonialism.

Neoliberalism continues and adds to the colonial legacy as can be seen in this age of liquid modernity (Bauman, 2013) in which globalization has meant the rise of standardization and colonization by the global elite, which includes individuals/corporations, such as Koch, Gates, Walton, etc. Knowledge is being produced under the crusader's aegis of No Child Left Behind (NCLB), Race to the Top (RTTT), and now Every Student Succeeds Act (ESSA), but the sanctity of these standards and high expectations must be further analyzed for what these values inculcate and silence. Coloniality of being (cf. Quijano, 2000; Mignolo, 2002) helps to frame youth within educational policies, such as school choice, Common Core, Zero Tolerance (ZTP), and English-only policies. These reign in schools under the pretense of being "for the children," working to provide *equal* standards of college and career readiness without thoughts to equity and access. However, this is a pedagogy of entrapment (Macedo, 1994) that masquerades as choice; it is a pedagogy of coloniality. Instead, critical transformative leaders need to be working towards a decolonial pedagogy that engages youth and educators in a learning process for social and cognitive justice.

Freire (2009) wrote that "[e]ducation is suffering from narration sickness" (p. 71). In an age of scripted teaching, standardized tests, and homogenized curriculum, educators can recognize the veracity of Freire's words; ironically, some U.S. educators reduce Freire's work to mere methods of critical pedagogy (Aronowitz, 1992). The conversation in educations functions as a narration of things that students, teachers, and administrators need to do as part of these educational reform policies that have been semantically reframed as "for the children" in order to hide their colonial heart. This colonial heart is connected to the colonization of the mind and soul in public education that appears benevolent, normalized through the curriculum of coloniality. Coloniality can be defined as "long-standing patterns of power that emerged as a result of colonialism, but that define culture, labor, intersubjective relations, and knowledge production well beyond the strict limits of colonial administrations" (Maldonado-Torres, 2007, p. 243). Although reductive, to help frame the argument, three types of coloniality have been theorized: (1) coloniality of power (cf. Quijano, 2000) as well as (2) coloniality of being (cf. Mignolo, 2002) and (3) coloniality of knowledge (cf. Mignolo, 2002). Maldonado-Torres (2007) attempts to succinctly provide an overview of these terms:

> Coloniality of power—complexities of exploitation and domination
> Coloniality of being—impact on language and experience
> Coloniality of knowledge—influence on the production of knowledge. (p. 242)

These brief definitions provide a platform for a deeper analysis of the complexities as applied not only to the traditionally theorized colonial spaces, such as Latin America, Africa, Oceania, and Asia as well as the indigenous populations of North America, but also to the often unnoticed or "unacceptable" colonial spaces within the U.S. We need to reframe the discussion as colonialities, instead of coloniality, in order to situate the analysis of coloniality within the numerous contexts that it can be seen or unseen. This is not to dismiss and/or occlude the atrocities and oppression of those who were subjected to these processes of colonization and to re-center the imperial U.S. However, to confine the analysis of colonialism within those traditionally seen parameters is a failure to go to the roots of colonialism. A child is not born a colonialist; he or she can be born into privilege, but that child is mis/educated to become a weapon of colonialism. The first lesson that I ever taught used a quote from *The Importance of Being Earnest* in which Lady Bracknell tells Jack,

> I do not approve of anything that tampers with natural ignorance. Ignorance is like a delicate exotic fruit; touch it and the bloom is gone. The whole theory of modern education is radically unsound. Fortunately in England, at any rate, education produces no effect whatsoever. If it did, it

> would prove a serious danger to the upper classes, and probably lead to acts of violence in Grosvenor Square. (Wilde, 1899, p. 96)

Lady Bracknell's words provide an inlet into the rationality of the dominant class's fear of education and the necessity to control it to maintain their power and status.

During the Industrial Revolution in the U.S., the primary reason that children left school was the need to work (Kliebard, 2004). The factories were dangerous places in which people were maimed, killed, subjected to unhealthy jobs, such as the "kiss of death" in which workers had to suck the thread through the shuttle inhaling lint and dust every 2 to 3 minutes, generally after two years operatives became sick (MacLaury, 2004). The kiss of modernity was one that educated the masses into the myth of meritocracy to only find that they had been sold into a system of servitude. As Melvin Dubofsky (1961) noted, they "exchanged the stagnation of a feudal society for the bondage of an industrial system. The riches of the new world were frequently a mirage, and the dream of American opportunity led often to the sweatshop, where laborers slept on upswept floors littered with work refuse while their worktables doubled as dining tables" (as quoted by MacLaury, 2004). This narrative has continued to the present in which we must recognize that the U.S. narrative is ironically not the narrative of the U.S. The former is the colonizer's curriculum and the latter is the silenced experiences of the subaltern as already pointed to by Howard Zinn's (2001) *A People's History of the United States*.

The U.S. tends to hold up a gleaming identity of freedom and equality to the world, proclaiming its superiority, but, as my students once asked, if almost one in four children live in poverty, "Why aren't there any [Save the Children] ads for the United States?" The utopian sanctity of the mythical U.S. thwarts the recognition and legitimation of oppression and coloniality (cf. Quijano, 2000; Mignolo, 2010; Dussel, 2005; Maldonado-Torres, 2007; Walsh, 2002). Colonialism and colonialities are based on a highly-racialized system of power as numerous scholars have noted, such as Quijano (2000), Césaire (2000), Fanon (1963), Mignolo (2010), Maldonado-Torres (2007), Walsh (2002), Wynter (2001), Darder (2015), and many others.

Racism has not dissipated in the shine of modernity, but rather it is hegemonic and legitimizes through neoliberalism as colorblind choice. Referring to the state response to the U.S. anti-racist movements after WWII, Omi and Winant (2014) explain how reforms were used to "substitute a system of racial *hegemony* for the previous system of racial *domination*" (p. 149). The racialized power of neoliberalism can be felt in schools through high-stakes testing, Zero Tolerance policies, and English-only policies. Rosa and Rosa (2015) describe how these equality alternatives in education, such as No Children Left Behind, are structures within a racialized narrative, terming them as 'cathartic policies' that are "designed not only to expand the wealth of the financial elite, but also to serve the existential function of redirecting and purging deep-seated public anger and dodging culpability" (p. 20). Race is at the core of colonial matrix of power as a mechanism of class exploitation but so is gender. If these reforms were examined through a lens of gender and Omi and Winant's statement was changed to a system of gender *hegemony* for the previous system of gender *domination*, we can see many reforms that inculcate hegemonic oppression through gender, such as through wage inequality and unpaid labor as well as the gendered division of the education workforce. The construction, manipulation, and exploitation of race and gender are critical to neoliberalism to frame choices of oppression, which ultimately is framed within a class analysis. hooks (2000) highlights how we can be taken in by the way the State can make a spectacle of race and gender, so we forget about class, but there is a need for us "all [to] be paying attention to class, using race and gender to understand and explain its new dimensions" (p. 7). The analysis of class takes us into the dark mechanisms of colonialities and colonialism that are hidden in the chiaroscuro shading of the world.

Race, gender, and class—nor should sexuality and religion be neglected—must all speak together about the colonial power network but not in reductive binaries. The detrimental effects of colonialism and colonialities are not only present in the global East and South. The challenge is to understand the way colonialism and colonialities can be understood in different contexts without trying to bind it in neat geopolitical or geographical parameters. The cartography needs to be deepened to understand who the lines define and who defines the lines. I must situate this research as not working to dismiss the importance of analyzing and fighting against colonialism and colonialities within other countries, but this study focuses on how colonialities can be understood in modern U.S. public education.

Fundamentally, I'm against putting these intellectuals into boxes, but, to help present the tools for this cartography, my theoretical sphere swirls with the concepts of anticolonial intellectuals (Nkrumah, 1964; Freire, 2009; Cabral, 1979; Machel, 1975; Sartre, 2004; Santos, 2005; Macedo, 2000), decolonial theorists (Césaire, 2000; Dussel, 2005; Grosfoguel, 2010; Maldonado-Torres, 2007; McClintock, 1995; Mignolo, 2010; Quijano, 2000; Walsh, 2002) as well as critical and post-structural scholars within and beyond Western epistemologies (Darder, 1991; Giroux, 2012; Gramsci, 1971; hooks, 1992; McLaren, 1993; Valenzuela, 1999; Wynter, 2001). To reiterate, my intention is not to box them within a specific theoretical label, but rather I am mapping them out this way as a form of theoretical systematization.

With this theoretical canvas, I analyze the impact of colonialities (Quijano, 2000; Mignolo, 2010; Dussel, 2005) within U.S. public education by examining the learning experiences that influence teachers' and students' spiritualties, affecting the construction and oppression of their identities. In order to support this analysis, I examine the complexities of the wrangle between colonialism and colonialities as well as how colonialities of being function within U.S. schools to create coloniality as a hegemonic philosophy of praxis that is perceived as liberatory instead of another oppressive system. Furthermore, I analyze the contested spaces in which spiritualties as connected with knowledges and languages intersect as a result of hidden, written, and performed curriculum. Through the use of decolonial autoethnography and decolonial processes, such as conscientização (Freire, 2009) and consciencism (Nkrumah, 1964), I examine my pedagogical role in colonizing and/or decolonizing the classroom, which functions as a political arena as well as a critical space of praxis in order to reveal how realities and knowledges are made nonexistent—an epistemic blindness and privilege.

This process of resistance, reproduction, production in which the system legitimizes and delegitimizes students for commodification through standardization and criminalization is what I will frame as the Pinocchio Effect. Although I will conceptualize this more in the theoretical framework, the Pinocchio Effect is a process by which some youth are trained to embody market values in order to become "real" as Pinocchio did, but others who resist are marked as deviant and are sold[4] into prison—consider the prison-industrial complex (cf. Hartnett, 2008; Meiners, 2010) and school-to-prison pipeline (cf. Advancement Project, 2010; Kim, Losen, & Hewitt, 2010)—or poverty (cf. Wacquant, 2009) as the necessary societal waste of U.S. capitalism. This is part of the colonization of youth.

Therefore, within U.S. public education, how can the effects of colonialities of being (Mignolo, 2002) and the construction and oppression of students' and teachers' identities be understood through the experiences that influence teachers' and students' spiritualties? These contested spaces in the classroom are fraught with challenges and contradictions that pedagogues must not only confront daily but also analyze and decolonize or else they shift into becoming trainers, doling out the knowledge and behaviors that are deemed legitimate.

Notes

1 In this book, names in the autoethnographic portions are all pseudonyms.

2 This was the case in Gloucester, Massachusetts. Chief Campanello wrote, "Any addict who walks into the police station with the remainder of their drug equipment (needles, etc) or drugs and asks for help will NOT be charged. Instead we will walk them through the system toward detox and recovery. We will assign them an 'angel' who will be their guide through the process. Not in hours or days, but on the spot" (https://www.facebook.com/GloucesterPoliceDepartment/posts/697808590329673).

3 "The Circumlocution Office was (as everybody knows without being told) the most important Department under Government. No public business of any kind could possibly be done at any time without the acquiescence of the Circumlocution Office. Its finger was in the largest public pie, and in the smallest public tart. It was equally impossible to do the plainest right and to undo the plainest wrong without the express authority of the Circumlocution Office. If another Gunpowder Plot had been discovered half an hour before the lighting of the match, nobody would have been justified in saving the parliament until there had been half a score of boards, half a bushel of minutes, several sacks of official memoranda, and a family-vault full of ungrammatical correspondence, on the part of the Circumlocution Office" (Dickens, 1868, p. 151).

4 Sometimes literally sold as was the case with Judge Ciavarella and his colleague Conahan (Hamill & Urbina, 2009). See www.nytimes.com/2009/02/13/us/13judge.html

CHAPTER 2

Need for Decolonial Autoethnography in Education

No Child Left Behind (NCLB) and Race to the Top (RTTT) have brought a wave of "innovative" and "research-based" practices that narrate the ways U.S. public education should run, but a critique of this research is needed—informed not only by views from the outside, but from those influenced most by these top-down policies. Creative destruction (Harvey, 2005) and shock doctrine (Klein, 2007) are at play within U.S. public education and its policies. Fear is fed to the masses and research-based solutions are applied that are "unbiased" scientific cures, which fail to value the indigenous knowledges and expertise of the educators, youth, and communities. Before I unfold my choice of research methodology, I must flag that the quest for legitimized research and methodology is one of white patriarchal privilege, and the fact that most of the authors whom I cite are white can in fact reveal the color of research in social sciences.

Tuhiwai Smith (1999) discusses the scope of traditional Western imperialist scientific research that cannibalized the indigenous cultures and knowledges for research. Anthropologists and scientists were the 'scholars,' which objectifies the 'Other' of these studies. Educators, who are under the microscope, also feel this as they are supposed to glean the knowledge of educational research experts in adherence to the national mantra of research based practices, but those research-based practices tunnel the mind to only see a heteropatriarchal capitalist vision that excludes other ways of being, seeing, and knowing. Smith (1999) claims that "[t]he problem is not just that positivist science is well established institutionally and theoretically, but that it has a connectedness at a common sense level with the rest of society who, generally speaking, take for granted the hegemony of its methods and leadership in the search for knowledge" (p. 189). Similarly seen in U.S. public education, research is something given to us as educators to learn and implement.

Authentic ways of researching are silenced. Knowledge only counts from above. We often mirror this patriarchal knowledge production to our students and continue this oppressive production of knowledge, failing to recognize the ways children are the best researchers. For instance, as I watched my nephews play on the beach with other children, the children experimented and tested things out, observing each other. If one experiment in building a castle fails, the others watch and apply their knowledge to change the consistency of the sand. In schooling, does an educator not engage in research every time he or she prepares a lesson? How about as they scour the internet for the best

 | DOI: 10.1163/9789004416048_002

resources by analyzing and evaluating them, or when they are at lunch and listen to their colleagues' pedagogical stories, evaluating what worked well and what didn't? Beyond the pedagogy of the official curriculum, we research ways of being for a pedagogy of humanity. This "we" is comprised of critical educators. Despite the rhetoric of bad teachers, there are many of us who fight every day for and with our students. We act as ethnographers and psychologists constantly listening, observing, evaluating, and reflecting. We are researchers, but we are public artists. We take what we learn and create a living space for our students in which we learn and transform as well. We must continue to decolonize research methodologies and fight for processes and products that speak with the work that we do as public pedagogues as a form of political art.

Research needs to be a dialectical process that engages all stakeholders in a dialogue that values their voices in policies that shape their reality, pushing toward a critical transformative education. This dialectical and dialogical research is a process of meaning-making and analysis, which I will be participating in through the use of what I have coined as *decolonial autoethnography*. Freire (2009) wrote that "[t]hey cannot sloganize the people, but must enter into dialogue with them, so that people's empirical knowledge of reality, nourished by the leaders' critical knowledge, gradually becomes transformed into knowledge of the causes of reality" (p. 134). Empirical data too often speaks in schools today without recognizing that human individuals are the source of those numbers and have identities, which cannot be negated by numbers or policies that ignore the social and psychological realities of both teachers and students, starving their spiritual needs.

Furthermore, educational research is often conducted but not made available for discussion with youth, educators, and guardians. If it returns, it returns as an instruction manual on best practices or as a textbook of scripted knowledge. Smith (1999) flags "[t]here are diverse ways of disseminating knowledge and of ensuring that research reaches the people who have helped make it" (p. 15). Academic research is increasingly being produced in different forms such as drama (c.f. Saldaña, 2005), novel (c.f. Leavy, 2011), and poetry (c.f. Prendergast, Leggo, & Sameshima, 2009), graphic novel (c.f. Sousanis, 2015), etc. To help unravel the complexities of spirituality under the current neoliberal colonizing standards-based testing regime, my methodology draws from critical, feminist, and decolonial terrains, using decolonial autoethnography with conscientização and consciencism in order to analyze my experiences and the discourses around and within me.

Autoethnography is, in a way, a response to the colonizing forces of research. Researchers often go to study someone in order to obtain more knowledge for themselves and to advance science. However, autoethnography calls for the researchers to be put into a vulnerable position in which their own knowledges and experiences are subject to analysis and questioning. For me as an educator and a researcher, this is crucial because too often research speaks about teachers and students without speaking with teachers and students. My locus of enunciation is in an English Language Arts secondary classroom—a classroom as noted earlier that is not contained in four walls but rather represents the political forces that environ me, my students, and my colleagues—which privileges me and curses me. I am subjected to research that pours down from corporate forces, such as the Bill and Melinda Gates Foundation, and *state* forces, such as the National Governors Association (NGO), the Council of Chief State School Officers (CCSSO), and Achieve Inc., and I am also the mercenary for that research, enforcing it within my classroom. My analysis must delve into a decolonial praxis that engages in the process of decolonial theory and practice. Autoethnography helps create a decolonial space for the analysis of this praxis as well as an avenue to understand how I interact with and how I am in/formed by colonialities and spiritualities.

1 Understanding the Foundations of Autoethnography

Autoethnography provides an opportunity to engage in research that is both enunciatory and liberatory for the researcher and for stakeholders when it is used to challenge assumptions and expose underlying sources of hegemonic power and reproduction of inequity. The ritual interactions and colonizing forces that educators and students' experience can be analyzed through conscientização that "refers to learning to perceive social, political and economic contradictions, and to take action against the oppressive elements of reality" (Freire, 2009, p. 35). Nkrumah (1964) describes how "[c]onsciencism, by avoiding the assertion of the sole reality of matter, prepares itself for the painless recognition of the objectivity of different types of being. Indeed, the conception of dialectic is itself connected with a recognition of different types of being" (p. 90). Acknowledging my subjectivity, I will use Freire's (2009) concept of conscientização and Nkrumah's (1964) consciencism to analyze how my emotions, past, perceptions interact with my words and paint a picture of *a* reality, which is a limitation not only of autoethnography but of any research. Although there is a danger in narration, as Said (1994) draws our attention to, "[t]he power to narrate, or to block other narratives from forming and emerging, is very important to culture and imperialism" (p. xiii). However, as an educator, the bigger power is the un-story; those stories that are never told and are never thought to be told.

Teachers consume, produce, reproduce, and resist stories all day. They carry them with them and their students do as well. We shoulder these and due to the quantitative push through Common Core, Race to the Top, and No Child Left Behind, the stories being told are not our stories. The indigenous of U.S. public education, educators and students, are left to be painted as lazy, dangerous, and re/formable. I remember talking to a colleague's mother who worked at an "underperforming" school in Fall River, and she commented on how the State brought in the men in black suits to fix the school, discounting the indigenous knowledge of veteran teachers who have been there and whose knowledge has value. It is easy to start to inferiorize yourself and to consider yourself unprofessional. Educators must approach their experiences with double vision to see the micro-politics of their realities with youth but also the macro-politics.

Boylorn (2013) discusses Alice Walker's (1983) notion of double vision and how she "use[s] autoethnography to see [her]self twice, talking back to [her]self and others at the same time. Autoethnography is particularly helpful because it is a doubled storytelling form and moves from self to culture and back again" (p. 174). This is engagement with conscientização and consciencism. Ellis, Adams, and Bochner (2010) describe how autoethnography confronts this subjectivity instead of hiding from it. Denzin and Lincoln (2011) add that "personal experience reflects the flow of thoughts and meanings persons have in their immediate situations .... We study the representations of experience, not experience itself" (p. 417). My words do not convey the only truth. These are memories and moments that I analyzed in order to unravel the contradictions and flaws within my own practices and consciousness, attempting to create a decolonial space for myself and my students. This connects to Denzin's (2006) claim that "research practices are performative, pedagogical, and political ... by enacting a way of seeing and being, it challenges, contests, or endorses the official, hegemonic ways of seeing and representing the other" (p. 209). Performativity "requires the performer of personal narrative to identify and critique the power relations rooted in the sociohistorical contexts of discourse that are occurring in the act of performing personal stories" (Spry, 2001, p. 718). In autoethnography, performativity is a crucial aspect when considering it as a part of a decolonial methodology. This involves understanding the sociohistorical roots of the present because "[a] mind that is adequately sensitive to the needs and occasions of the present actuality will have the liveliest of motives for interest in the background of the present, and will never have to hunt for a way back because it will never have lost connection" (Dewey, 2004, p. 73). A critique of the sociohistorical context and analysis of power relations within a colonial matrix complexifies the dialectical nature of the classroom(s) of which I am a part. Autoethnography "embraces uncertainty and emotionality, and it attempts to make sense of the ways in which our identities are raced, gendered, aged, sexualized, and classed. Researchers impact what we see, do, and say. Autoethnography thus breaks the silences embedded in traditional research; the method conceives of humans as possibly-patterned-but-unpredictable beings and not static and stoic machines (Soukup, 1992; Ellis, 1991)" (Jones, Adam, & Ellis, 2013, p. 35). Autoethnography allows me to engage in questioning ways of seeing, hearing, feeling, and being as I decolonize my pedagogy and ask, how does spirituality manifest under the current neoliberal colonizing standards-based testing regime?

Serving as an educator under this regime means constantly having to question my role in facilitating knowledge production and epistemicides. Furthermore, Sousa Santos (2014) explains how "the result of the destruction of all alternative knowledges that could eventually question such privilege [is] a product of … epistemicide. The destruction of knowledge is not an epistemological artifact without consequences. It involves the destruction of the social practices and the disqualification of the social agents that operate according to such knowledge" (p. 153). The killing of knowledge has a price beyond the present. Paraskeva (2011) discusses how an epistemicide occurs within the curriculum and how it a "human rights issue" (p. 11). As an educator, I attempt to decolonize and rupture these epistemicides (Santos, 2007b, 2014; Paraskeva, 2011, 2016a, 2016b, 2017).

My mind is a contested space in which I must use conscientização to critique my presents, pasts, and futures. I could have used autobiographical writing, narrative inquiry, etc. for this study, but autoethnography provides a framework for me to engage in understanding the dialectics of coloniality of being and spirituality. Auto ethnographers must take seriously Chang's (2013) question: "Does the knowledge that autoethnography produces privilege the perspectives and experiences of academics? If the reaches of academics stop at their own worlds, who will bring out the perspectives of non-academic persons to publications from which all can learn?" (p. 120). Through this study, I do not intend to explore what privileges my perspective to the exclusion of others, but I intend to use my writing and analysis as the beginning of a much-needed dialogue amongst educators, parents, administrators, politicians, and youth. The process of writing and describing my experiences is in a way about decolonizing. As Richardson (2000b) explains, "[w]riting as a method of inquiry, then, provides a research practice through which we can investigate how we construct the world, ourselves, and others, and how standard objectifying practices of social sciences unnecessarily limit us and social science" (p. 926). My intention is to craft a narrative that integrates theory and experience in a way that crystallizes for the public an understanding of colonialities of being as well as spiritualities within U.S. public education.

There are several different types of autoethnography, including performance, interpretive, evocative, and analytical. Ellis (1999) describes how in autoethnography, "concrete action, dialogue, emotion, embodiment, spirituality, and selfconsciousness are featured, appearing as relational and institutional stories impacted by history and social structure, which themselves are dialectically revealed through actions, feelings, thoughts, and language" (p. 673). Interpretive autoethnography "allows the researcher to take up each person's life in its immediate particularity and to ground the life in its historical moment. We move back and forth in time … interrogating the historical, cultural, and biographical conditions that move the person to experience the events being studied" (Denzin, 2014, p. x). Evocative autoethnography or he*art*-ful autoethnography involves writing with passion to cultivate emotion in the reader, to connect with them (Ellis, 1999). Analytical autoethnography entails "(1) complete member researcher (CMR) status, (2) analytic reflexivity, (3) narrative visibility of the researcher's self, (4) dialogue with informants beyond the self, and (5) commitment to theoretical analysis" (Anderson, 2006, p. 378). Anderson (2006) conceptualizes analytical autoethnography as a way of bridging the gap more with traditional social research.

Finally, performance autoethnography stems from performative ethnography and involves the analysis of the dialogical body. Spry (2001) explains how "[t]he purpose of dialogical performance is to embody an intimate understanding of self's engagement with another within a specific sociocultural context. In autoethnographic performance self is other. Dialogical engagement in performance encourages the performer to interrogate the political and ideological contexts and power relations between self and other, and self as other" (p. 716). Evocative and performative are best aligned to conscientização and conscien-cism and encompass what analysis of decolonial pedagogy would need to be or perhaps be better conceptualized as decolonial autoethnography.

2 Mapping Decolonial Autoethnography

When we write and tell our stories, we are not only evoking emotions, but, through performing, we can engage in a decolonial analysis of our bodies as text. As Spry (2001) states, "[t]he autoethnographic text emerges from the researcher's bodily standpoint as she is continually recognizing and interpreting the residue traces of culture inscribed upon her hide from interacting with others in contexts" (p. 711). Autoethnography is research done through and by the body; it cannot be disengaged from you. Stacy describes how autoethnography involves "telling our stories [which] is a way for us to be present to each other; the act provides a space for us to create a relationship embodied in the performance of writing and reading that is reflective, critical, loving, and chosen in solidarity" (Adams, Jones, & Ellis, 2014, p. 5). All of our lives we are engaged in performances and hear scripts that stay with us.

Boylorn (2013) describes how much of what she knows is through "sayin's" that she grew up with and shaped her identity. Boylorn (2013) speaks to her reality as a black woman, but, as a white female, I have felt the veracity of her words. The power of sayin's that hit you and morph you. Boylorn (2013) brings up "Sit with your legs closed," which I remember getting lectured on by my aunt at *Beauty and the Beast* in a chiffon bottom sundress as I put my feet on the railing. The irritation and aggravation that boys could do it because they wore pants. Coupled with "Not bad for a girl," or being crushed against a wall in preschool after asking to play with the boys and being refused as a girl. I spurned my identity as a female. Being a female meant being hurt, meant oppression. I grew tough. Then, I learned the power of being a girl, in being sweet and delicate. I played both sides. There's another sayin': Southern Belle. As I went down to speak to my evaluator, I called over my shoulder to my colleague, who was telling me to be careful, "I'll pull my Southern Belle." In order to be heard, I have to submit to my gender and ask for help, appearing unthreatening. The veracity of my knowledge and words has no value unless it is recognized. I am nonexistent until He recognizes me and legitimates me.

This was something I learned in school through other sayin's. I think about how sayin's in school defined me as a child of the imperialism of standardization. "Pencils down"—everything is finite, and you don't control time. "Keep your eyes on your own paper"—don't work with others; remain individualistic. "Eliminate two answers and choose the best answer. Remember process of elimination"—the best answer for whom? Not my answer, but *His* answer. I use He/His to represent the White, patriarchal, capitalist dominator, not because females are not a part of this. I am a part of this through my submission, resistance, and reproduction. Furthermore, the He can be a political space of power that can be filled by male, female, transgender, corporation, etc. He is a Panoptic-body that looks out:

> This [conquering] gaze signifies the unmarked positions of Man and White, one of the many nasty tones of the word "objectivity" to feminist ears in scientific and technological, late-industrial, militarized, racists, and male-dominant societies, that is, here, in the belly of the monster, in the United States in the late 1980s. I would like a doctrine of embodied objectivity that accommodates paradoxical and critical feminist science projects. Feminist objectivity means quite simply *situated* knowledges. (Haraway, 1988, p. 581)

Haraway capitalizes Man and White, which for me is a crucial point and relates back to my explication of He/Him. These words are metonymic of positions of power. When I capitalize White in this study, it is to connote an imperial dynamic that is built on white, heterosexual, patriarchal power and wealth. Not every heterosexual white male can assume this power because they are within the subaltern. As Freire (2014) noted, "Besides skin color, or sex differentiation, ideology, too, has its 'color'" (p. 136). It's the color of His ideology through racialization and genderization. The objectification of His gaze is a coercive assault on the spirit, body, and mind. Decolonizing that gaze involves unraveling the ways we are tethered to it as well as how we have been shaped by it; that is an individual we and a sociocultural we. This gaze is a panopticon that follows us everywhere.

The notion of the panopticon must be seen beyond prison through the way we are in a prison of a colonized mind, understanding the panopticon as "at once surveillance and observation, security and knowledge, individualization and totalization, isolation and transparency" (Foucault, 1995, p. 249). This is the gaze that we feel as we walk through corridors that have security cameras and have to use transparent grading available for students and parents to see with cell phone apps that notify immediately when grades are put in. This is also the eyes that we don't feel watching us from the screens beneath our fingertips or in front of us. This is part of the colonialities of being. Foucault (1995) further discusses how there are two images of discipline in which one is the "discipline blockade" and the other panopticism, which is "a functional mechanism that must improve the exercise of power by making it lighter, more rapid, more effective, a design of subtle coercion for a society to come" (p. 209). We are constantly being in/formed by dominant ideologies as well as in/forming the dominant class with every click we make, exposing more and more of our identities to be exploited for their sake. How many think twice before agreeing to the access request of the latest app that they install? Quickly, we give up information and bits of our identities while also consuming new identities. There is a need for conscientização and consciencism, for a critical mind to analyze the knowledge networks around us and engage in decolonization.

This is both individualistic and collective. We must examine our individual actions but also frame them within the cultural, social, and political forces that create the currents that we are swept up into. Discussing the importance of analyzing the micro- and macro-politics of everyday life, Mohanty (2003) claims, "[t]he link between political economy and culture remains crucial to any form of feminist theorizing—as it does for my work. It isn't the framework that has changed. It is just that global economic and political processes have become more brutal, exacerbating economic, racial, and gender inequalities, and thus they need to be demystified, reexamined, and theorized" (p. 510). A decolonial praxis that engages with a feminist praxis "that builds on the understanding of difference and translates these insights by emphasizing the importance of taking issues of power, authority, ethics, and reflexivity into the practice of social research" (Hesse-Biber, 2012, p. 17).

Decolonizing our beings and mentalities is an incessant movement of being within oneself and on the outside. We are the performer and the audience. Madison (2004) describes how "performance asks the audience to 'travel' empathetically to the world of the Subjects and to feel and know some of what they feel and know, two life-worlds meet and the domains of outsider and insider are simultaneously demarcated and fused" (p. 478). As critical transformative pedagogues, this is something that many of us do every time that we interact in the classroom.

Reed-Danahay (1997) discusses the dualism within autoethnography of self and society in which "the autoethnographer is a boundary-crosser, and the role can be characterized as that of a dual identity," but, in the present context, there is a need for a multiplicity of identities (p. 3). The pedagogue is not always the performer; it becomes hard to tell what you are because there is a fluidity. Part of you is teaching with your mouth and hands while your eyes and ears are translating what your audience is doing, but your audience is also a part of this drama.

There needs to be an "emphasis on personal narrative as a situated, fluid, and emotionally and intellectually charged engagement of self and other (performer and witness) made possible in the 'evolving, revelatory dance between performer and spectator'" (Miller, 1995, p. 49; Jones, 2005, p. 773). This entails constant reading of body language as well as analyzing your words and youths' words, which can be understood through Santos' (2014) intercultural translation, "a living process of complex interactions among heterogeneous artifacts, both linguistics and nonlinguistic, combined with exchanges that be far exceed logocentric or discourse-centric frameworks" (p. 215). The discourse today imperializes science to the point of blinding us from other realities. However, "[f]eminism loves another science: the sciences and politics of interpretation, translation, stuttering, and the partly understood" (Haraway, 1988, p. 589). Intercultural translation also engages in this stuttering and interpretation; it's a decolonial process, not a scientific method of replicability.

A pedagogue does not have a supreme knowledge nor do the students. It's about ecologies of knowledges and dialogues that unfold. Multiple beings, identities, spiritualities, and knowledges are carried out through languages. The meanings of which may be analyzed with each other and our selves. To ignore the fact that in the classroom, or in life, I am a composite of multiple identities would be erroneous. My identities are not my own and others are constantly seeing me in different ways.

My students may see me as a "bitch" in one moment while in the same moment others thought I was "chill." Identity is a dialogical process. My spirituality speaks with my students, and my consciousness is constantly transforming. If I don't analyze and decolonize, then I will become who I am not; this has happened too many times. A pedagogue's body is constantly being read by themselves and others. It is a vulnerable openness that doesn't allow you to hide much. A teacher can, but a pedagogue cannot.

When I come into the classroom and I'm quiet, unsmiling, my students read me—"Miss J, are you OK?"

The whispers surrounding that question multiply its caring invasiveness. You are supposed to perform. The script of curriculum has been written by your district as ordered by the federal government and your performance has been written by societal expectations, *but* you are also human. The fluidity of this identity leaves me open to different currents of knowledge, and I cannot live under the dictates of scientific replicability and researched-based practices. I can exist and survive, but not live. We must struggle to find ways to break out of those chains and decolonize the imperial view that He knows best:

> Science becomes the myth, not of what escapes human agency and responsibility in a realm above the fray, but, rather, of accountability and responsibility for translations and solidarities linking the cacophonous visions and visionary voices that characterize the knowledges of the subjugated. A splitting of senses, a confusion of voice and sight, rather than clear and distinct ideas, becomes the metaphor for the ground of the rational. (Haraway, 1988, p. 590)

Science can fill the space of He and has filled that space. The work of feminists helps us decolonize its imperialism to find a pedagogy that engages youth and understands the cacophony of languages, knowledges, and spiritualities.

Autoethnography provides a methodology that allows us the space for reflection to grapple with decolonization and our experiences. As Ellis, Adams, and Bochner (2010) stated, "autoethnography is one of the approaches that acknowledges and accommodates subjectivity, emotionality, and the researcher's influence on research, rather than hiding from these matters or assuming they don't exist." Denzin and Lincoln (2011) clarify this further: "Lived experience cannot be studied directly, because language, speech, and systems of discourse mediate and define the very experience one attempts to describe. We study the representations of experience one attempts to describe. We study the representations of experience, not experience itself" (p. 417). Consequently, this autoethnographic study is not *the* truth but *a* truth, which must be critiqued for not only what it explicitly and implicitly denotes but also for its silences.

Autoethnography benefits the researcher and readers and "refers to writing about the personal and its relationship to culture. It is an autobiographical genre of writing and research that displays multiple layers of consciousness" (Ellis, 2004, p. 37). Through decolonial theory, I will analyze those layers of consciousness as well as the contradictions within me and my words. Acknowledging my subjectivity, I critiqued it through Freire's (2009) concept of conscientização. My emotions, past, and perceptions are the force behind my words and paint a picture of *a* reality, which is a limitation not only of autoethnography but of any research.

Denzin and Lincoln (2011) add that "personal experience reflects the flow of thoughts and meanings persons have in their immediate situations .... We study the representations of experience, not experience itself" (p. 417). My words do not convey the only truth. Too often, researchers study data and *objective* facts about students, teachers, and schools, seeing it as truth, not as *a* story. Numbers are a language capable of telling a story, yet probably have more power to misrepresent the facts through their denial of the narrative.

Educators often are asked to tell a story, using only numbers or excel sheets—quantifiable realities. A child is not a quantity, nor is a teacher. Their bodies may be, but not their spirits and minds; we cannot calculate the value of a human being without engaging in dehumanization. Data and "evidence" not only speak, but silence and occlude. Watts (1966) discusses how what we notice or what we have an *ignore*ance about has to do with what language or symbols we have based on our experiences. In this process, we determine not only the meaning but also the value. What is worth sharing, what is worth translating, and what is worth hearing?

In order to shake the monocular view of education as it perpetuates a concealed hegemony and silence, this decolonial autoethnography applies decolonial theory to help me discover my complicity and responsibility as a critical transformative leader in education. To be a critical transformative leader, you need to be a decolonial pedagogue. You must not only resist the dominant narrative but unhinge it, decolonize it. You must not engage alone but through a process of enunciation with youth, educators, parents, and administrators.

Education appears to be the retelling of Polyphemus and Odysseus. In a cave with a giant boulder blocking the entrance, we are trapped by a one-eyed giant that is further blinded by its own insatiability for more human capital. The only possibility seems to be our demise. However, the story of Odysseus teaches the power of words and intellect to survive a fated end. Critical transformative leaders need to keep working towards an emancipatory and decolonial education beyond common sense, realizing that spiritualities and identities must be dialectically engaged in education. My experiences as an educator continually open my eyes and close them as I have to maintain a double consciousness to survive in the neoliberal rule of education in which by staying it is hard to decipher when I'm resisting and reproducing imperial discourses and knowledges of oppression. Autoethnography allows me the space to navigate this to deepen our "understanding of social realities through the lens of the researcher's personal experiences" (Chang, 2013, p. 108). Personal stories are often dismissed in education in favor of so-called hard facts.

The production of truth is seen as a neutral enterprise in which the emotional and personal have no value. Much of education is deaf to the sexist and racist colonial undertones of knowledge production, even in the roots and origins of language. When speaking to administrators about an alumnus' complaint, due to my class's critique of the racist use of language in his Twitter comments, I explained how I engaged my class in discussing the undercurrents of language and how the arguments used against me as "emotional" were sexist, as could be traced back through the word hysteria. They looked at me, confused, and one asked, "I don't understand. What is sexist about hysteria?" I felt myself questioning the validity of my comment but explained briefly how society used to believe that a woman's uterus floated about her body making her overly emotional and irrational, incapable of being a *logical* male. Despite the befuddled looks, the conversation moved on. Logic hides a hegemonic form of masculinity that dismisses the sexist and racist roots as crazy or non-rational. This must be part of decolonizing the curriculum, which obliterates knowledges through the control of language and memory.

Emotional and personal knowledge must be reclaimed as valuable. Chang (2013) claims, "[p]ersonal stories become vehicles for social critiques through which readers gain understandings of autoethnographers' social realities and of the social forces contextualizing their experiences" (p. 109). Personal stories allow us to decolonize the curriculum that is performed, written, and hidden within public education to analyze colonialities of being as well as the silencing or anesthetizing of spiritualities. These are interconnected, and, "[b]ecause autoethnography presents a person's experience in the context of relationships, social categories, and cultural practices (or the violation of these relationships, categories, and practices), the method revels in sharing insider knowledge about a phenomenon" (Jones, Adam, & Ellis, 2013, p. 34). My position as an educator in English Language Arts, a high-stakes testing subject, as well as my own educational experiences as a youth and a female under the neoliberal momentum for standardization and privatization of knowledge, enables me to have an insider's view of this phenomenon.

Janesick (2000) discusses crystallization (cf. Richardson, 1994) instead of triangulation in qualitative research. In her view, "crystallization incorporates the use of other disciplines, such as art, sociology, history, dance, architecture, and anthropology, to inform our research processes and broaden our understanding method and substance" (Janesick, 2000, p. 392). When considering autoethnography, crystallization provides a way to understand the multiple fragments, refractions, reflections that create the mosaic of reality. As Spry (2001) notes, "[a]utoethnographic texts reveal the fractures, sutures, and seams of self, interacting with others in the context of researching lived experience. In interpreting the autoethnographic text, readers feel/sense the fractures in their own communicative lives, and like Gramsci's notion of the organic intellectual, create efficacy and healing in their own communal lives" (p. 712). I discuss colonialities of being in the classroom, but that classroom exists in a world with a history that is steeped in colonialism, capitalism, and imperialism, and each must be complexified from a psychological and sociological lens.

My analysis cannot be purely hermeneutical phenomenology or meta-theory. It must pull from multiple disciplines to analyze the classroom as contact zones, which act as "social fields in which different cultural life worlds meet, mediate, negotiate, and clash" (Santos, 2014, p. 218). These decolonial contact zones are spaces in which colonialities, beings, spiritualities, knowledges, and languages collide and interact.

As a critical transformative leader and educator, I have to navigate this socio-political field not merely through the cartography of sight but through feeling, hearing, smelling, and tasting; sometimes these senses are metaphorical and other times they are literal. The heat of the room mixed with the sound of raised voices as well as the scent of lunch mean I must analyze it all and translate it into the mentalities of the students that I have. It could mean a fight or it could just mean that they are excitable and anxious for lunch. I am seeing and interpreting. Vision must be decolonized in research, and we must not see with just our eyes. Haraway (1988) calls our attention to the need to not giving in to the tempting myths of vision as a route to disembodiment (p. 582).

There has been discussion to take a performative turn in research to go beyond representation, as it is "understood that experience exists only in its representation, it does not stand outside memory or perception," and that, through performance, researchers are asking the audience to join in reliving the experience and re-interpreting (Denzin, 2000, p. 905). In fact, "[t]he performative turn responds to the twin conditions of bodiless voices, for example, in ethnographic writing; and voiceless bodies who desire to resist the colonizing powers of discourse" (Langellier, 1999, p. 126). The question of "[w]ho gave us permission to perform the act of writing?" (Anzaldúa, 2005, p. 81) connotes the revolutionary action of writing in an age in which educators are told to keep silent and be grateful to have a job.

I have heard this too often, and why wouldn't it make me want to fall to my knees and thank Him, my patriarchal master for his charity in allowing me to teach? I shouldn't "whine" as the *females* of my department have been told. I shouldn't question as *I* was told. Performative autoethnography is a way for me to speak out, exposing myself and making myself vulnerable, but, if I don't speak, who will? How long will silence gag public school educators? How do we even find our own words when for so long we have been colonized through education in schools and in public discourse of a monocultural way of being and knowing. Epistemicide has to coincide with linguicide because, when we lose our knowledge, we lose our voice, and, when we lose our language, we lose our knowledge.

We must find our words and speak from our soul where the memory still lives. This in itself is a revolutionary act for educators and students. According to Macedo and Bartolomé (1999), "[t]o tell 'a story in one's own words' not only represents a threat to those conservative educators who are complicit with dominant ideology but also prevents them from concealing. According to Václav Havel, 'their true position and their inglorious modus vivendi, both from the world from the selves'" (p. 56). I don't want to speak through just the ways that He has granted. Consequently, I would like to borrow from how performance ethnographies intend "to explore bodily knowing, to stretch the ways in which ethnography might share knowledge of a culture, and to puzzle through the ethical and political dilemmas of fieldwork and of representation" (Jones, 2002, p. 7). Writing an autoethnography is a dialogical process. What I write becomes a conversation for tomorrow ....

I stood outside the door of my classroom as students passed by, and I grimaced as I heard the cacophony inside my room. I had intended to read the narrative piece I was presenting on Saturday to my kids. It was written about Talia, their classmate. It occurred when they were freshmen, and many of them had been touched by her death. They had shared their personal narratives with me, and I thought it would be good to hear their reaction to my words. Did I liberate the story or had I enslaved it within my position as teacher? I took a deep breath and walked in. This was a battle with a lion. Last period on a Thursday. They were all riled up. I walked to the epicenter of the room. The small curve of students to my left toward the back liked to keep to themselves, choosing when to join in. On my back right were the dynamic trio of boys who eagerly engaged in conversation. In front of me, the girls who could either make or break this classroom.

"Alright!" I boomed. The noise started to quiet. "I was going to read you a piece that I had written about Jalissa. But, I don't think that this is a good day." I shook my head feeling the giggles and fervor of the room. At her name, several eyes looked up. Anne looked at me.

"You are going to read us a piece about Jalissa?" she asked, looking back at Mercedes.

"Hey, guys shut up!" said Mercedes. The group arched their eyebrows at her, thinking who are you to call rank at this moment in which we are having a conversation. "She's going to read something about Jalissa."

"No, no, I don't think so. Maybe tomorrow. You guys aren't in the right state of mind."

June shook her head. "No, you have to read it." She was a formidable force in herself. Her words were cold not angry just cold. I should have known, but I didn't.

"Which one do you want me to read? The one about her funeral? The other one I wrote first and it's about the day she told Mr. Marcus to f-off."

Mercedes' shoulders were tense she put her hands to her lips. "That one. The one you did first."

"Both!" exclaimed Anne and Ariana.

"Start with the first one," said Mercedes.

I nodded. "You guys are all about to do your Capstone project, and there's different ways to do research. One way is use stories to help explain what your research shows."

They all waited eager for the real meal; skip the intro they were saying.

"So, I wrote this to talk about how we silence students' identities and spiritualities in school. We teach the standards that the federal government want, and, as teachers, we're forced to pay attention to that. It blinds us sometimes to the knowledge that we are teaching beyond that. It has to do with a story about Jalissa."

Vivian shivered. "I got goosebumps guys," she said nervously.

I turned to look around the room, and they were all waiting. I felt nervous. These are not the easiest kids to read to. They don't all like the same things and will often turn their attention to their cell phones or start talking. What if they thought it sucked? There was technical language in it. Should I stop to explain or just read it? Would they understand?

I took a deep breath and began, "Some people have their day start off with warm, welcoming greetings, and others have their day start off with hearing their sweet little freshman scream, 'Fuck off' as the administrator escorts her into his office. The sounds of joy within schools. The day before that same girl, Jalissa," I paused, having to switch out the pseudonym for Talia, "had written on our class goal's poster that she was going, 'To leave all the drama behind her.'" Looks of remembrance and small smiles flitted amongst the girls. I was facing them not looking at the wings of students on my sides. "Despite her vow to leave the drama behind, Ta-Jalissa had center stage that morning as she screamed 'Fuck off.' I had been in the copy room, and I watched her walk with him. She was walking in an arrogance of pain. She was bothered by it, but she was acting for her captive audience of gawking high schoolers as if she didn't give a 'fuck.' I saw her soon after sitting in the office at the 'discipline table.'"

I paused here unable to keep switching. They were looking at me with anxious eyes.

"I'm going to use her pseudonym for the rest, which is Talia." I continued on telling the story of how I had left Talia alone in that room and how I had screamed, "Fuck you" to her by leaving her. I explained how easy it is to get wrapped up in the craze of federal mandates and that we forget the hidden curriculum. This was the first time I had read directly a piece of research that I had done, and I was surprised to see that they understood. I ended with "U.S. youth soon learn which knowledge/language is legitimated and which knowledge/language is delegitimized and consequently who has value and who does not. The oppressor is oppressed but feels freedom through the oppression of others."

"You wrote that, Miss J?"

"Yes, I did." I looked down. Still a school girl at heart who hates to read in class, to be noticed. I blushed.

"Read us the other one," said Mercedes.

June had the tissue box in front of her, but her eyes weren't too wet yet.

"I don't know," I said.

"Read us the other one!" they exclaimed. "Please," a few added.

I went over and got my laptop, hearing them whisper and talk and fearing that my administrator would come in to evaluate me. I could relate this to the standards. It wouldn't be a problem. Despite my self-reassurance, I still looked at the door and listened to hear for the sound of the door knob turning.

"So, this is the introduction to my dissertation. It is my way of hooking the reader. I start off at the funeral procession, and," I put the laptop down on the center table, so I could use my hands. "I start off with the word. Kneel. Then, rise," moving my hand through the air straight and then up, "Kneel," I added, dipping my hand low and repeating the words, drawing the heartbeat in the air until it flatlined. "To represent an ending heartbeat."

"That's cool."

They were eagerly sitting forward.

The boys to the side back with heads propped on hands. As I read the introduction, I didn't look at any of them. I just read.

My own heart beating faster and my voice catching as I relived the memories, feeling my own guilt. After I ended, I saw June sobbing.

"Oh no," I said unsure of what to do. "I'm sorry. I shouldn't have read it."

"No, no, you had to," they said.

The conversations that happened were with me and not at the same time. Some were directed to me others to themselves.

"When she moved to Wren, she changed her name. It was as if she didn't want to be her anymore," said Mercedes.

Rudy shook his head. "That's so messed up."

"If it had been Sara Mello, this would have be so different," said Cara.

Dennis shook his head too, his shoulders tensing. "Nobody would care if I died."

Rudy looked at him. His face a mixture of shock and understanding. "Yea, that shit's messed up but true. No one would care if we died."

The girls were having their own conversations. "They didn't even say her name on the morning announcements."

"They didn't care. They didn't want to talk about it."

"But, if it had been Sarah Mello, or somebody else they would have."

"Jalissa was a bad girl though. She didn't count."

June dried her eyes with tissues. "I asked why they didn't say anything, and they said it was too sensitive a subject."

"Isn't it important to talk about it?" I asked.

"Yea, we needed to."

"How else do you have closure?" I questioned. "I think we need to talk and feel that connection."

As I looked around the room, even kids who I didn't think would be affected were all crying or looking morose. Losing Jalissa had impacted many of them. I also knew others within the room had lost loved ones due to overdoses.

Their words would echo in my ears, "No one would care if I died." It wasn't the first time that my "low-level" kids had expressed how they felt second class. Even this year, the "low-level" seniors were not invited down for the college and career software training. Some of them wanted to go to four year schools, so I took my kids down anyway. My colleague's section of "low-level" seniors asked, "Why are all the upper level seniors going? What are we second class citizens?" They knew their place too well.

They reaffirmed for me the need to engage in dialogue about Jalissa's story and to write her story. They needed someone to speak up with them, so that they could be heard.

At Christmas, they did a balloon launch in her honor, Mercedes asked me if I got their email. I shook my head. I had sent a prayer up on Christmas Eve at four when I knew they were releasing the balloons. I didn't think that they would have thought of me, but they had.

"We released one from you, Miss J," said Mercedes. "Cara emailed it to you. I don't know what happened." Mercedes pulled up the image on her phone of the balloon with my name on it. We had established a bond, and we perform our narratives within and beyond these pages.

The performative aspect of ethnography and autoethnography is a way of engaging the readers and the text and is essential in my approach of decolonial autoethnography. When I teach *The Grapes of Wrath* to my students, we always discuss Steinbeck's belief in the writing trilogy of the reader, writer, and text. This trilogy represents unfolding engagement of the audience with the writing and the writer.

For each person, there will be a different response, a different line remembered, but this dialogical nature of performance is what makes it meaningful. Furthermore, "[t]he aim of dialogical performance is to bring self and other together, so that they can question, debate, and challenge one another. It is a kind of performance that resists conclusions, it is intensely committed to keeping the dialogue between performer and text open and ongoing" (Conquergood, 1985, p. 9). Conquergood (1985) created a box divided into four corners (Sensationalism, Selfishness, Superficiality, and Cynicism) to explains dialogical performance.

Conquergood (1985) refers to the corner boxes as "'dangerous shores' to be navigated, binary oppositions to be transcended" (p. 5). He applies this diagram to relationships with the other. But, I would like to use this as a visual cartography of the *Discourses* (Gee, 2005) that we see within the classroom. As educators, engaging in a decolonial praxis, these are areas that we must navigate, but we must not transcend these areas but delve into them with students. We must not be afraid to dialogue with those who exist in the spaces of Sensationalism, Selfishness, Superficiality, and Cynicism. We can see the Superficiality of ideas toward the other, but we can also see the superficiality toward the self because we are in a culture that thrives off the superficiality of ideas and aesthetics; a trip to the supermarket checkout line with the tabloids on the side and magazines of doctored photos provides a glimpse of this. The space of genuine conversation is made by reaching out or going to those who are still colonized within these spaces. For me, this is part of being and teaching within a decolonial contact zone (Santos, 2014). It means exposing ourselves as not only educators but as learning humans. By putting dialogical performance in the center and considering the outlying boxes as binaries to transcend, the performer would actually re-inscribe those within these spaces into a colonizing dichotomy.

Ongoing dialogue is necessary when considering how to engage in decolonizing practices and knowledges in the classroom. Jones (2005) claims that "performance ethnography seeks to implicate researchers and audiences by creating an experience that brings together theory and praxis in complicated, contradictory, and meaningful ways" (p. 770). In order to enliven democracy, we must remain open to contradiction especially in contact zones, such as the classroom. As a pedagogue, I engage in dialogical performance, which "is a way of understanding the intersections of self, other, and context passionately and reflexively. It offers a critical methodology that emphasizes knowledge in the body, offering the researcher an enfleshed epistemology and ontology" (Spry, 2001, p. 716). The colonial matrix of power makes this process even more complicated, and we must decolonize the colonialities of being. Santos (2014) adds that "Ortega y Gasset teaches us that the human being is the human being and her circumstance. I think we must go beyond and say that the human being is also what is missing in her circumstance for her to be fully human" (p. 114). How have neoliberal discourses and colonialities dehumanized individuals? To fight against the standardization of the spirit involves decolonization, which can be done through analysis of performance and performative writing:

> Performative writing brings the performance-performativity dynamic to the moment of texting in which identities and experiences are constructed, interpreted, and changed. It occurs when we encounter the page with the intention of entering into a discussion marked by contest and negotiation, embodied knowledge and vociferous exchange, emotional and intellectual charge. It occurs when we invite an audience into dialogue as we write, speak, and perform the words on the page, in our mouths, on our bodies, and in the world. Because the performance-performativity dynamic asserts that performances are inseparable from performers and that performativity is inseparable from politics, autobiographical performance, personal narrative, and performative autoethnography enmesh the personal within the political and the political within personal in ways that can, do, and must matter. (Jones, 2005, p. 774)

There is no way to separate pedagogy from the personal or the political. Even if we relinquish our autonomy and appear neutral, we still made a political decision. Every action we take is political, and "it is already within a set of norms that are acting upon us, and in ways that we cannot always know about" (Butler, 2009, p. xi). As educators, we are environed in sociopolitical and cultural factors that shape what we are allowed to teach, how we are allowed to teach, etc. We may resist these factors, but, even in doing so, we are taking a personal and political position. Writing our narratives becomes part of the analysis of colonialities.

The art of writing is a spiritual practice that enables us to hear ourselves and others while constituting different forms of being until we uncover our truth. Anzaldúa (2005) claimed that "[t]he act of writing is the act of making soul, alchemy. It is the quest for the self" (p. 84). Bochner and Riggs (2015) discuss Heidegger's work on how human beings are always living in a questioning form, which is why autoethnography can help with this questioning through the writing and performance, allowing us to dialogue about the complexities of being. In addition, Langellier (1999) explains, "approaching personal narrative as performance requires theory which takes context as seriously as it does text, which takes the social relations of power as seriously as it does individual reflexivity, and which therefore examines the cultural production and reproduction of identities and experience" (p. 128). Crafting these narratives through deep analysis and reflection is important because "voice is an embodied, historical self that constructs and is constructed by a matrix of social and political processes. The aim is to present and represent Subjects as made and makers of meaning, symbol, and history in their fullest sensory and social dimensions" (Madison, 2004, p. 473). Consequently, experience is tied to the *performance of possibilities*, which "centers on the principles of transformation and transgression, dialogue, and interrogation, as well as acceptance and imagination to build worlds that are possible" (Madison, 2004, p. 472). Madison (2004) discusses the interrogative field, which is similar to Santos' decolonial contact zones and intercultural translation, "where the *performance of possibilities* aims to create or contribute to a discursive space where unjust systems and processes are identified and interrogated" (p. 476). These decolonial contact zones can be analyzed through performativity that "points to the impossibility of separating our life stories from the social, cultural, and political contexts which they created and the ways in which performance as a site of dialogue and negotiation is itself a contested space" (Diamond, 1996, p. 2; Jones, 2005, p. 774).

Although there are a multitude of autoethnographic approaches, I will be using decolonial autoethnography that draws from the dialectics of performance and performativity as well as the philosophy of praxis. Interpretive autoethnography is unsuitable as a decolonial approach because, in the process of interpreting we are othering and removing the subject from within the body. As autoethnographers, we can never disengage our body/soul but must always speak with our beings, the ones within and the ones outside. Our bodies are texts constantly being produced, created, and interpreted. In decolonial autoethnography, we are analyzing the dialectics of our beings in the world through a performance of possibilities, which is "the active, creative work that weaves the life of the mind with being mindful of life, of 'merging text and world,' of critically traversing the margin and the center, and of opening more and different paths for enlivening relations and space" (Madison, 2004, p. 471). The performance of possibilities can be used as a decolonial approach but not for emancipation, rather for enunciation. Autoethnographers must strive to enunciate their beings in a political place of decolonial praxis. We must be conscious of how neoliberal spaces seek to colonize our political places, especially our bodies. Walt Whitman wrote, "I sing the body electric" to which I say, "I be the body politic." He asks, "Was it doubted that those who corrupt their own bodies conceal themselves? … And if the body does not do fully as much as the soul? And if the body were not the soul, what is the soul?" The soul is another way to understand our being and can be an embodiment of spirituality. The spirituality of the body for youth and educators in U.S. public schools is shaped by the religious zeal of the capitalist market but also its spirituality, neoliberalism.

Using decolonial theory along with the concepts of conscientização (Freire, 2009) and consciencism (Nkrumah, 1964), this work deconstructs the layers of critical consciousness and action to understand the way hegemony (Gramsci, 1971) and epistemicides (Santos, 2007b, 2014; Paraskeva, 2011, 2016a, 2016b, 2017) are reproduced, resisted, and produced within U.S. public schools. The neoliberal is for reproducible consistency that is managed through privatized sources. Gee (2014) claims:

> The need to "manage uncertainty" was created, in part, by the fact that mounting "observations" of nature led scientists not to consensus, but to growing disagreement as to how to describe and explain such observations (Shapin & Schaffer, 1985). This problem led, in turn, to the need to convince the public that such uncertainty did not damage the scientist's claim to professional expertise or the ultimate "knowability" of the world. (p. 66)

As a teacher in an ever-present curriculum of data mining and "seeing" students' progress and charting it for others to see with transparent grading, etc., it is the visible within the invisible and the invisible within the visible with which I attempt to uncover through decolonial autoethnography. We should be less consumed with seeing and more opened through feeling. The metaphor should be of sensing. As an equestrian, I learned to feel my horse's thoughts as well as hear them, from the stomping of the hoof, to the twitch of the ear, to the tensing of the body; this is something as a pedagogue I try to constantly be aware of. I try not to only listen and see but use all of my senses to understand where I am located, whether it is in a space of privilege or as the oppressed, depending on the situation, to consciously situate myself and connect with my students and colleagues. We must decolonize how we relate research and experience, recognizing that "[t]he eyes have been used to signify a perverse capacity—honed to perfection in the history of science tied to militarism, capitalism, colonialism, and male supremacy—to distance the knowing subject from everybody and everything in the interests of unfettered power" (Haraway, 1988, p. 581). Decolonial autoethnography provides a methodological space to situate myself within a network of beings and identities to decolonize the culture around me. From the time that I learned how to engage in academic or formal writing, I have fought to keep myself out of it. I was taught that my voice didn't belong, and I was to keep my writing formal and impersonal. Langellier (1999) explains how "[w]hen we move between narrative and literary performance or between narrative and scholarly discourse—what Merleau-Ponty would call a move from one order of expression to another order of expression—we do not leave our bodies behind to enter a separate realm of aesthetics or academic but rather extend and transform embodiment" (p. 140). We cannot separate our academic selves from our pedagogue selves from our maternal selves from our student selves.

We are always present just acting and consequently being heard and sensed in different ways. Each year as an educator, I have formal narratives written about me and who I am as a teacher, judging me. In addition, my students say, "Miss J, I was tweeting about you last night" or "J, I texted Kalie about you this weekend." Parents write emails to my principal. Students write narratives about me during class. The narratives written about me are also narratives about them. Yet, how much is forgotten in these narratives? How much is written in a way that I never intended? More directly, my decolonial autoethnographic writing is an attempt to speak what is un-spoken by Him. Checked boxes don't narrate the classroom that I am engaged in. Therefore, "I write to record what others erase when I speak, to rewrite the stories others have miswritten about me, about you" (Anzaldúa, 2005, p. 84). When I was told to write without me in my research, it always seemed like a lie behind an unbiased voice because "[l]anguage is a constitutive force, creating a particular view of reality and of the Self" (Richardson, 2000a, p. 925). An unbiased voice that was really just the legitimization of a Western, white patriarchal colonial power matrix, His voice. Autoethnography allows us to situate ourselves and be honest about our subjectivity as researchers and to stop hiding from our biases and confront them. Harding and Norberg (2005) relate this to feminist theory:

> In challenging conventional epistemologies and their methodologies, both of which justified problematic understandings of research methods, feminists have contributed to the epistemological crisis of the modern West, or North. No longer is what the ruling groups in the North think and do regarded as the legitimate standard for what the rest of the world should think and do, if it ever was so regarded anywhere except among such groups. The epistemological crisis is also a political, economic, social, and ethical crisis. (p. 2010)

Decolonial theory can dialogue with feminist theory in order to analyze how we need to challenge the construction of modern North-South and West-East to see the Norths within the Souths and Souths within the Norths and to see how local realities of oppression are often varnished with the gleam of Northern/Western modernity. We must deepen our construction of power, which in education is needed more than ever. Autoethnography should analyze "the visual, linguistic, and textual bias of Western civilization and our attention to an aural, bodily, and postmodern expression of culture and lifeworld, fieldwork and writing (Conquergood, 1991, p. 189; see also Tyler, 1986)" (Jones, 2008, p. 213). Decolonizing our culture is one of the first steps in analyzing our beings and spiritualities. Gee (2005) explains how "we are all, in fact, 'colonized' by a good many cultural models that have come to us without much reflection on our part about how well they fit our interests or serve us in the world. They use it, a model which actually fits the observations and behaviors of other groups in the society, to judge themselves and lower their self-esteem. But, as we have seen, since they fail to identify themselves as actors within that model, they cannot develop the very expertise that would allow and motivate them to practice it" (p. 68). These cultural models can be seen in schools on television that engage people in self-depreciation. It requires conscientização to help decolonize the mind and spirit from oppression. The ideology of inferiority due to individual fault is rampant in the cult of neoliberalism. Giroux (2001) calls for, "[i]deology critique as a form of critical consciousness opposes the knowledge of technocratic rationality, and implies instead a dialectical knowledge that illuminates contradictions and informs critical judgments needed for individual social action" (p. 155). Pedagogues are in a colonized space that needs this critique and can also be a space for decolonial praxis.

I teach in an era in which everything must be quantified equitable bias. We have DDMs, evidence binders, TPA, PPI, CCR, CCW4, [1] need I go on? Yet, the unquantifiable is often the memory champion. A colleague asked me last year, "What is the most memorable thing a student has said to you?" I wanted to answer, "How did you lose your virginity? I bet it was a big black man." Fear of being shamed kept me from saying that. I could have also responded with a student's response to a discussion on drugs, "Yes. I do understand. My mother chose crack over me." But instead, I gave a comical response quoting a sophomore girl, "Wait .... There was a prompt [referring to MCAS long composition]?" My colleague laughed hysterically and kept walking. I have no clue what prompted his question. But, as I thought about my response and his laughter before and after the question, my mind was more focused on how the most memorable moments were at times what students did not say and sometimes couldn't be explained.

Year two of teaching, I sat on top of a desk discussing, "Where Are You Going? Where Have You Been?" Four girls were seated close to me with numerous other students in the circle, but, at that moment, the conversation had been between me and those girls. I shared with them the moment in college when my creative writing professor got a lesson in the unpredictable while discussing this story. A couple of boys in my college class had said that protagonist had been asking for it (rape). I flipped out on the boys. As I was normally a quieter student in that class, my professor never expected the passion that erupted, the seething anger. I told them that shame of rape is often what keeps us girls silent. I have discussed this story numerous time and recounted this tale, but rarely have had the silent conversation that ensued. Other students may have had this conversation with me, and I was deaf to it. But that day, as I looked at those four girls' eyes, and their eyes turned to speak to each other, one broke group contact to speak with me. One girl, who was so polite and reserved generally, had the noisiest conversation in silence with me. Romeo asks while looking at Juliet, "She speaks, yet she says nothing; what of that? Her eye discourses, I will answer it" (2.2.13–14). This girl said nothing, and I said nothing. The other girls around her said nothing. But, there was a palpable discourse. This was immeasurable. Literally, nothing uttered to count or to record. However, this is part of the languages of spiritualities. The languages of spiritualities are heard in the silences as much as in the noisy chaos. These girls chose to do their research project at the end of the year on child sexual abuse. I was emailed the night before their presentation because Kara wanted to tell her story of being sexually abused by her grandfather, of being spurned by her grandmother, of the awkward reality of living with that. I silenced her. I said to tell the story in the third person. I explored this narrative more in detail in a previous study, but my point here is that I silenced her, saying, not now, maybe your senior year.

Senior year came, and this time I fought for her to be able to tell her story. Counselors, teachers, and administrator were against it. We couldn't know the damage her story could do. What if other girls heard it and did *something*?

Something like cut themselves? I went down a month later with another girl who wanted to interview another girl about cutting for her Capstone project. The answer was again no, that this wouldn't be a good plan. When I brought up this was a problem that youth were facing, the counselor smiled kindly and said that they (the counselors) were aware and had been to two conferences and that there was a box under her table with the curriculum for helping students deal with this. It was a sensitive issue that they needed to begin carefully.

I sat looking at her, a woman with an enormous heart who is always there to listen to youth, and I thought back to my high school's adjustment counselor when I had been called in. She had asked me if I knew about these girls cutting themselves. I had looked at her and thought, *Of course*. And, I *had* responded with yes, girls were carving boys' names that they cared about—requited or unrequited love—into their arms. She had made some comment about how it was just terrible that they needed some other outlet. I remember looking at her through a haze, as she asked me about what my career plans were, etc., and thinking that she was a good-natured idiot. As I write that word, I think ignorant may be better, but, as an adolescent, I thought idiot. She was so oblivious to what girls were going through.

When we had to show a video[2] about bullying and self-harm as part of a student advisory, I was once against confronted with the same ignorance as Tray remarked, "If you're going to kill yourself do it right. Why cut like that?" Other male students joined him remarking on the stupidity of this kid. Immediately there were other students on the defensive attack, including a boy. They tried to talk, but these boys wouldn't listen. I turned to Tray, Rick, and Nate. "Cutting isn't about killing yourself. Cutting is about feeling physical pain instead of emotional because the emotional is worse than the physical. The cut makes you forget for a minute about your mind."

"Well, that's stupid, just get over it!"

Molly and two other girls rolled their eyes and continued to file their nails or stare into space. The bell rang as we continued to talk it out. Molly approached me. "Miss J, they're just so stupid. Why do we even talk about this stuff with people like that?"

"They're just blinded by ignorance. We have to try and talk it out. Some people don't understand until it happens to them."

Willful ignorance is related to the need for education to engage with spiritualities. To understand another, we have to understand our connections and decolonize our ignorance, (re)engaging with ourselves and others. My school counselor had lost her son, but that grief wasn't translatable apparently to the mind and pain of adolescents. As I look back at my close circle of friends in high school, and I think about those four students whose eyes discoursed, I think about the spirituality that was within and between them as it had been for us.

Yet, for the majority of educators, and guidance counselors are educators as are parents, there is a world on mute that is coexisting with the steady stream of hegemonic discourses, the acceptable and prescribed pain or violence. Violence wears spiked collars, black shirts and pants. Violence doesn't dress in a polo and jeans. Pain doesn't wear a cheerleading skirt. Sadness doesn't wear a soccer jersey. Or, does it? The ones who were forced to the ground in the woods assaulted by a cousin whom they have to see every holiday, told to smile, sleeping with scissors under the pillow, hiding in hanging clothes, having loving-raping boyfriends. Different stories, different curses, different memories, different youth, different clothes. These are the stories told and un-told that must be analyzed and engaged through dialogue to be decolonized to understand the violent and exploitive nature of U.S. public education. The classroom can be a decolonial contact zone in which decolonial pedagogues may engage with youth, understanding the complexities of spiritualities as well as the way that colonialities of being are at work, which can be better understood through decolonial autoethnography.

Notes

1 DDM (District Determined Measures); TPA (Teacher Performance Assessment); PPI (Pupil Performance Indicator); CCR (College and Career Readiness); CCSSW4 (Common Core Writing Standard 4).

2 See "Jonah Mowry: 'Whats goin on'" at www.youtube.com/watch?v=TdkNn3Ei-Lg

CHAPTER 3

Colonialism, Colonialities, and Imperialism within and beyond U.S. Education

> In fact, civilization has reached the point where the frontier now lies in the mind itself. Americans must conquer knowledge as formerly they conquered the wilderness. Bacon's saying, 'the mind is the man' is now literally true for each man and for all of mankind. Our future depends squarely on how well we succeed in developing the minds of our young men and women.
>
> RUSSELL (1921, p. 160)

•••

> It is only on condition of perfect submission and stillness that I shall liberate you then.
>
> BRONTË (1859, p. 7)

∴

Drawing from critical, post-structural, anti-colonial, feminist, and decolonial approaches, I will lay out colonialities, spiritualities, and technicalization of language in relation to the neoliberal momentum within U.S. schools. In using de/colonial theory to analyze the dialectics amongst teachers and students, I am not attempting to compare this to the continuing struggles of those who are oppressed in abject poverty, have experienced and are experiencing linguicide, genocide, epistemicide, and other violent forms of oppression. Rather I'm asking us to think of Constantino's (1966) discussion of the Philippines and the U.S. decision to use the school as its intellectual oppressor, something that is stronger than a gun. Kill a man and he is of no use to you, the colonizer, but destroy his spirit and colonize his mind, and you just gained an intellectual slave.

I do not seek to equate the real of colonialities for different people across the world. I cannot compare the experiences of Pacific Islanders, Native Americans, South Americans, Africans, etc. to myself, teachers, and youth in U.S.

 | DOI: 10.1163/9789004416048_003

public schools today. Instead, I attempt to engage different theories, experiences, knowledges, and voices in what Santos (2014) calls intercultural translation in which, "[i]t is imperative to start an intellectual dialogue and translation among different critical knowledges and practices: South-centric and North-centric, popular and scientific, religious and secular, female and male, urban and rural, and so forth" (p. 42). Intercultural translation requires decolonization as well as going beyond binaries. Analyzing colonial power in different spheres of the world creates a theoretical space to aid us in analyzing the colonial power network that shrouds their realities as well as analyze the colonization of the minds that is occurring to U.S. youth *and* U.S. educators.

I must situate myself as a speaker within this text before I continue. At times, I will use "we," it is not meant to be a forced inclusiveness but rather an invitation to join in the analysis. I do not claim to have all the answers and struggle with my students and colleagues as well as family to further understand how this colonial matrix of power is shaping our youth. The "we" is meant to be an invitation into a dialogue with not just me but the text, the reader, the community, society, etc. A poster hangs in my classroom with a quote by John Donne (1839), "No man is an island entire of itself; every man is a piece of the continent, a part of the main; if a clod be washed away by the sea, Europe is the less, as well as if a promontory were, as well as any manner of thy friends or of thine own were; any man's death diminishes me, because I am involved in mankind. And therefore never send to know for whom the bell tolls; it tolls for thee." Every action and inaction in the world affects us as we affect the world. The "we" is meant to be porous to allow those who wish to come in and out as the text speaks to them or not.

I write as a U.S. public high school educator, but I also write as a former student of this education system; I have the privilege of helping to bring my nephews up, so I write as "Auntie," who gets to see how elementary education has dramatically changed, criminalizing youth as young as four.[1] I write as a counselor, mentor, defender, community member, sister, daughter, friend, etc. For me, the arms around all these beings is female. In *The Grapes of Wrath*, Ma Joad comments, "woman got all her life in her arms. Man got it all in his head." Ma Joad's words speak to how, as females, we are constantly working to care but feeling and being present in joyful and painful touch with the world. As I stood filling up water balloons for my nephew's end of the year party, I listened to the moms talk about how the school fired the teacher aids. "They'll just get more moms to come into the classroom," one said. My eyes jumped up at this. This was the deskilling of teacher aids, which a teacher should know is not a job that any person can do. There was a class issue because how many females worked night shifts or no shifts that could fulfill this job as well as a gender issues via the exclusion of room dads. Females make up a huge portion of the capitalist market through unpaid work.[2]

The construction of female is related to the white heterosexual patriarchal capitalist vision and privilege. Lugones (2008) discusses Oyěwùmí's analysis of the biological duomorphic assignment of gender as a Western construction for capitalism and colonization as well as explains that gender was "introduced by the West as a tool of domination that designates two binarily opposed and hierarchical social categories .... Women are those who do not have a penis; those who do not have power; those who cannot participate in the public arena" (p. 8). Oyêwùmí (2002) discusses how in the Yoruba family there was no gender distinction, as could be viewed in lack of differentiation in roles and power for males and females. The colonialist quickly shifted women from power and cultivated a gender disparity. Capitalism's needs "shaped the particular ways in which colonial domination was effected" (Oyěwùmí, 1997, p. 123). It was through colonialism fed by capitalism that the division of labor was needed, which is part of the coloniality of power.

Lugones (2008) highlights how indigenous people before colonization were not subject to this binary of gender, and thus the discussion should not be focused on "'light' side" of modern/colonial construction of gender but going "outside the coloniality of gender so as to think of what it hides, or disallows from consideration, about the very scope of the gender system of Eurocentered global capitalism" (p. 9). Her focus is on the intersection of race and gender in the third world context, and her analysis is extremely important in understanding the nexus of race and gender with colonial and capitalist exploitation. However, I would also suggest that we consider that the world wasn't born capitalist, and that women in the global West at one point were seen as equals in relation to males, such as the Viking females in the 9th century (McLaughlin, 1990) or Gallae, transgender[3] priests/priestesses in ancient Greece as well as in the global East, including transgender individuals in African, Native American, South American, and Asian cultures (Feinberg, 1996). Feinberg (1996) notes that it was in Deuteronomy somewhere between 11th and 7th BCE that laws began to forbid cross-dressing and sex change that "reflects the deepening of patriarchal class divisions among the Hebrews, who lived in and among communal societies" (p. 50). It is not my purpose to explore the acceptance of different sexualities and/or genders within the "West," but rather to highlight that capitalism needs the exploitation of power through the gender binary. However, Wynter (2003) claims, in agreement with Quijano (2000), that "race—unlike gender (which has a biogenetically determined anatomical differential correlate onto which each culture's system of gendered oppositions can be anchored)—is a purely invented construct that has no such correlate" (p. 264). Race was an important construct of the colonial model, but Wynter and Quijano fall into the modern Western trap, as Lugones (2008) flags, that gender is a binary that is determined by biological parts alone. Biologically determined sex is different from socially constructed gender. In this way, I would join Lugones and say that Wynter and Quijano should decolonize their construction of gender. Failure to analyze the socio-political nexus between gender-race, gender-class, gender-sexuality, gender-coloniality, etc. paralyzes the decolonial movement by casting race into modernity's shine and gender into its shadow. The world is not a chiaroscuro painting of dark and light. There are a plurality of colors, lights, and shadows. We have to clearly understand what we are struggling against. Cabral (1973b) remarked, "We have to combat the material reality that produces the shadow" (p. 77). Hegemony works to conceal from us the different layers of reality. The most perfect example for me was while watching Trotro, a British toddler cartoon, my nephew remarked, "But why are all the fishes blue?" I didn't understand. "They're not. They're red, white, and green." Then, I saw what he saw. The water had turned the fish blue. I didn't even see the water because rationally I knew that when objects went in the water they changed, so I saw beyond the water. But, he was right. The fish had turned blue. I didn't see the water though until he called my attention to it. Hegemony controls how we see or un-see. It is only through conscientização and questioning that we begin to unravel the different layers of reality. Our ideological waters determine what ideological colors we see. The hegemony of the capitalist divisions of labor and construction of identities must be problematized.

The coloniality of gender and the subsequent disempowerment of females was something that was necessary for the success of capitalism. As a female educator, in a highly gendered public service—I would add that perhaps it is better to note teaching is treated as a public servitude, instead of service, considering the number of hours teachers spend unpaid after their workday finishes, correcting, copying, preparing, tutoring, which must be coupled with the de-professionalization of the field. Although, after reviewing the history of teachers, one has to wonder if we ever had professionalism. Teachers claim to have professional status, yet 62% still work a second job (Eggers & Calegari, 2011). Teaching comes from an oppressive past with Roman educators often being captured slaves of war in which they "furnished a ready supply of adult educated slaves equipped to meet the insistent demand for the instruction of the youth of the Roman upper classes" (Westermann, 1984, p. 127). Gender is a critical component of the analysis of teaching i.e. females comprise 84% of the teaching workforce (Feistritzer, Griffin, & Linnajarvi, 2011, p. 12) but only 13%

of superintendents (Gates, Ringel, & Santibanez, 2003). The gendered nature of the teaching profession comes from a long history of females and capitalism, drawing to the complexities of gender beyond cultural and societal construction through the need to "be treated as a specification of class relations" (Federici, 2004, p. 14). I am a part of this gender, but I am also privileged to understand my own colonial chains—those that oppress me and those chains that I have that oppress others. My education, my job, etc. is part of White privilege. Although teaching is a highly gendered profession, it is also a highly racialized profession with the majority of teachers being white; consider that less than 20% of teachers are classified as racial/ethnic minorities (Feistritzer, Griffin, & Linnajarvi, 2011, p. 12). We need to decolonize the teaching profession, which begins with decolonizing ourselves, but we also must recognize that the distribution of gender and race in teaching is to do with larger societal factors that inculcate where a white woman's place is and is not as well as whose place it is not.

hooks (1994) writes that it is a privilege to be able to decolonize, and she is right. I announce that privilege and rattle its bars and attempt to decolonize my being as well as enunciate myself. My mind might still have been trapped if it weren't for amazing educators, professors, youth, friends, and family, who have helped me to see my position of privilege as well as to see how that privilege has come at a price for others as well as myself. My rural childhood, education, and my teaching position were all opportunities afforded to me by White privilege. That privilege has a history of violence against others and self. To be legitimated, white immigrants had to give up their languages and culture to be absorbed into the hegemonic power. My tongue speaks English because my ancestors were kicked out of Ireland, but, even before that, they were forced to speak English through the Penal Laws of Ireland that deemed them an inferior breed of human. I do not speak Portuguese either because my father's grandmother refused to speak it to them, only whispering it on the phone when her sisters called. Everything must be forgotten except White assimilative power. My identity has been whitewashed. Although my skin speaks ... I hate to say it, but my skin speaks. It not only speaks of privilege, which I can never deny but try to rupture this privilege in society, but it also speaks of self-contempt, which I often have tried to hide. Here we invite body-politics (Mignolo, 2009b) into the dialogue to discuss manufacturing of beauty that has racial, class, and gender ties, which reveals the way colonialities of being becomes a silencing slaughter of selves.

My sister was blessed with the Portuguese and French olive skin tone. I was cursed with the Irish complexion. In seventh grade, my history teacher looked at me while he was teaching a lesson, probably on Ireland, but I don't remember—the explicit content was not as important as the performance and hidden content.

He said, "The only two in here that really look Irish are," he addressed some boy and then addressed me, "and you, Elizabeth." His eyes roamed me. I was a quiet student, always attempting to blend in with the desk and the white walls. "You look Irish with those freckles." His examination of me stopped, and his gaze hardened. "Except ... except for your eyes .... What are your eyes?"

I was blushing and embarrassed, wishing I could scrub my freckles off. Despite the myth, lemons don't erase them. Why were they there? Then, inwardly, I reached for my eyes as if they were foreign, as if I had never felt them resting in my head before. My eyes? He wanted to know what *my* eyes *were*? My body became not my own, and my eyes weren't me, and my skin wasn't me. As I teach *Purple Hibiscus*, I sympathize with the young female protagonist, Kambili, who is similarly befuddled after her father chastises her for possibly eating pagan food and desecrating her "Christian tongue" (Adichie, 2012, p. 69). Kambili freezes and thinks, "I did not know that tongues could be Christian, too" (Adichie, 2012, p. 69). That realization that your body isn't you; it's a piece of a *what*. For me that day, I was in the limelight all kids turned to me, studying my face and waking out of their sleepy boredom. I was a spectacle for their curiosity. Suddenly, I was othered. I couldn't hide under a white-washed identity. In that moment, I was no longer one of them but a specimen for examination. Every inch of my being examined in zoological curiosity.

"Your eyes ...."

My heart was pounding, and my eyes charring a deeper brown from the force of heat from my skin. Tongue speak. "My father's part German," I offered. "Take it, please take it" was the whisper unheard.

"No, no that's not it. What else?" Finger wavering ... poking at my genetics .... As if my body was a dish that he was savoring, calling out the flavors.

"He's also part Portuguese."

"Yes, yes," he drew out the words as if he had finally found my inner secret with a satisfied grin that made me want to disown my body, "that's it." I had been consumed.

I looked over to my best friend who was in the back desk—hidden. I envied her. She was much more "Irish" than me. She had the freckles and dark hair but also the iconic, striking blue eyes. In fact, we look so alike that, when we were little, people used to mistake us for twins. I coveted her back hiding spot. I felt the burning sensation of my skin. The pale whiteness that wouldn't hide my embarrassment but would make it glow. This was my conscious beginning of understanding body-politics (Mignolo, 2009b). Yet, in agreement with Deleuze (1988), there is no beginning for it is the middle that then can be analyzed to an earlier beginning. Similarly, there is no end but just the middle of the infinity of humanity.

My teacher in his moving obelisk of White patriarchal privilege thought of the analysis of my body without thinking of the person within it; the quiet girl who did not want attention. I was an object for his lesson. Our exchange is not the beginning, but the middle of a history of White male dominance. I was a white, little girl in a country that has never ratified the Declaration of a Child's Rights in which the Bill of Rights has no place in the public school, as the principal maintains supreme, oppressive, power for the safety of the children, *in loco parentis* .... Big Brother is watching .... His obelisk of power gave him the right to use me as he would a map. My body a cartography. Consciously or not, he had drawn my attention to the body-politics (Mignolo, 2009b) and biopolitics (Foucault, 2010) of beings. Since I was a teenager, I have felt the reoccurring shame of my skin as I became a woman and was judged for my beauty—intelligence is not woman; beauty is woman. My sister sternly told me before my junior prom that I needed to go tanning because my dress was white, and I was too white. Sibling animosity surged.

"I'm white, and I'm proud of it!" I yelled at her.

Hearing those words, out of context, I feel my cheeks burn and think that I should have had a white Klu Klux Klan hood on; yet that is a corrupt White patriarchal power that I would not have been welcomed into, no matter how white my skin. But, my words weren't meant as a pronouncement of white superiority but rather came from a defense against societal inferiority. It was a defense of aesthetical whiteness that had been attacked at that time. That white/pale was so bad that we should go tanning and apply bronzers; it was an attack fueled by class difference. It was a dominant male attack on femininity that was corporately driven, as can be seen in the U.S. through the $5 billion industry of indoor tanning (Brooke, 2014) as well as the additional $763.4 million spent on self-tanning products; conversely, the skin lightening industry has a global market of about $10 billion (Rolfes, 2012). The message: we need to change our skin. Who has the capital to change his/her skin? This is a class issue and a race issue. I would situate it as body-politics, which is intimately connected with the colonialities of beings and spiritualities. The constant rhetoric that inferiorizes our being in order for capitalist exploitation anesthetizes spirituality and consumes our identities. In order to try to blend with society's norms, we erase or silence who we are, yet are we ever truly with the dominant power? We can't escape how others view us.

Quickly as a teen, I learned how to apply makeup to cover my "blemishes" (i.e. freckles)—I can't deny having tried rubbing lemon on my face to get rid of them, to erase my skin. I thought that as an adult I had finally escaped my skin, until I was hired and my principal made my password freckles. My cheeks burned, and I quickly touched my face, looking in the mirror. Were they so pronounced that even he saw them? Hadn't I hid them? I say this because society constructs what is Europerfect, the ideal for women. This has to do with Mignolo's (2009b) discussion of biopolitics (Foucault, 2010) and body-politics:

> [B]ody-politics is the darker side and the missing half of bio-politics; body-politics describes de-colonial technologies enacted by bodies who realized that they were considered less human at the moment they realized that the very act of describing them as less human was a radical un-human consideration. Thus, the lack of humanity is placed in imperial actors, institutions and knowledges that had the arrogance of deciding that certain people they did not like were less human. Body-politics is a fundamental component of de-colonial thinking, de-colonial doing and the de-colonial option. (p. 16)

In Mignolo's (2009b) work, biopolitics and body-politics has to do with race and religion (he discusses how body-politics came to Europe through the Holocaust), but as he notes with the Civil Rights Movement women were instrumental. I would say the argument is interconnected with gender, as can be seen through beauty for women in which biopolitics is at play. With $5 billion spent on indoor tanning in the U.S. in which 70% of consumers are Caucasian females and the use of indoor tanning correlated to the ever increasing cases of melanoma for those under 35 (Kite & Kite, 2014), one has to wonder why women are willing to give up their lives for the sake of their bodies being deemed beautiful by that White patriarchal gaze. For a female, beauty is what she is; cue Daisy Buchanan who said at finding out that she gave birth to a daughter in *The Great Gatsby*, "And I hope she'll be a fool—that's the best thing a girl can be in this world, a beautiful little fool" (Fitzgerald, 2010, p. 13). Be beautiful and stupid. In high school, when tanning became the social ritual of one's existence—that is, until my best friend's cousin died of melanoma—my friends and I discussed how un-tanned skin had been in vogue previously due to the class distinction; if you were tan, then you were a farmhand, lower class. Unknowingly in line with the epistemic de-linking of body-politics, we hypothesized that tanning was now "in" because it meant you had the money to vacation; hence, the sayin' "Where did you go [on vacation]? You look so tan!" Apparently, this is true, and we can thank Coco Chanel (Kite & Kite, 2014) for inspiring this carcinogenic ritual of dying one's skin.

To reflect back on the biopolitics of this, the ideal of light skin was also strengthened from the force of Europe pushing away from the South whom they racialized and inferiorized for their dark skin. Mignolo (2009b) claims, "the colonies were not a secondary and marginal event in the history of Europe but, on the contrary *colonial* history is the non-acknowledged center in the making of *modern* Europe" (p. 16). The $10 billion spent on skin lightening in which people are willing to buy skin whitening *candy* (Oaklander, 2014) and swallow this to stop producing melanin in order to bleach their skin reveals the ongoing coloniality of being as does the charring of one's skin. Both done to match the color of power. The confectionary delight of oppression .... Yes, the color of power ....

I remember sitting in English class my junior year, and the girl in front of me telling me how she couldn't go tanning for a bit because she had a dance competition, and they all had to be the same shade to appeal to the judges. I thought that she was kidding, but she was serious. The girls that were light had to go tanning to try to match the darkest girl, and the darkest girl had to avoid light. It seemed ludicrous, but the image was more important than art; we are within an imagocentric culture (Santos, 2014) online and off-line. In my seventeen-year-old mind, I started to understand the push for homogenization for us all to think, look, and act the same. For the most part, I joined this bacchanal of homogeneity, trying to hide as much of me as I could. This is part of female biopolitics. However, let me reiterate, while I felt shame for my skin, and it disqualified me from being Europerfect, I have maintained my White privilege. I pass. I have the privilege of hegemonic invisibility. If I keep my eyes down and my face hard, I can pass through the streets in a cloak of White privilege, having to deal with my sexualization and objectification, but not eliciting fear from my community as Brent Staples talks about in "Just Walk on By" or facing police brutality as exemplified by Tamir Rice, Michael Brown, Freddie Gray, and the list unfortunately goes on. On the street, I may be eye raped, a prop in a man's fantasy world, and I may be stalked by males at work or followed to my car with a white male arm and body threateningly blocking my escape, but it is different from what African-Americans and Latinos face. I do not want to compare the experiences. The purpose of discussing body-politics and biopolitics of females is not to deny the increasing issue of racism, Islamophobia, ethnocentrism, homophobia, or linguaracism; rather, it is to begin this intercultural dialogue by situating myself within a socio-political framework. These body-politics and biopolitics reveal the colonial power matrix that subjugates even those within the dominant class who also live within a sexual, classed, and racialized market. Colonialism feeds off self-depreciation.

Machel (1975) asserted, "Colonialism is a crime against humanity .... Colonialism is a cancer that destroys humanity, it is a cancer that feeds from blood.

Killing, massacring, assassinating, humiliating—it destroys the lives of human beings" (pp. 72–73). Colonialism is a system for the exploitation of humans and resources in order to create market gain. The destruction of life as well as knowledges, languages, and identities is still sentient today. Neoliberalism continues and adds to the colonial legacy in this age of liquid modernity (Bauman, 2013) in which globalization has meant the rise of standardization and colonization by the global elite. Common Core and high-stakes testing policies are colonizing forces that inculcate the hegemony of neoliberalism that belies choice without acknowledging its racialized and class-based agenda that further exploits subaltern[4] youth for the sake of the U.S.'s position in the global economy. Nkrumah (1964) claimed, "the basis of colonialism is economic, but the solution of the colonial problem lies in political action, in a fierce and constant struggle for emancipation as an indispensable first step towards securing economic independence and integrity" (pp. 98–99). Educators must engage in political action and engage in decolonizing the curriculum. However, an anesthetizing positivist culture thrives in U.S. schools and society through the colonization of youths' minds. Therefore, it is the decolonization of the mind that critical transformative educators need to fight for in part by uncovering the *epistemicides* (Santos, 2007b, 2014; c.f. also Paraskeva, 2011, 2016a, 2016b, 2017) that are destroying and occluding knowledges. Educators must struggle for social and cognitive justice, shaping practices and policies while decolonizing the curriculum.

The current educational reform initiatives, i.e. Common Core and Race to the Top, seek to standardize knowledge as part of a renewed rigor and competitive edge in the global economy and in so doing reinforces a dangerous subjectivity. Tero Autio (2009) argues that

> by psychologizing subjectivity and the curriculum, stripped out of metaphysical, moral, or political considerations, the Tyler rationale would form a kind of circular reasoning in curriculum planning ("Curriculum Development"), where educational-psychological goals are constantly revised and shaped along with the most recent empirical findings and empiricist fashions ("brain-based," "evidence-based," "research-based," etc.) and crossed with the current "needs" of society. (Autio, 2009, p. 10)

Educators must work to decolonize how these policies are enacted within the classroom and through them by creating a counter-curriculum and critical space for dialogue and decolonizing knowledge. It is important to note that the classroom as referred to in this study does not mean an isolated four-walled compartment within the public school. The notion of a classroom must be decolonized as well, in a system in which "the vast majority of teachers re white, despite an increased number of diverse students" (Jupp, 2013, p. 2), which makes schooling an "ugly de-facto re-segregation process" (Jupp, 2013, p. 2). Furthermore, public education extends beyond public schooling into the interactions and rituals that youth have with their families and communities, which should be a dialectical education for youth and adults. Although this study focuses on public education within the "classroom," the classroom must be seen as a liquid space. We must decolonize our notion that the classroom's borders are physical borders, but rather these are interlaced with that of youth and educators' lives as well as larger socioeconomic and political veins as well as the media.

Even the notion of *a* classroom does not convey the multiple classrooms that I have with my students. Every time, a student and I enter into a dialogue or two students enter into a dialogue, a learning experience is occurring in a physical space. This human connection represents political space for decolonial praxis. Furthermore, curriculum must be decolonized in order to understand that the traditional notion that the educator brings the curriculum to the students even in a "critical" fashion within the physical walls of a classroom during the class period is colonial conception of educator and student as well as curriculum and learning.

The U.S. public schools are built on the colonial legacy of Britain's public education, which is why educators and youth must work to decolonize the classroom. U.S. public education is an arena for the coloniality of knowledge, power, and being. Although this study will focus on coloniality of being, coloniality of knowledge and coloniality of power are interconnected with coloniality of being. It is like an oceanographer studying the coral without paying attention to the water and/or the other life forms; their relationship cannot go unnoticed as they are part of the same ecosystem, or in this case socio-cultural, political system. In fact, Mignolo (2003) asserts that

> 'Science' (knowledge and wisdom) cannot be detached from language; languages are not just 'cultural' phenomena in which people find their 'identity'; they are also the location where knowledge is inscribed. And, since languages are not something human beings have but rather something of what humans beings are, coloniality of power and of knowledge engendered the coloniality of being [colonialidad del ser].' (as quoted in Maldonado-Torres, 2007, p. 242)

Their interconnections relate to the spirituality and its epistemic and discursive power. In this study, language will not be seen as the technical code as it reigns in U.S. education today, but, as a form of expression for the imagination, ideologies, and knowledges.

The standardization of knowledge is also the standardization of language, and, in the classroom, we must navigate how to standardize and imagine, teaching two discourses. To constantly aid students in learning the mandated standard without succumbing to the standard requires my students to challenge me and for me to challenge them. This is not walking on a tight rope. In fact, it is more walking on water, sinking, splashing, swimming in liquid modernity, and feeling spirituality within this dance requires analyzing the web of interactions that occur. Currently, educational policies, such as RTTT and NCLB, are technologies for the colonization of the mind, which narrows the possibilities for knowledges, languages, and ideologies that compose an individual's spirituality, connecting to the colonialities of being. Spirituality in its nature is an enigma, fitting well within the intricate web of colonialities. But, how can spirituality be understood within the current neoliberal colonizing standards-based testing regime? Coloniality of being is interconnected with spirituality in U.S. schools and impacts the development of self, which must be resisted as part of a need for social and cognitive justice, a democratic responsibility. Through this study, I seek to analyze my experiences as a pedagogue in navigating the tensions and contradictions of decolonizing knowledges and experiences while also being caught in a web of neoliberal policies that seek to standardize, dismembering teachers and youths' spiritualities as part of coloniality of being.

Spirituality does not have to be a religious term, but, when my students hear it, they often conflate it with religion. I try to explain to them that it has more to do with the connection with others and self, a form of expression that is not about reproduction but about understanding and creativity. Spirituality is intimately connected to language as the oppression of language is in a way the oppression of spirituality. In addition, Palmer (1999) noted that "[s]pirituality—the human quest for connectedness—is not something that needs to be 'brought into' or 'added onto' the curriculum. It is at the heart of every subject we teach, where it waits to be brought forth" (pp. 2–3). Spirituality as a "human quest for connectedness" can be felt often within youth and educators, but also at the heart of the content curriculum as prescribed by the Common Core is an anesthetization or a distancing technicalization of knowledge and language, which bypasses the heart to the nonrational brain; it is the silencing of body-politics. In many instances, this results in an anxiety in youth, a distrust of their being because they have been produced as a nonbeing by being seen in society as a number or a blue and orange circle on a screen. My administrators can click on Edwin analytics and reveal the MCAS (Massachusetts

Comprehensive Assessment System) scores for my students that can pull up the *legitimated* factors such as race, gender, socioeconomic status, but what about illegitimate factors, only some of which can be measured, like peer relationships, lack of parents, emotional wellbeing, hunger, fear, etc. Even the statistics teacher sat with me at the introduction to Edwin and questioned how this can be used to evaluate a child's growth and concomitantly a teacher's "effectiveness." This is part of the colonialities of being, the power to decide which parts of you count and which parts don't, which parts should be cultivated and which parts should be wasted. The "effectiveness" of teachers and "growth" of youth. Human beings are not blue and orange dots. They are not. These are symbols of the production of beings as nonbeings. Consequently, "[n]onbeing is depending on the being it negates" (Tillich, 1952, p. 40), which can be connected to anxiety of the being that is under threat or attack through standardization, performance indicators, etc. When looking at the colonialities of being, it is also important to consider the colonialities of nonbeing as well. This is framed under a colonial process of violence against individual's beings. To more fully understand the colonial process, the differences between colonialism and coloniality must be highlighted.

Despite their intimate relationship, colonialism and coloniality are different. As Maldonado-Torres (2007) explains:

> Colonialism denotes a political and economic relation in which the sovereignty of a nation or a people rests on the power of another nation, which makes such nation an empire. Coloniality, instead, refers to long-standing patterns of power that emerged as a result of colonialism, but that define culture, labor, intersubjective relations, and knowledge production well beyond the strict limits of colonial administrations. Thus, coloniality survives colonialism. It is maintained alive in books, in the criteria for academic performance, in cultural patterns, in common sense, in the self-image of peoples, in aspirations of self, and so many other aspects of our modern experience. (p. 243)

By focusing on coloniality, I am not interring colonialism and eulogizing that we live in a post-colonial world, despite the post-colonial writings that seem to suggest that. Coloniality and colonialism sew an intricate tapestry of modernity/civilization in which we live. The omnipresence of coloniality is the stitching that transforms the fabrics of knowledge, power, and language into the tapestry of the neoliberal empire, while colonialism still cuts and adds new pieces or cuts the old in order to reform and recreate. Coloniality is the progeny, the legacy and living memory of colonialism, and it is evolving through neoliberal hegemony that functions as a pervasive colonial power that has strong epistemological ties. So much so, that we, as educators, may not perceive its power, instead see our position as one without agency and never realize how much of the world we do not understand since we lack the language and knowledge, relating to Mignolo's (2010) call for epistemic delinking.[5] In addition, as related to the current educational reform initiatives that seek to standardize knowledge as part of a renewed rigor and competitive edge in the global economy, "'[c]oloniality of knowledge and of being' is hidden behind the celebration of epistemic breaks and paradigmatic changes" (Mignolo, 2010). This market mentality reflects dominant interest of the global elite that flows seamlessly due to the *celebrated* act of globalization. Quijano (2000) claims that "Europeans imagine themselves as the exclusive bearers, creators, and protagonists of that modernity ... they were capable of spreading and establishing that historical perspective as hegemonic within the new intersubjective universe of the global model of power" (pp. 442–443). As an educator, I am continuously confronted by the miseducation (cf. Constantino, 1978; Chomsky, 2004) or *schooled* ignorance of youth. As Santos (2014) notes, although "Ortega y Gasset teaches us that the human being is the human being and her circumstance[,] I think we must go beyond him and say that the human being is also what is missing in her circumstance for her to be fully human" (p. 114). Our geopolitics of location may also mean a geopolitics of negation. The fact that U.S. youth may not even acknowledge their role in the production of "civilization" and "modernity" demonstrates ongoing colonization of minds.

Countries colonized geographic spaces. Now, in the age of "liquid modernity" (Bauman, 2013), the land colonized is the ridges of the brain and the waves of the soul. This does not mean that geographic colonization has ended but means that, with time, it has multiplied to the point where it is perceived as a past state or is only visible through militancy. Contrary to this analysis, Quijano (2010) claims that "coloniality, then, is still the most general form of domination in the world today, once colonialism as an explicit political order was destroyed" (p. 24). But, colonialism is not dead. It has just complexified. Colonialism feeds off a system of exploitation to which Césaire (2000) demands that we admit, "without flinching at the consequences, that the decisive actors here are the adventurer and the pirate, the wholesale grocer and the ship owner, the gold digger and the merchant, appetite and force, and behind them, the baleful projected shadow of a form of civilization which, at a certain point in its history, finds itself obliged, for internal reasons, to extend to a world scale the competition of its antagonistic economies" (p. 33). To extend and complexify Césaire's argument, not only have geographic spaces, people, time been colonized for production but also for consumption. When people would rather go hungry than not buy the next iPhone, the earbuds that dangle from their ears can be seen as the modern whips of the colonizer and oppressor. It begs the question: Who owns what?

Grosfoguel (2010) points to the fact that "the old national liberation and social strategies of taking power at the level of a nation-state are not sufficient because global coloniality is not reducible to the presence or absence of a colonial administration (Grosfoguel, 2002) or to the political/economic structures of power. One of the most powerful myths of the twentieth century was the notion that the elimination of colonial administrations amounted to the decolonization of the world" (p. 73). Although often seen as Eurocentric, colonialism and coloniality need to also be seen through the new world power of neoliberalism, which is the imperial power above dichotomies that is often perceived as capitalist and communist divide. Perhaps like Pope Alexander VI through the Treaty of Tordesillas, this neoliberal emperor and pope has divided the *world* under the same "religion" just two different "nations." The world system regulates and enslaves through neoliberal policies that provide choices but are in fact feeding into the capitalist system. However, "[t]o call 'capitalist' the preset world-system is, to say the least, misleading. Given the hegemonic Eurocentric 'common sense', the moment we use the word 'capitalism' people immediately think that we are talking about the 'economy'. However, 'capitalism' is only one of the multiple entangled constellations of colonial power matrix of the 'European modern/colonial capitalist/patriarchal world system'" (Grosfoguel, 2010, pp. 72–73). As part of the colonial structure that is racialized and gendered, the current capitalist system is within a neoliberal hegemony that contributes to a biopolitics (Foucault, 2010) of choiceless choices (cf. Macedo et al., 2003) that engenders a rationalization of the supremacy of science under the regime of truth (Foucault, 1980) that legitimizes knowledges and identities within U.S. education. The hegemony of science as truth is reified in youth. Chelsea, my biology teacher colleague, and I have discussed the need to de-deify science. Science does not have all the answers, as one of our junior students presented on for her end of the year research project. Since she had both local and national accolades as a young, scientific scholar, another sophomore student was flabbergasted by her presentation and believed that "science could prove everything." In his words, "Miss Science presented on how science can't prove everything?" He shook his head, bewildered. Chelsea and I discussed how this is the beauty of science; it's not black and white. He was still skeptical. His skepticism is natural as he is a good student who earns As and Bs. Science has been constructed as a monolithic truth, which is readily imbibed by certain youth and educators.

This hegemony (Gramsci, 1971) continues through the people's acceptance and reproduction of *rationality* despite resistance. Quijano (2010) adds to this by explaining that "Europe thought of itself as the mirror of the future of all the other societies and cultures; as the advanced form of the history of the entire species. What does not cease to surprise, however, is that Europe succeeded in imposing that 'mirage' upon the practical totality of the cultures that it colonized; and, much more, that this chimera is still so attractive to so many" (p. 30). The "West is Best" motto continues to be perpetrated through global discourse. Even when the word "West" is left from discussion, its presence is felt since the best way has become synonymous with the global "West," ignoring, killing, and/or enslaving other forms of knowledges. This ethos of superiority shadows the lived experiences of suffering and oppression faced by the subaltern. The colonial matrix of power "did not only entail militarily subjugating the indigenous peoples and dominating them by force (colonialism); it also attempted to radically change their traditional knowledge of the world, to adopt the cognitive horizon of the dominator as their own (coloniality)" (Castro-Gómez, 2008, p. 281). The "cognitive horizon" is now measured under pseudo-neutrality and objectivity. We must disrupt or decolonize the "the masculist truth-claim to universality or academic objectivity" (Spivak, 1999, p. 148). Achievements and statistics are only markers of a deeper system of coloniality that permeates the U.S. educational system. By educational system, I do not mean only schools. The school is an ideological State apparatus as Althusser (1984) noted, but let's not forget the media, which may have no box to confine individuals in like a school; it is much more *sophisticated, modernized.* The box is constructed of sound waves and pixels in which an individual creates his or her own box without even knowing it. As Constantino (1978) wrote:

> We see our present with as little understanding as we view our past because aspects of the past which could illumine the present have been concealed from us. This concealment has been effected by a systemic process of mis-education characterized by a thoroughgoing inculcation of colonial values and attitudes—a process which could not have been so effective had we not been denied access to the truth and to part of our written history. As a consequence, we have become a people without a sense of history. We accept the present as given bereft of historicity. Because we have so little comprehension of our past, we have no appreciation of its meaningful interrelation with present. (p. 1)

Coloniality in the U.S. is not necessarily the physical force and takeover witnessed with colonialism. Coloniality is intricate. It runs on multiple planes; it can be seen in the subtle hegemonic way that it forms identity for the proletariat or *precariat* (Bauman & Donskis, 2012), and it can be seen in the brutal force that rules the prisons, which have become commercial colonies, social inequality that criminalizes the poor (cf. Wacquant, 2009), while making profits off the suppression and dehumanization of these humans as "capital"—captives of capitalism. Coloniality can be felt in the violent language of schools, which marks some as inferior and some as superior, while never even acknowledging others—the mark of invisibility. The discussion of coloniality must be viewed as interconnected with colonialism and imperialism as can be seen through the U.S. McClintock (1995) points out that the *U.S. imperialism-without-colonies* has been maintained through its financial power and corporations that are able to exploit the world's populations through knowledge and labor, "exert[ing] a coercive power as great as any colonial gunboat" (p. 13). Furthermore, the U.S. imperial armada includes education in which it exports its pedagogical and curricular knowledge to other countries through programs like IREX and ILEP (cf. Janson, 2015). An epistemicide can be more powerful than a gun. Constantino (1966) noted that one of the first things the U.S. military did when it took over the Philippines was establish schools. General Otis almost immediately assigned men as superintendents of schools and teachers (Constantino, 1966, p. 2).

This mis-education (Constantino, 1978; cf. Chomsky, 2003) and guilty ignorance is central to coloniality. U.S. educational policy is shaped and is shaping the hegemony of neoliberalism within this globalized economy. As Darder (2002) states:

> [with] the disastrous implications of an intensifying 'globalized' political economy, both locally and abroad, educators need to understand the impact of capitalism around the world and link it to the local conditions that exist in their schools and communities ... capitalism is advanced upon contradictory terrain, and does not function as a simple imposition. Instead, the notion of society as a collection of possessive individuals is reinforced and any serious sense of the common good is marginalized. This is advanced efficiently through the dynamics of the 'free market' ideology. (p. 11)

This globalized political economy will be analyzed further through colonialism and imperialism later on, but it's important to note how neoliberalism paints the parameters of what is considered legitimate within U.S. education as well as what should be considered outside and delegitimized, while promoting the liberty of choice. This *ethics of neoliberalism* "emphasizes the significance of contractual relations in the marketplace. It holds that the social good will be maximized by maximizing the reach and frequency of market transactions, and it seeks to bring all human action into the domain of the market. This requires technologies of information creation and capacities to accumulate, store, transfer, analyse, and use massive databases to guide decisions in the global marketplace" (Harvey, 2005, p. 3). These technologies are what we see in public schools, including scores from SAT (Scholastic Aptitude Test), AP (Advanced Placement), PARCC (Partnership for Assessment of Readiness for College and Careers), MCAS (Massachusetts Comprehensive Assessment System), ritualized benchmarks that have become easy to administer and assess through Scantron devices or other technologies—slide it through, like a rapid fire machine gun, red slashes, as the student's identity emerges, riddled or safe. Teachers are evaluated on how well they use these data coffins that inter the beings of youth. It is through this data that teachers are supposed to be getting students "college and career ready," making them good citizens for the U.S. market.

This functions through what Harvey (2010) calls creative destruction, claiming "innovation waves in technological and organisational forms are associated with crises of 'creative destruction' in which one bundle of dominant forms is displaced by another" (p. 100). The innovation of teaching switched from open classrooms of the 1970s to the highly compartmentalized education of today or from student-centered to test-centered. As I walked into Thyme Elementary School in Massachusetts, I noted the lack of walls except for the one glass wall classroom jutting out from the second floor. Yet, the teachers were closed off from one another. They had made their own classrooms by putting dividers up, moveable partitions. When I asked the teachers why the open classrooms didn't work, they explained that there was a lack of resources, too many children, the kids found the noise distracting, etc. The teachers seemed to envy that glass classroom, the fishbowl, which perhaps was a semi-panopticon but at the very least a symbol of power as it reflected light out.

My current high school is a former open school, but our district paid to have sheets of metal put up to make walls. Now, there are numerous classrooms without windows—we don't want openings in education, we want walls—to the point which my program supervisor during my practicum complained, "There's no windows in this school. I've never been in a school with so few windows." Innovations to build and to destroy and to build. Students lose freedom and teachers and administrators gain control. Creative destruction is linked to accumulation by dispossession (Harvey, 2005) but also the shock doctrine (Klein, 2007). In 1984, A Nation at Risk (ANAR) sent a shock through the country to radically transform education, the beginning of the innovative switch from student-centered to test-centered as U.S. citizens were fearful of keeping up with other countries. Reducing a child to a number is irrational. Expecting a child who has only known English for a year to take a high-stakes test in English is irrational. But, in actuality, this is all rational in the public education crisis where there are high expectations for all. Harvey (2010) explains, "[c]rises ... are the irrational rationalisers of an irrational system" (p. 215). The harnessing of fear is a powerful motivator that feeds off people's emotions in order to provoke change.

However, these reactionary changes are not what we need to decolonize our minds and to have sustainable and authentic transformation in society. Nkrumah (1964) stated, "[t]o declare a political war on religion is to treat it as an ideal phenomenon, to suppose that it might be wished away, or at the worst scared out of existence. The indispensable starting point is to appreciate the sociological connection between religious belief and practice on the one hand, and poverty on the other" (p. 13). Neoliberal patriotism is a religion in the U.S. The free market mentality for the sake of the good country is hegemonic and shields U.S. imperialism from a critical public consciousness. The U.S. declared the separation of church and state, wedding instead corporation and state. However, to declare a political war against the socio-industrial complex that has taken over public education, social services, prisons, etc. would be to only see half of the problem.

In order to decolonize mentalities, we must understand how this requires fighting with knowledge, and it begins with ourselves. Human conscience is shaped by sociopolitical forces and in many instances anesthetizes. As educators, we need to decolonize our minds and work with youth to create decolonial spaces for them to critique their world and discover their identities while also analyzing the factors that they have resisted, reproduced, or produced, which can be theorized and unraveled through understanding colonialities. It is important to understand that the psyche is not separate from physical nor can they be disentangled from the socio aspects as well. Fanon (1952) describes a study that analyzed how, when couples married at some point, they had a biochemical change, and "there are subjectively experienced processes taking place, whose functioning cannot be explained in the terms of only the natural sciences, of only physical laws" (Wynter, 2001, p. 36). Relationships and human contact not only affets our mentalities but also our bodies. Fanon's (1952) findings draw our attention to the way that body is not separate from the mind, which speaks to spiritualities and colonialities. In addition, Wynter (2001) explains:

> The implication here is that the biochemical events taking place in his being as he reads the evidence of his own mutation, his power in the others' eyes (and thereby the evidence of his own recognition in the terms

> of the dominant culture and its bearers) are determined by the change in his cultural situation: the shift from an amputated experience of being to the experience of almost 'full' (that is, almost white), almost French bourgeois, being. (p. 38)

The problem comes from decolonizing the notion of an amputated being when not assimilatedly "full" in the bourgeois culture and power. In order to be, we often feel that we have to give up who we are to that White heteropatriarchal power. We give ourselves to His being in order to feel a spirituality that is colonized and connects us through exploitive and seductive ways. This attempts to silence the plurality of beings and epitomizes the colonialities of being. Furthermore, to think that by rejecting assimilation will be whole or "full" is erroneous as well. We are forever changed by the interactions we have with colonial powers. We must decolonize our minds in order to complexify our understandings of our positions and identities within the colonial matrix of power and consequently our connections to others. Liberation does not mean that we have gained freedom of mind and spirit. It is through consciencism and conscientização that we begin to decolonize our mentalities and understand our spiritualities in order to enunciate our beings and identities.

Spirituality is the human ability of expression and connection. The power of language is one of the greatest colonizing forces and vehicles of coloniality. Fanon (1952) claims, "[e]very colonized people—in other words, every people in whose soul an inferiority complex has been created by the death and burial of its local cultural originality—finds itself face to face with the language of the civilizing nation" (p. 9). A civilized tongue has been mutilated until it forgets the body and mind that houses it. This spiritual amnesia does not deny humans agency but requires an awakening, a rupture of this anesthetized consciousness to remember that humans are not rooted in the constraints of the physical present. Rather, they "participate in the creative dimension as well, men can intervene in reality in order to change it. Inheriting acquired experience, creating and re-creating, integrating themselves into their context, responding to its challenges, objectifying themselves, discerning, transcending, men enter into the domain which is theirs exclusively—that of History and of Culture" (Freire, 2013, p. 4). As decolonial educational leaders, we must consider the psychological, social, and cultural factors of youth, educators, guardians, and communities. Studying psychosocial laws gives "insights into the laws which govern the realm of lived subjective experience, human and non-human: which govern, therefore, the interrelated phenomena of identity, mind and/or consciousness" (Wynter, 2001, p. 3). The psychosocial laws are in a way spiritual destruction and part of the colonialities of being, which oppress humans' spiritualities and identities.

Spirituality is intimately connected with the colonialities of being. Dantley (2005) wrote, "critical spirituality allows for not only a grappling with our individual sense of being and purpose but it also grounds our work in interrogating those social and political contexts within which we find ourselves" (p. 503). I would claim that we need a decolonial spirituality that not only interrogates those social and political contexts but also engages in intercultural translation (Santos, 2014) as well as considers whose knowledge defines spirituality. Spirituality for liberation can be a mechanism of seduction in neoliberalism in which knowledges, identities, and relationships are orchestrated by "choiceless choices" (Macedo, 2003).

When viewing the social and political effects of neoliberalism within school as well as the sanctity of the new standards for college and career readiness (i.e., Common Core) as assessed through PARCC, we see that the commodification of knowledge is also the commodification of students through criminality and disposability. Furthermore, this is done through the control of youth's body from the ubiquitous Zero Tolerance policies that have no official definition but are felt throughout schools in which it is legitimate to take a six-year-old out in handcuffs for having a temper tantrum,[6] or, on a more personal note, the determination of the superintendent that if my seven-year-old nephew play-acted with imaginary light sabers at recess, the police were to be called and he would be similarly disposed of.

These school rituals (Quantz, 2011) are not democratic but are part of colonization into capitalist system in which students may resist or conform. The contradictions and the subtractive effects on students' identities and spiritualities from the positivist culture of standardized practices within schools function "under the guise of neutrality, scientific knowledge and all theory become rational on the grounds of whether or not they are efficient, economic, or correct" (Giroux, 2001, p. 16). This secularization and stupidification of knowledge to the realm of the rational and replicable thwarts innovation, which is exactly what Common Core and Race to the Top claim to want.

This transformation of knowledge is part of the colonialities of being. Much of the rationalization comes from the knowledge put forth by the Enlightenment in contrast to the previous knowledge of man being connected to religion. Wynter (2003) discusses the secularization of man in the Enlightenment, stating:

> While, if this redescription was effected by the lay world's invention of Man as the political subject of the state, in the transumed and reoccupied

> place of its earlier matrix identity Christian, the performative enactment of this new "descriptive statement" and its master code of symbolic life and death, as the first secular or "degodded" (if, at the time, still only partly so) mode of being human in the history of the species, was to be effected only on the basis of what Quijano identifies as the "coloniality of power," Mignolo as the "colonial difference," and Winant as a huge project demarcating human differences thinkable as a "racial longue durée." (p. 263)

Man was "degodded" and defined by the principles of reason that were soon based on market mentality. Yet, the secularization of man was really just switching the Christian God with a neoliberal god that functions through national pride and economic development. In addition, there remains "the radical separation produced between reason/subject and body ... in Eurocentric rationality the body was fixed as object of knowledge, outside of the environment of subject/reason. Without this objectification of the body as nature, its expulsion from the sphere of the spirit (and this is my strong thesis), the 'scientific' theorization of the problem of race (as in the case of the comte de Gobineau [1853–1857] during the nineteenth century) would have hardly been possible" (Quijano, 2000, p. 555). Santos (2014) adds that, "[t]he centrality then assumed by class and the psyche is now being assumed by the body (corporeality), itself now converted, like enlightened reason before, into the roots of all options" (p. 84). Today, we no longer need minds to think science does and tells our bodies what to do.

There is an automatization (animation of the corpus) and the anesthetization/euthanization of the mind. The body under the hegemony of Western knowledge is needed as a vehicle for production and/or destruction. Spivak (1988) claims that "the subtext of the palimpsestic narrative of imperialism be recognized as 'subjugated knowledge,' 'a whole set of knowledges that have been disqualified as inadequate to their task of insufficiently elaborated: naive knowledges, located low down on the hierarchy, beneath the required level of cognition or scientificity' (Foucault, 1980, p. 82)" (pp. 24–25). The scientificity is what drives the rhetoric of modernization and the rise of a liquid modernity (Bauman, 2013) in which nations have become transnational and neoliberalism seems to be a nation that has imperial and colonial power.

The imperialism of Western knowledge and the dismissal of the knowledge of the body and experience for science and rational knowledge was part of the theo- and ego-politics of knowledges (Mignolo, 2009b). Mignolo (2009b) explains how "[b]y locating knowledge in the mind only, and bracketing 'secondary qualities' (affects, emotions, desires, anger, humiliation, etc.), social actors who happened to be white, inhabiting Europe/Western Christendom and speaking specific languages assumed that what was right for them in that place and which fulfilled their affects, emotions, fears and angers was indeed valid for the rest of the planet and, consequently, that they were the depositor, warrantor, creator and distributor of universal knowledge" (p. 19). This production of the superiority and universality of Western knowledge is reproduced in the U.S. public schools today through Common Core and assessments, such as PARCC. The reduction of students' spiritualities to mechanistic consumption and reproduction of knowledge via standardized assessments—from multiple choice tests to rubrics—is dehumanizing and oppressive. Freire (2013) explains, "[b]y requiring a man to behave mechanically, mass production domesticates him. By separating his activity from the total project, requiring no total critical attitude toward production, it dehumanizes him" (p. 31). Unfortunately, the quest for the replicable and research-based teaching is hegemonic in schools.

This is part of the banking style of education that contradicts the push for personalization and differentiated instruction that I also hear in schools. Banking education is inherent in the U.S. public educational system through the demands for information retrieval and standardized testing. Multiple choice tests are just prepping them for the market in which there is a selection of possible choices that do not require a critical mind, just a credit card. As Darder (2015) states, "banking educational objectives emphasize to what extent students have the potential to participate as consuming citizens of the empire" (p. 31). Ironically, students often complain that they have no fiscal knowledge or perhaps fiduciary knowledge. They know how to buy, but they do not understand what their responsibilities and consequences are of their purchases.

Quantz (2011) refers to the national objective that teaching be based on "research" and adds that "such research only seems to matter when the research supports what policymakers want" (p. 167), neglecting a needed "culture of care" (Noddings, 2005). This is crucial in an age of "innovation," which seems to mean the devolvement of our identities and spiritualities. One must ask, "Whose interests are served by schools that provide well-trained young adults able to read and follow directions and apply techniques but unable to read and critique the world and apply moral and political reasoning?" (Quantz, 2011, p. 166). This anti-intellectualism plagues schools, denying teachers and students the right to question, yet consensually constructing hegemony (Gramsci, 1971). Macedo et al. (2003) adds to this that

> the current 'crisis of critique' signals the cessation of questioning and the suffocation of critique. This general failure to question is a direct

> by-product of neoliberal ideology, which has managed to produce a powerful myth about itself that it does not need to be interrogated .... Neoliberal politics pretends to provide the answers for concepts and ideas that should remain perpetually open and be constantly questioned and redefined if they are to contribute to a vital political cultural and a process of democratization. (p. 111)

This critique is a dialectical and dialogic process, which involves educators and students researching and discovering, pushing the spaces of innovation. Even though educators are in the bowels of neoliberalism with privatized choices and reforms constantly invading the public school, Branco (2015) found that the majority of secondary educators in her interviews with teachers did not know what the word neoliberalism meant. It means going beyond the canon of orthodox knowledge and providing a space for students to be able to see words and works that will allow them to read worlds. Youths' lives are full of texts that they, or we, never even recognize.

Once I pulled out a Gap advertisement for my students to analyze, and they passed it around wondering what was wrong with it. In the advertisement, one little girl was black and the other was white, so they immediately thought that it had to do with race. I said, "No, look beyond their skin color. Analyze it." Both four-year-old girls were wearing makeup, sitting on a bench posing. The dialogue began.

"Look at their body language .... What are they saying?" I asked.

"Like her shoulders?"

"Yes. What else?" I poked.

"They're not smiling."

"But they're wearing makeup."

"They are!" exclaimed another. "They're just little kids."

"I didn't even notice the makeup."

"Why?" I asked. "Are we so used to everyone covering their face and advertisements being airbrushed that we fail to even see the un-reality?"

Things that are so hegemonic that they never consider how this is forming what we think a child should be. Even a child must be dolled up? We discuss their videogames and texts. There is so much for them to read that they read without critically analyzing. This is part of Freire's conscientização and Nkrumah's consciencism for educators but for students as well. As an educator, I was introduced to Freire's work early in my pedagogical education, but Freire was not alone in his conceptualization of conscientização. Nkrumah's theorization of consciencism should be in dialogue with Freire. Failure to do so would be a hollowing of their concepts.

Freire is often heroified as *the* critical pedagogue within the U.S. While his work cannot be diminished and his words speak to the realities that, as teachers and/or pedagogues, we live daily, critical pedagogy does not begin or end with Freire, it exists with Freire; as Carlos Albert Torres remarked, "we can stay with Freire or against Freire, but not without Freire" (as quoted in McLaren and Leonard, 1992, p. 1). I would not say that we are working through Freire because that would seem antithetical to his work, but rather with him.

Although Darder (2002) notes that Freire speaks of reinventing, recreating, and rewriting his ideas in particular, she focuses on reinventing as being "true to the spirit of a liberatory pedagogy" (p. 151). I do not disagree that students and teachers are often reduced to producers and reproducers due to the fact that "reproduction is more sought after, leading to 'teacher-proof' methods and the standardization of knowledge. These are antithetical to the creativity inherent in reinvention, for reinvention entails imagination" (Darder, 2002, p. 151). However, it is the "re" that needs to be problematized. If we are re-creating/inventing/writing/etc., then that means that we are limiting critical pedagogy, knowledge, language, etc. to begin from what was, and, in a way, rewriting those ideas and words decontextualizes from their historicity.

Critical pedagogy is within the waters of decolonial pedagogy, but it must be disrupted in order to go further. Freire's language in *Pedagogy of the Oppressed* has evident sexist undertones, but, as he later reflects, it must be contextualized and analyzed within that historical moment (Freire & Macedo, 1992). But, that historical moment needs to also be analyzed—as I will discussed earlier—for the making of the sexist undertones constructed by the colonial and capitalist expansion that obliterated the gender fluidity that many indigenous cultures had (cf. Oyěwùmí, 2002; Lugones, 2008). The challenge is not to "reinvent" but to continue the dialogue in which we envision and create new theories that honor the work of others, such as Freire as well as other critical/anti-colonial/decolonial pedagogues and previously silenced or excluded voices, by challenging it and creating new worlds. The words of Cabral (1973a) in which he asks to "return to the source" but not necessarily to traditions; rather, he conceptualizes this as a "reply to the concrete need" (p. 67). His words embody a decolonial pedagogy that is "not a voluntary step, but the only possible reply to the demand of concrete need, historically determined, and enforced by the inescapable contradiction between the colonized society and the colonial power" (Cabral, 1973a, p. 67). We must not return to the replicative process of colonial pedagogy, nor must we *re*claim public education as it has been, returning to a colonial apparatus.

We must envision and build a public education that is a response to the needs and contradictions of the public and for its enunciatory and liberatory potential. Through the praxis of teaching and theorizing, as pedagogues we must deepen and complexify critical pedagogy with decolonial pedagogy. By its nature, critical pedagogy (cf. Freire, Giroux, hooks, Darder, McLaren, etc.) cannot be static and immutable, it is through the constant dialogue and dialectics with people, engaging spiritualities, languages, and knowledges. Without this critique and engagement, epistemicides (Santos, 2007b, 2014; Paraskeva, 2011, 2016a, 2016b, 2017) are propagated in unconscious and complicit silence that scourges.

The romanticization of meritocracy seen within U.S. schools reflects a culture that believes in the "American" dream but ignores the culture of violence that it cloaks. The sense of culture that I have observed is not one of solidarity but of solitary with occasional spurts of "solidarity on demand" (Bauman & Donskis, 2013, p. 114). Darder (2002) addresses the fact that teachers with students must recognize the privileges and entitlements that are associated with the dominant culture; failing to do so

> perpetuates alienating beliefs within the educational system of what is legitimate knowledge, classroom practice, and teacher-student relationships. To be considered a legitimate or valuable educator or student requires the willingness to conform to a standard and protocol rooted in the dominant cultural and class values of the educational system. It this set of values which also then determines whether a student or teacher will be considered a "good fit" within many institutions. (p. 21)

It is this legitimacy and illegitimacy that, as decolonial pedagogues, we must consider as well since students navigate the school system environed in these political dimensions of power. This is connected to biopolitics (Foucault, 2010) and body-politics (Mignolo, 2009b) and the Pinocchio effect, which I will be discussing in the subsequent chapters.

Notes

1 The U.S. Department of Education Office for Civil Rights (2014) reported that approximately 5,000 preschoolers have been suspended once, but 2,500 have been suspended more than once (p. 7). Furthermore, 79% of those suspended are boys, and 48% of these suspensions are black children despite the fact that they only comprise 18% of the preschool population (U.S. DOE, 2014, p. 1).

2 In the United States, females do 60% of the unpaid work and have less leisure time than men according to an OECD report in 2011, "Cooking, Caring and Volunteering:

Unpaid Work Around the World." For the full report, see http://thinkprogress.org/economy/2014/03/14/3399641/oecd-housework-women/

3 Note that this is modern Western terminology that did not exist in these cultures but is used for classification purposes.

4 I use subaltern youth instead of "minority" youth because I feel "minority" hollows the politics and power involved in the classification of youth as minority as well as occludes how in fact many times these youth are the majority of the population, but they are the minority power.

5 Delinking changes "the terms of the conversation, and above all, of the hegemonic ideas of what knowledge and understanding are and, consequently, what economy and politics, ethics and philosophy, technology and organization of society are and should be, [then] it is necessary to fracture the hegemony of knowledge and understanding that have been ruled, since the fifteenth century and through the modern/colonial world by what I conceive here as the theo-logical the ego-logical politics of knowledge and understanding" (Mignolo, 2010, p. 313).

6 This was the case in Georgia where a six year old girl was handcuffed and removed by police from school, which police defended as necessary and legal measure (Campbell, 2012).

CHAPTER 4

Canary in the Mind: Colonialities, Biopolitics, and Body-Politics

> There can be no more urgent task than to come to understand the mechanisms and practices of indoctrination. These are easy to perceive in the totalitarian societies, much less so in the propaganda system to which we are subjected and in which all too often we serve as unwilling or unwitting instruments.
>
> CHOMSKY (2003, p. 212)

"*We're*—we're the canaries in the coal mines," my colleague told me as I coughed.

My doctor had informed me that the thirty or forty year old carpets in my classroom and the ceiling tiles that had mold on them were the likely source

FIGURE 4.1 Canary in the mine at Cross Mountain mine explosion (from MSHA, December 9, 1911)

 | DOI: 10.1163/9789004416048_004

of the severe allergic reaction I was having. "It's slowly killing me," I sputtered. The joke falling flat.

"Yes, yes it is," Colleen said, my colleague and mentor for the past six years.

I breathed out, catching a solid wave of oxygen. "It's not the room," I said sitting on a desk. "I can't stand the policies anymore. I can't stand the lack of respect. We know what is best for our kids, but we keep going down the same path. I'm so tired of fighting." I look up at her feeling the exhaustion streaking my face. I feel as if teachers' faces are tattooed with the years that they have served. The way their spirit is whipped until they moan like His bitch. I turn my back toward her. "Just let us be the whipping girls again. My back is covered."

What do I care?

"I wish I had taken a picture of you when you first started and now. You've aged fifteen years."

I weep sometimes for that girl. The one who believed in the utopian possibilities. I was going to come in and connect with my kids, and everything would work itself out. Fight the system! How do you fight the system when youth and your colleagues are so readily consuming the White heterosexual patriarchy? They feel their oppression as liberation, rubbing against it like sandpaper until their ridges that define them are made smooth in the symmetrical oppression of systemic beauty. Every piece of wood the same. Those who do this are made real. The Pinocchio effect.

They get to be in the world without realizing that there may be no strings, but their actions and thoughts have been colonized by hegemony, mental puppetry. Then, there are those who resist. You have those students with such critical or wounded minds. Their stories so long silenced.

When you try to reach them, it can seem impossible, but then you do. Your hand in theirs until you have to let go in 45-minute increments. Bell. The fight is over. Just hang on until tomorrow. I'll be here. Just hang on. Ok?

Did you hear?

What?

She dropped out. She signed herself out this morning.

The anger builds. Does no one think to call teachers down to counsel these kids? Does no one think of the work that we do in keeping these kids in school? Four years of work gone in the month of April, three weeks from graduation. All that remains is her letter to you that stays in your planning binder of her childhood memories of forgetting but embodying. A traumatic past fled from memory but lived.

The disdain when kids want to share their stories of sexual abuse, mental illness, or pornography. A gendered oppression. Student research on hip hop also foul in the mouth, illegitimate knowledge. A racialized oppression. Mocking of public university as not prestigious to a group of youth who cannot afford the Ivy League caviar. A classed oppression. Yet gendered, racialized, and classed they are all intertwined. How can I box these experiences into categories? Or, perhaps the better question is why did I? This question is part of consciencism (Nkrumah, 1964) and conscientização (Freire, 2009). The decolonial momentum cannot concern itself with stopping thoughts falling into the neoliberal hand of oppressing our tongues whilst our colonized thoughts continue to direct neutral actions under oppressive rationalities that legitimize violence as can be seen within the racism in the colorblind war on drugs (Alexander, 2011).

We must not fall prey to political correctness for the sake bourgeoisie gentility. Our thoughts must be challenged because we live in a violent system of neutrality that produces rampant systemic inequalities. To not recognize the number of people who are being killed as a public health crisis is an example of how we are shocked by the flu epidemic but not by the lives killed by police violence. Using data collected by researchers in the United Kingdom on the U.S., a report from the Harvard T. Chan School of Public Health found that "[a]s of September 19, 2015, the cumulative 2015 total of 842 U.S. persons killed by the police notably exceeded the corresponding totals reported for the 122 cities' 442 deaths under age 25 (all causes) and also 585 deaths (all ages) due to pneumonia and influenza" (Krieger, Chen, Waterman, Kiang, & Feldman, 2015, p. 2). Challenging what the media chooses to highlight and not highlight is part of decolonizing the mind. Decolonizing thoughts cannot be about silencing the mind or quartering off, which world needs decolonial thinking and which does not.

The decolonial momentum must understand that although coursing through different limbs of the body, this oppressive blood carries the autoimmune virus of colonial power that contains the necessary oxygen along with the destructive cells. However, this oppression will eventually asphyxiate us as there are no cells left to carry the oxygen since the autoimmune virus kills our own cells.

The decolonial momentum cannot only be a Southern or Eastern world concept. If it is, then it has already failed. The decolonial momentum must concern itself with biopolitics (Foucault, 2010) and the new rationales in all spheres, complexifying the distinctions of East vs. West or North vs. South. This is not to say we live in an objective or neutral world without location. Our viewpoint cannot be without a locus of enunciation because this would be what Castro-Gómez (2008) describes as the *hubris of zero degrees*. Rather, traditional cartographies and conceptions of boundaries fail to sufficiently theorize and depict the provinces of power.

The geographic map of the world is not the modern world. Modernity makes geography an antiquity as in reality East, West, North, South are all parallel planes of diverse experiences that run along and through each other. Each experience impacts the other with lightning speed. However, each experience, each location is not blended into a universal experience and description. Each location has its own history and knowledges, but isolation will thwart decolonization. We must see deeper into spaces of wealth and spaces of poverty, while not forgetting those who may be schooled and mis-educated and living within a poverty of experience. Material wealth and spiritual poverty is not un-problematic; it enables a disconnection from the world that dehumanizes and strips humans of agency. Similarly, poverty is not an "Other" problem.

A child starving and freezing in the once thriving city of New Bedford is no less a consequence of capitalism's colonial assault as a child in a favela of Rio de Janeiro. After studying the "universal soul" in *The Grapes of Wrath*, I reiterate to my students the words of Donne (1839), "Ask not for whom the bell tolls, it tolls for thee." A simple expression that stands for the relationship that we have with others as well as ourselves, which we often forget in an era of data processing. Postman (1993) explains how William Carrish in 1792 was the first to grade students' responses. This assignment of a numerical value to student knowledge is using the number as technology, and that "quantitative value should be assigned to human thoughts was a major step toward constructing" (p. 13). The ubiquity of grading today makes it nearly impossible to imagine how we would assess students without grades.

What makes an A so much better than a B? When I whip through a batch of MCAS essays, do I think about where that child was with his or her writing in Septemeber and where he or she is now? If I do, I am failing to be objective. We have pushed toward "a mathematical concept of reality … [in which people] believe that without numbers they cannot acquire or express authentic knowledge" (Postman, 1993, p. 13). Reality can be defined by math, but then what of the real is left out because it cannot be made into a number?

Children become numbers. Teachers are numbers. But, where are the bodies? Where are the minds? How can they be dismembered from each other? Body and mind are together. However, the sustenance we derive from food and water or the creams that we rub into our skin to heal the cracks do not heal the cracks within our selves. Where is the self? We live in an age when you can walk into a store, and it'll have different sections of how to make a better you and take care of you, from creams to vitamins to drinks to foods, but the body is not the self. Foucault (1988) detailed how "[w]hen you take care of the body, you don't take care of the self. The self is not clothing, tools, or possessions. It is to be found in the principle which uses these tools, a principle not of the body, but of the soul" (p. 25). The soul is the nexus of the mind and body. Make the mind and body fear, and you oppress the soul as it cowers from its dialectic engagement with mankind, oppressing spirituality. The body-mind becomes subject to a new reason, governed not by laws but by rationalization of oppression. The false division of soul and body was part of colonization particularly in relation to Christianity:

> The process of the separation of these two elements (body and nonbody) of the human being is part of the long history of the Christian world founded on the idea of the primacy of the soul above the body .... The body was and could be nothing but an object of knowledge. From this point of view the human being is, par excellence, a being gifted with reason, and this gift was conceived as localized exclusively in the soul. Thus the body, by definition incapable of reason, does not have anything that meets reason/subject. The radical separation produced between reason/subject and body and their relations should be seen only as relations between the human subject/reason and the human body/nature, or between spirit and nature. (Quijano, 2000, pp. 554–555)

Disconnection of body and soul is nonrational for many; they are deemed as separate. Yet, if a body sustains sexual abuse, does not the soul, spirit, and/or mind transform due to this? If a body is starved of food does not the soul and mind transform? If it is starved of love? We know that it does. Human babies can die from lack of love and human contact (Szalavitz & Perry, 2010).

To dismember the body from the soul is part of biopolitics (Foucault, 2010), a concept which I will examine further later. In addition, this is "thingification = colonization" (Cesairé, 1963), in which the colonized mind treats the body as an instrument of the societal norms and standards of production. Fanon (1963) explained, "the spirit of discouragement which has been deeply rooted in people's minds by colonial domination is still very near the surface. But we must not overlook the fact that victory over those weaknesses which are the heritage of the material and spiritual domination of the country by another is a necessity from which no government will be able to escape" (p. 194). We become *objects* of the world instead of *agents* in the world. Humans have their place and are subject to the *naturalized* reflexes of society, which leaves an air of hopelessness about changing society. It is *natural* for there to be poverty. It is *natural* for people to go to prison for being addicted to a drug because they deserved it. And, it is *natural* for a man to be addicted to money, even stealing others' because he earned it. Students fall prey to predatory universities that saddle them with a *natural* debt. Man is free. Man is indebted. The contradiction of those two sentences is normalized out of our memories:

> You are free insofar as yon assume the way of life (consumption, work, public spending, taxes, etc.) compatible with reimbursement. The techniques used to condition individuals to live with debt begin very early on, even before entry on the job market. (Lazzarato, 2012, p. 31)

Children are ritualized into debt, watching their parents garner it. Parents, to make their children happy, often swipe their credit cards. In a survey of mothers, 46% have gone into debt raising their kids and "53% said they're stressed out by trying to create 'perfect' childhoods for their kids" (DiGangi, 2015). Commercials and advertising make parents feel that they need to give their children perfection with a beautiful bow. This is part of the mass production of consciousness that has roots in the Industrial Revolution.

People who had been working in factories under grueling conditions were acquiring the ability to buy luxuries that gave them something to work for beyond living necessities. People began to have the power to buy and with that came the realm of advertising as well as its ability to shape public consciousness and its economic responsibility to mold the minds of the masses with this economic liberation. Ewen (1977) describes how "[w]ithin the vision of consumption as a 'school of freedom,' the entry onto the consumer market was described as a 'civilizing' experience" (p. 30). This was the re-shaping of cultural knowledge and rationalities, inculcating a desire to consume where "[t]he social perception was one in which people ameliorated the negative condition of social objectification through consumption—material objectification" (Ewen, 1977, p. 36). Harvesting social perception is a colonization of the mind that requires education. Advertising is a tool of colonization through education.

In President Calvin Coolidge's (1926) "Address Before the American Association of Advertising Agencies," he juxtaposed advertising and education, explaining that "[a]dvertising ministers to the spiritual side of trade. It is a great power that has been entrusted to your keeping which charges you with the high responsibility of inspiring and ennobling the commercial world. It is all part of the greater work of the regeneration and redemption of mankind." This redemption and ennoblement is at the crux of the colonial ethos, which I will discuss later in this chapter.

The morality of consumption is part of the technologies that produce consciousness and cultural knowledge—a regime of truth. Foucault (1988) detailed the need to question knowledge as to whether it is ordained under scientific truth or not because these are part of the "truth games" that shape our perception of self:

> [W]e must understand that there are four major types of these "technologies," each a matrix of practical reason: (1) technologies of production, which permit us to produce, transform, or manipulate things; (2) technologies of sign systems, which permit us to use signs, meanings, symbols, or signification; (3) technologies of power, which determine the conduct of individuals and submit them to certain ends or domination, an objectivizing of the subject; (4) technologies of the self, which permit individuals to effect by their own means or with the help of others a certain number of operations on their own bodies and souls, thoughts, conduct, and way of being, so as to transform themselves in order to attain a certain state of happiness, purity, wisdom, perfection, or immortality. (p. 18)

When I saw the commercial for the dystopian movie, *In Time*, I discussed the premise with my students who were eager for its release. Here was a perfect allegory of how technologies are the gatekeepers of our lives. In the movie, money is time. As you buy things, you give up hours, days, years of your life via the clock on your arm. Yet, there are those who have millions of years to themselves, while the poor are dying in the streets. As an educator, an aunt, a community worker, etc., how many times have I muttered, "Why aren't there more hours in the day? I need more time" (Niccol, 2010). Time *is* a luxury. Will Salas, a working class young man, is stealing time from the super-rich Weis's safe in order to try to restore balance to society, but Phillippe Weis tells him, "But don't fool yourself. In the end, nothing will change. Because everyone wants to live forever. They all think they have a chance at immortality even though all the evidence is against it. They all think they will be the exception. But the truth is, for a few to be immortal, many must die" (Niccol, 2010). The concept of immortality mixing with meritocracy and equality is important in understanding rationalities in modernity.

Many people believe that everyone has an equal chance or at least a chance that is the same as everybody else. People consume and buy new things relating back to Ewen's (1977) research and consumerism, marketing for mass consumption. In addition, Davies (2011) writes about the political economy of unhappiness and that "[advertising] acts as capital's own trusted moral and artistic critic in order to inspire additional psychological engagement on the part of ordinary worker-consumers. Dissatisfaction is reduced to a psychological tendency to be fed back into processes of production and consumption" (p. 73). My father told me that he had a hole in himself that church, or rather Christian faith, filled for him. It made him whole. His brother filled that hole with drugs, alcohol, food, etc., but it never was enough. Consuming isn't the same as communing.

In a previous piece, I have written about the image of my uncle's arms with tattoos all the way up, which as a child fascinated me. However, I remember as I got older how his arms would be riddled with "moons of pain"—places where his skin was seared out by cigarettes that he fell asleep holding, burning his skin. Pieces of him gone even though those pieces had already been inked. Was the scar more him or was the dyed skin? Did he even know? What mattered him or the next hit? Why did he feel the need to dye himself? To get high? To change himself? What does consuming drugs do? Was he consuming identities or escaping from realities?

hooks (2000) writes, "Widespread addiction in both poor and affluent communities is linked to our psychotic lust for material consumption. It keeps us unable to love. Fixating on wants and needs, which consumerism encourages us to do, promotes a psychological state of endless craving" (pp. 110–111). Those who have so much are still longing for more. Do mountains of dollar bills warm a soul? There is always something better, but it further disconnects people from others.

I turned to the class as we were going over the notes. "Why is Uncle John drinking so much?" The habitual silence echoed. Nothing like the sound of "Please don't make me speak" ringing in the classroom.

Finally someone spoke, "To escape his guilt."

I looked at the faces, and they were half glazed over. Many I assumed had not read. Others didn't care. The reading I couldn't tackle, but the apathy … *that* I could possibly assuage. I tried to connect to them, and maybe un/consciously tried to provoke them.

"Yes, most people who use drugs or alcohol are trying to escape something, right? When people smoke a joint, they are doing it to escape reality. Alcohol and drugs are used to dull pain."

"Not necessarily. Some people, some people smoke weed because they just like the feeling. It makes them happy."

"YEAH! Weed just makes people happy!"

I give a slow nod of understanding. "OK, so if weed makes people happy, what does that make them when they aren't smoking weed?"

The boys go to argue but then stop.

I repeat, "If you are happy when you are high, what are you when you aren't high?"

"Huh," they said. Their minds were churning the rationality of my question.

"They are escaping reality. If you are smoking weed to get high and to feel something, that means you don't feel that happiness without the drug? Drugs represent people's inability to own their own bodies and emotions." The bell rang soon after, and they left deliberating my statement.

To be frank, I was still questioning it as well. People have told me that they are truly themselves when they are high or drunk. Alcohol and weed the great liberators from the societal construction of consciousness .... Is it a true freedom of self? Foucault (1988) asked, "First, what is the self? Self is a reflexive pronoun, and it has two meanings. *Auto* means 'the same,' but it also conveys the notion of identity. The latter meaning shifts the question from 'What is the self?' to 'What is the plateau on which I shall find my identity?'" (p. 25). What holds us from knowing our identities? Is it others' perceptions of us? Who oppresses our knowledge? Who has the privilege of that knowledge? Why are we so violent against our selves?

Rudy, one of my senior students, came into my classroom late, and I looked at the Christmas bag in his hand. He was wearing that goofy smile of his, which suited his imperviousness to the demands of the world. "Aww, Rudy. You brought me a Christmas gift! How sweet!"

"Naw, Miss J." He laughed. "This is mine from Mr. L."

I smiled, happy to see a smile on his face again. The day before he had been upset over his girlfriend 'dropping him' because she said that she thought too much. He ended up punching a wall in my classroom and going for a walk. Today, his face was bright. "That was nice of Mr. L. You are one of his favorites."

"I know. I don't know why!" he said, shrugging and sitting down. He opened his gift, which had a blue Chaps sweater inside.

As he held it up, the girls exclaimed, "Those are expensive!"

"Aww, Rudy. That's so you," said one of the girls.

He grinned and held it up to himself.

"They are *really* expensive, Rudy," said another girl.

"I know." He said looking at it and eagerly pulling it on over his shirt. In fact, I don't think I have ever seen him in a sweater like it. "Miss J, I'm going to go change. I can't wear it with my shirt underneath."

"Go ahead, Rudy."

After the class, I went up to him as he stuffed the tissue paper back into the Christmas bag.

"That was really kind of Mr. L. He thinks you're such a nice boy."

I hear in my words the power of educating through rewards and the materialism that youth learn to equate things with love. Yet, this object was not about materialism but more a symbol of gratitude and love. It was not the possession of the item that matter but the action of giving.

He shrugged off the compliment from one of the most beloved and oldest teachers at Clayton.

"I did an oil change in his car and fixed ...." His voice trailed off, and he shrugged again.

"A nice present after a bad day. It must make you feel special …." I decided to brave it and ask, "Is it a better day?"

"Aww Miss J … I was so mad yesterday." He shifted, his hands moving, reminding me of a boxer in a ring before a fight. "I almost gave myself a concussion. I slammed my head into a locker." He shook his head. "When my head came back, whoa. I was all dizzy and …."

I had my arms crossed against my chest, ready to scold. "You have to learn to deal with your anger in a different way though. It's not good—."

He interrupted quickly. "But I didn't hurt anybody. I mean I don't hurt people. I just—" His own past creating a defense of his present.

My turn to interrupt. "You got hurt. Aren't you somebody?"

He laughed, shaking his head.

"Aren't you somebody? You're a human, no?"

"Naw, I'm nobody, Miss J. I'm nobody." He laughed.

I shook my head. "That's not true." What I should have said, was you're somebody to me. You're somebody to Mr. L. You're somebody to your peers. "Hurting yourself is as bad as hurting someone else."

"It's okay."

I walked with him toward the door of my classroom. "This is what we were talking about today. Are we ruled by self-hate or self-love?"

"I don't know." He laughed it off as he walked out the door. "See you tomorrow, Miss J."

As an educator, I stand in the middle of selves, feeling the different veins of oppression and violence. Whether it's class, race, gender, sexuality, religion, dis/ability, they're all around. Those whose privilege triumphs while others are crushed under the victory. At times, you can put your hand down to cover theirs before it's stepped on, but, under that boot, both hands are crushed. You hold their hands with broken fingers, muttering that it's going to be okay. They see the inequity. They see the violence. They see you whipped. You see them whipped. Their spirits are slowly crushed and so is yours, but you must still fight, even with your hands behind your back. You use your teeth to bite onto whatever scraps of hope that remain. Teeth leave marks. The clock was ticking, and I was back to Colleen's classroom.

My mind went back to her words: "I wish I had taken a picture of you when you first started and now. You've aged fifteen years."

"I still fight for my kids. I still love teaching," I said, hopping off the desk, ready for the bell to sound. She smiled in a way that made me wonder … were my own words getting weaker?

She looked at me and chirped, "It's best job in the world! Go get'em, Janson!"

I smile. "All that matters is my classroom."

How many times had she told me this? It was a mantra, a rhetorical palladium from the onslaught of toxins that came at us via reforms, or deforms, in public education.

She nodded, typing away at her computer.

I walked back out as the bell tweeted. I repeated to myself: We are the canaries in the mine. National teacher shortages could substantiate this (Westervelt, 2015). The high turnover rate could substantiate this (Ingersoll, 2011). The levels of stress and mental health issues for teachers could as well (American Federation of Teachers, 2015). If we are the canaries, who is our miner: principals? Are the children coal?

Guinier and Torres (2002) use the metaphor of the miner's canary to talk about race and how "it is easy to think that when we sacrifice this canary, the only harm is to communities of color," but this ignores the "problems that converge around racial minorities at their own peril" (loc: 134). Their discussion deals with political race that "[a]t its core it does not ask what you call yourself but with whom do you link your fate. It is a fundamentally creative political project that begins from the ground up, starting with race and all its complexity, and then builds cross-racial relationships through race and with race to issues of class and gender in order to make democracy real" (loc: 131). Their notion of political race is beyond hegemonic conceptions of race and deals more with the color of one's ideology, to return to Freire's words. Furthermore, it brings in the concepts of biopolitics (Foucault, 2010) and body-politics (Mignolo, 2009b). I will conclude this chapter with a discussion of how biopolitics and body-politics are at tension and there is a need to analyze them with and through the decolonial momentum.

However, for now, let me define biopolitics as the way in which government no longer uses laws or physical force but rather government is the mechanism by which reason or truth is generated to in/form our subjectivities, which is a colonization of the mind that employs the body as its agent for the modes of production. Body-politics involves a decolonial praxis in which individuals become aware of how their bodies are part of the colonial and imperial narratives—the subjectification and objectification of their mind and bodies.

Body-politics means finding authentic ways of enunciating one's self and spiritualities. Walsh (2002) notes, "authentic is an oppositional and politically strategic term, a way to articulate what it has meant to be culturally and epistemically dehumanized by colonization and a way to reorganize 'national consciousness' in the struggles for decolonization" (p. 67). Governance in modernity has to do with sophistication of violence, wrapping violence up in a velvet bow and declaring it a gift of freedom and prosperity. It is the receiver's fault if he or she fails to understand how to take care of herself/himself or cannot escape his or her circumstances.

This creates a stratification of society in which there are those with the knowledge, discourses, privileges, and power that is enshrined in the sanctified oppression of others. Kelly (2004) writes that "[a] state with biopolitical aims—the aim of improving the material well-being of the population—but which also in the name of this project eliminates vast numbers of its own people, needs a 'social-racism'" (p. 61). This is rationalization of the stratification of populations.

Quijano (2000) discusses the formulation of race and how in the colonization of America it re/shaped identities as well as provided a rationale for colonial dichotomies of oppressed and oppressor, "granting legitimacy to the relations of domination imposed by the conquest" (p. 536).

These relations of domination are still felt today. For instance, they are normalized, manifesting in the way an educator says he still believes in the power dynamics of master and learner with other teachers not disagreeing. U.S. public schools are inherently oppressive. The system is designed to manufacture youth into societal norms.

While discussing a prisoner who broke parole in order to go back to prison during the Great Depression, I asked the students to look at this image on the right and to think about Tom's statement, "Jus' laid there waiting for the bell to go off." In order to connect with them, I asked them to think about how they feel sitting in a classroom "waiting for the bell to go off."

"Why do you need a bell to tell you to move?" I asked. "In college, there are no bells, class ends, and you leave."

"Really?" Noah asked. He leaned back in his seat. "I guess they did that in middle school."

"So why use bells? Look at this image. How are schools and prisons similar?"

"It's a factory," said Kayla.

"Exactly! There's a profit to be made. Remember how the sheriff got 75 cents per day for each prisoner, but it only cost 25 cents to feed them?" They all nodded. "So what can we *infer*?" MCAS buzzword inserted … check … language, language, everywhere ….

"They're making money off the prisoners."

"It's a business. So do you guys know why we have bells in schools?"

They looked at the loudspeaker and at me, running possibilities through their heads. I smirked, waiting for them to figure it out.

"They put the bell system in to get you used to working bell to bell based on the factory model," I remarked.

Every person has a different reaction to this knowledge, but Dakota and Luke were immediately in a rage.

"Miss J, that's messed up!" exclaimed Dakota.

Initially, Noah's mouth was practically open, and then he scrunched his face to say, "I don't like that."

Kayla shook her head. Some students accept this revelation as practical and logical without any kind of resistance. Others find it extremely unnerving as they realize that they are being programmed. A month later our administrator decided to have a Friday with music instead of bells. The theme songs to *Jaws, Star Wars, Indiana Jones, Mission Impossible, Rocky*, and *James Bond* played. It was something that he wanted to try.

"What's with the music?" they kept asking me.

Some liked it, and others hated it. It was so loud that having a conversation with students between classes was impossible.

When Noah came into my class, he asked, "Is this resisting the whole bell thing?"

Was it resistance? "Perhaps, it was something he wanted to try. But, if it was that, shouldn't we have talked with all of you, and why not do it all the time? It's just for today."

This was the spectacle of critical transformative change. It had the potential to be decolonial, but, instead, it was a shiny bauble to entertain or confuse the masses. All the songs had a strong discourse of White heteropatriarchy, which I didn't realize until I typed out the names, so I shouldn't have been surprised when the day before winter break we had Christmas songs all day.

Enya, who isn't a strong student, but she has critical potential, shook her head as she entered my classroom.

"Why are they all Christmas songs?"

"I don't know. I keep expecting to hear at least the Dreidel song? Or, kwanza … or something else. The next one has to be," I said.

"It better!" she said, nodding with animosity toward the loudspeaker. Class continued and ended. The music came on … a Christmas song.

Enya got up. "Why!" she exclaimed with a shake of her head.

"I know." I shook my head and sighed. "You're going to lunch. He'll be down there. Why don't you bring it up to him?"

"OH, I *will*. I have a friend who is Muslim. This has to be difficult for her. I don't know how she feels about this. This is stupid." With that she walked out, flipping her hair over her shoulder and working the discourse of "I'm done with this world."

Youth in schools are subject to so much knowledge that they may reject, but they have to be surrounded by. Prison bars of words. Students who voice their opinions and are told they are ignorant. Students who are told flappers were promiscuous or in the student's words "sluts." Students who are taught racism as an issue to be studied, but not engaged?

When I introduced *A Raisin in the* Sun, I talked about how it was a huge moment on Broadway for the first African American female playwright and how previously African-Americans had been featured in minstrel shows or black face comedy.

"I remember during Spirit Week one year, on Blackout Day, a group of students had done blackface with the wigs. I think they got in trouble, but I don't think they understood what their costumes were about."

"How could they not know?" asked Noah.

"It's not necessarily the cultural knowledge that you are taught in school. It's not part of the generic history."

Nathan asked, "How come we don't learn about this stuff in history?"

Kiera laughed under her breath as if to ask, "You're really wondering why?"

"We cover racism."

"Yea, but we didn't learn this," said Kayla.

"It's probably not in the textbook," I said.

"But, why?"

"A lot of stuff isn't. There's a great book called *Lies My Teacher Told Me* … it might be behind …." I looked at my little line of books by my window behind Noah and Kiera's heads. "Nope. It goes through all the mistruths in how U.S. history is taught to American kids."

"That sounds cool!" exclaimed Kayla.

"It's a good book."

"Can you show us a video of Blackface comedy, so we can see what it is?"

I put up a black face comedy video from YouTube, and we watched it. I didn't want this to be an act of voyeurism. It needed to be an act of decolonizing history and media, helping them learn to use the analytical tools within them. "Look in the background, see all their faces are painted black. Notice how the female in this is white and portrayed as a sophisticate while they make the man in blackface seem stupid."

"This is so bad," said someone as we were watching.

One did laugh. "It's bad but it's funny." Looking around at the other sullen faces, he quickly shut his mouth.

Then to the side of the video we saw, "The Most Racist Cartoon Ever,"[1] which was "Scrub Me Mamma with a Boogie Beat."

"Can we watch it please?" asked Nathan.

I went and got the lights. "Now, do some discourse analysis on this again. Watch how they portray African Americans and see if the stereotypes still persist today." As it came on I talked with them, "Notice how they are portraying them as monkeys."

"Those lips are ridiculous!" someone shouted.

"They're making them seem lazy."

"Yeah, it's 'Lazytown,'" I remarked. "Now look at how they're sexualizing the female and making the men react."

I cut it off just before the end. Kayla shook her head. "That's so wrong."

"Now, you can see people's comments in the present. I love analyzing these because people just reveal their un-censored thoughts." We stopped at one comment, which stated, "if really i dont wanna [sic] be racist but they look like monkeys o.O." One particular excerpt is important to reflect on for the intricate body politics it reveals. I'll transcribe here. User 1 said "Omg have you never seen a black person before? They look and act like monkeys IRL." This was followed by User 2 responding, "User 1 Racist Fuck." User 1 responds back, "How is the truth racist." User 1 then adds, a few responses later, "Relax, atleast [sic] you are not so much as a threat as the muslims today, who cannot integrate into western civilization." User 3 responds, "Are you doing this on purpose? Out of sarcasm? Because I'm really confused ... You can't be serious can you ?" User 4, then states "yawn, you're (User 1) trying so hard to be a troll. Clearly your girlfriend left you for a black man or some other race with bigger dicks lol." User 1 responds to User 4, "Hate when that happens... Once you go black, you're a single mom."

I read through the comments to a multitude of responses that, to be honest, I didn't process beyond their shock factor at how violent and ignorant people are. Then, I stopped as I got to the "... with bigger dicks" comment. I saw it and quickly shut the screen .... Dangerous language in a school setting ... or perhaps dangerous knowledge? Sex language not allowed, never mind coupling it with profanity. However, we did discuss the hatred for Muslims, the negative stereotypes of class and race, the violent responses, assimilation. But, also we discussed the idea that "truth" can be used to justify violence against others via the question of "How is the truth racist?" We can justify violence and discrimination as long as it corresponds to veridiction and societally produced knowledge. Foucault (2008) discusses the practices of veridiction created within penal institutions:

> that were fundamentally linked to a jurisdictional practice, and how this veridictional practice—supported, of course, by criminology, psychology, and so on, but this is not what is essential—began to install the veridictional question at the very heart of modern penal practice to the extent of creating difficulties for its jurisdiction, which was the question of the truth addressed to the criminal: Who are you? When penal practice

> replaced the question: 'What have you done?' with the questions: 'Who are you?" you see the jurisdictional function of the penal system being transformed, or doubled, or possibly undermined, by the question of veridiction. (pp. 34–35)

The action that is committed becomes less significant and the person's status in society whether due to class, race, gender, sexuality, religion, dis/ability, etc., determines how or if they are punished. In schools, we see this. I can remember my first year teaching, two boys who were best friends. One dressed as a prep and the other as punk. Both would walk in with baseball caps and Dunkin Donuts iced coffees, contraband in school.

"I walk in," said Jay, the punk dresser. "And it's take the hat off and throw that away. He walks in next to me, and they don't even say anything!"

He was understanding the politics of his being. It angered him. Although this argument could be expanded to beyond schools, I want to look at how youth and educators are governed within a panopticon. Foucault (2008) described how "Panopticism is not a regional mechanics to certain institutions; for Bentham, panopticism really is a general political formula that characterizes a type of government" (p. 67). He is always there behind me, even when I don't feel his hot breath on my neck or his hand over my mouth. He is always there. That panopticon of White male heteropatriarchal surveillance. The *He* does not need to be a physical body but the ideological corpus is just as strong. Teachers and students are under the panoptic gaze.

Students exist in a panopticon, but it is hegemonic to be under this cult of surveillance, unnoticed until you are targeted. This hegemonic panopticon is sensed through experiencing its violence, which involves education and engaging in conscientização. Revealing to youth different layers of the world and analyzing *with* them is part of decolonizing. Jay was beginning to understand body-politics and struggle against biopolitics. There were the same rules for everybody, voted on by school committee, sanctioned democratically. However, this was not a democratic process for all. Quijano (2000) explains

> the institutions of public authority and its specific mechanisms of violence … is exercised in every sphere of social existence linked to the state and thus is accepted as explicitly political. But such a sphere could not be democratic (involving people placed in unequal relations of power legally and civilly equal citizens) if the social relations in all of the other spheres of social existence are radically undemocratic or antidemocratic. (pp. 557–558)

Democracy can be used as a mechanism of biopolitics. Bodies ruled by the mechanisms of social life as decided by the greatest power. In addition, if we have been looking at the bio of politics, what is the politics of the bio? If we look at body-politics, what are the politics of the body?

1 Colonialities: Tensions between Biopolitics and Body-Politics

Biopolitics (Foucault, 2008) when theorized within power networks of colonialities provides a conceptual tool for understanding how individuals become part of a system that schools them into learning a hegemony that oppresses them in the blindness of liberation. In addition, Foucault (2008) warns us of the dangers of liberalism: "Liberalism formulates simply the following: I am going to produce what you need to be free .... Liberalism must produce freedom, but this very act entails the establishment of limitations, controls, forms of coercion, and obligations relying on threats etcetera" (pp. 63–64). Foucault in *Security, Territory, Population* says that he is going to talk about biopolitics but rarely ever mentions the word; but, instead he talks of liberalism and the new government. To combine decolonial thought with Foucault's (2010) conception of biopolitics, I would define biopolitics as the way in which government no longer uses laws or physical force, but, rather, government is the mechanism by which reason or truth is generated to in/form our subjectivities that is a colonization of the mind that employs the body as its agent for the modes of production. The modes of production may be for the production of wealth, production of violence, or the production of human waste. Capitalism needs production as much as it needs destruction—creative destruction (Harvey, 2000). Davies (2011) explains that "[c]apitalism's gravest problem is then how to maintain governments or consumers in a state of dissatisfied hunger, and how to find ever more credit through which to feed that hunger" (p. 71). There are several points of analysis here. One is to understand the production of truth because this process is not only a form of production of knowledge but also in the killing of knowledge or an epistemicide (Santos, 2007b). The creation of what we know is not considered in today's high speed consumption through lens of why or how we know it. People hear reports all the time that detail how coffee is good for them and then coffee is bad for them. This basically delegitimizes the value of knowledge so that people have no solid ground of knowledge. Their minds pliable to the hyper-consumption of knowledge to whatever is the newest version of truth. Foucault (2008) explains "how a particular regime of truth, and therefore not an error, makes something that does not exist to become something" (p. 19). In the age of globalization, the world can make a place appear and disappear with the click of a mouse.

Biopolitics involves a new governmental or a new governmental reason that "does not deal with what I would call the things in themselves of governmentality, such as individuals, things, wealth, and land .... It deals with phenomena of politics, that is to say, interests, which precisely constitute politics and its stakes; it deals with interests, or that respect in which a given individual, thing, wealth, and so on interests other individuals or the collective body of individuals" (Foucault, 2008, p. 45). The ability to create a place and destroy a place involves the colonization of the mind. This involves the colonialities of knowledge, power, and being. Fanon (1963) describes how "colonialism is not simply content to impose its rule upon the present and the future of a dominated country. Colonialism is not satisfied merely with holding a people in its grip and emptying the native's brain of all form and content. By a kind of perverted logic, it turns to the past of the oppressed people, and distorts, disfigures, and destroys it. This work of devaluing pre-colonial history takes on a dialectical significance today" (p. 210). Biopolitics includes the manipulation of memory and the denial of histories.

History occurs in the present at the whim of the elite; it is produced with new meaning. The elite act as the colonizers deciding which knowledge counts and whose knowledge counts. The attacks on La Raza studies in Tucson, Arizona are an example in which then Superintendent Horne remarked, "They are teaching a radical ideology in Raza, including that Arizona and other states were stolen from Mexico and should be given back" (Lewin, 2010). The teaching of a history that disenchants the romanticization of U.S. history is considered dangerous contraband and an illegitimate knowledge. The American Dream is full of cultural values of a white picket fence, husband and wife, children, good job, etc. Youth may want these things and more. They want the life of the rich and glamorous, but they also recognize their place. Youth receive an education in public school that teaches them content often at the expense of meaning. This is part of the educational game of colonization:

> The colonizer also imposed a mystified image of their own patterns of producing knowledge and meaning. At first, they placed these patterns far out of reach of the dominated. Later, they taught them in a partial and selective way, in order to co-opt some of the dominated into their own power institutions. Then European culture was made seductive: it gave access to power. After all, beyond repression, the main instrument of all power is its seduction. (Quijano, 2010, p. 23)

Education lives in the lap of seduction. Constantly schools are seduced into new reforms that promise change and also money. Curriculum is transformed. Time from helping and teaching students is taken to prepare evidence binders that purport to provide a more effective public education system. These are "the ideational traps constructed by colonial modernity that diluted the liberatory ethos of decolonization and channeled it towards emancipation that did not question the alienating logic of modernity itself but called for reforms within the same system" (Ndlovu-Gatsheni, 2013, p. 66). Modernity and progress seduce and leave little time to think as life and change happens rapidly. The colonial power networks surround us and run through us.

This conceptualization of political race is linked to intercultural translation (Santos, 2014). We must engage in a decolonial thinking, which rips off modernity's mask to see that we do not live in a colorblind world in which race, gender, class, ability, sexuality, etc. exist in peaceful equality. To begin' decolonization, we must start with conscientização or consciencism.

The other day, I walked out of my room to see a senior student, Dana, talking with Colleen. Dana's eyes are downcast, but then she would perk up as she said something .... All the symptoms of Capstone. The excruciating process for seniors when they have to choose their own research and think for themselves. I had already talked with her during my lunch duty the other day. But, she was a student with such self-doubt. Ironically, she and her partner wanted to do a research study on doubt and integrity by conducting experiments where people would have options such as to return money they found or to tell the teacher if the answer key to a test was visible in the room. However, her friend's teacher thought it wasn't scholarly enough. Now, she had a new topic that she was more interested in. She wanted to look at the hyper-security of terrorism post-9/11, but in particular she wanted to interview her mom's friend, a Muslim who worked in the airports. However, after conversations with her at lunch, it seemed she wanted to look more at the fear of Muslims and stereotypes.

"Do you want to look at how youth of today's world is full of fear? People didn't have to worry twenty years ago about studying abroad and a bombing," said Colleen. "Do you feel safer at the airport with all these security measures?"

She laughed. "No!"

Colleen nodded. "See, Miss Janson ... Dana wants to do her Capstone looking at the fear of terrorism and security."

I nodded. "When I talked to you, it seemed like you wanted to look at Islamophobia."

"I do." She put her hands to her face, and then put them down. "I don't know where to begin!"

"So, that's why you need to do a little research. You'll start to know what you want to look at," said Colleen.

"I mean if you want to look at fear and terrorism. You should look at how language is codifying that fear. Terrorism is a coded word for Islamophobia. It's a neutral word that allows us justification for targeting Muslims without saying we are. People fear Muslims, but who has done most of the mass shootings and bombings?"

"White males." She stepped side to side uneasily, moving her thoughts from foot to foot a soccer ball of questions.

"Sandy Hook, Aurora Theater, the Amish school, Columbine, Virginia Tech, Oklahoma City."

She looked up. "That Newtown one, right?"

I nodded, not bothering to correct that Newtown and Sandy Hook were the same. "They never called those acts of terrorism."

"But then what are they?" she asked.

Colleen nodded. "It's language. They tried it with acts of domestic terrorism, but it didn't work. They call them mass shootings instead. They don't call them acts of domestic terrorism even though they are."

She was having trouble processing. "But, they're—" She paused. "But, then what do they call them?"

"Mass shootings or bombings," I repeated. "You have to see how terrorism justifies Islamophobia. It's a colorblind ideology. We say we live in an equal society and that we're attacking *violence*. But, this is the same rhetoric that is used against black males. One out of four black males will end up in prison."

"Really?" she asked, shaking her head.

"If you surveyed the kids in this school and asked them how fearful are they of being attacked by a black male, their responses would be significantly different than if you asked them about a white male .... Maybe I'm wrong though." A qualifying clause at the end of most sentences, one of feminine humility.

"No. You're right." She shifted and thought. "That could be cool."

"There's tons of things you can do. You just need to start researching."

She nods, still unsure but gaining confidence to explore. "Can I have a pass?"

"I'll take you. I'm going that way anyway," I said.

She pulled her backpack higher on her shoulders. "I hate Capstone. I hate it."

I laughed, feeling my energy rise. "I love it! You just have to start searching and figure out what you are interested in."

"It's hard. I don't know what to do."

"You'll understand once you start. It's fun to explore. You need to find what gets you curious. You have a great topic."

"I know. I'm really interested in it. I just—I just *need* a research question."

"You need to do some research first before you can nail down the question. But you're on the right track." She looks straight ahead in complete automization. The walls a burnt red. For me, it's the color of Bedadine when it gets on your skin. Antiseptic walls against rogue creativity. The part that was scaring her was the fact that for the first time she had no track. She had to build it. I told her, "It's going to work out. You all get nervous, but then you do great!"

The corner of her lips curls up in a familiar smile and nod. "Alright, Miss J." The unspoken, "If you so say so" contained in that smile. I watch her enter math, where they are all quietly taking a quiz. Heads down. Pencils to paper. Some look up to see who enters. The rest just keep working. The quiz more important than curiosity in one's surroundings.

Education maintains the modes of production for standardized consumption. The equality is there. You choose to accept or not, but the choice is A or nothing. We are in the bowels of violent neutrality. The danger is there of losing our identities and humanity in the age of liquid modernity under the pretense that the world is blind—to pretend that we are not oppressed and manipulated. Lazzarato (2012) describes our relationship with consumption and the debt economy: "We carry within us the creditor-debtor relation—in our pockets and wallets, encoded in the magnetic strip on our credit cards. Indeed, this little strip of plastic hides two seemingly harmless operations: the automatic institution of the credit relation, which thereby establishes permanent debt. The credit card is the simplest way to transform its owner into a permanent debtor, an 'indebted man' for life" (p. 20). Our hyper-consumption of goods in the U.S. is of our own choice; no one is coercing us with advertisements built on psychology. The stagnant real wage is not oppressive as living costs rise. College debt is a necessary burden for college students. These are all things that *you*, the individual, must overcome; the choice is always yours. If you want more, then you take the risk and you take the consequences. We dream of liberation, and we fight for liberation, but whose liberation? Liberated into what?

The universality of liberation is a ritualized regime of truth. Government produces what is freedom. Freedom to buy, to consume, to dispose. On September 20, 2001, President Bush addressed the U.S. after the 9–11 terrorist attacks. The usual patriotic lingo of U.S. greatness and strength is present. He remarked, "Americans are asking, 'What is expected of us?' I ask you to live your lives and hug your children … I ask your continued participation and confidence in the American economy. Terrorists attacked a symbol of American prosperity; they did not touch its source" (Bush, 2001). The mixture of family and nationalism coupled with economic patriotism is cultivated. This is an example of biopolitics at work.

Our freedom is constructed as being built on prosperity. The freedom to buy. After addressing the needed U.S. vigilance and perseverance to help those "ordinary moms and dads across the Middle East who want the hope and opportunity for their children," Bush explained that "[a]s we work with Congress in the coming year to chart a new course in Iraq and strengthen our military to meet the challenges of the 21st century, we must also work together to achieve important goals for the American people here at home .... The recent report on retail sales shows a strong beginning to the holiday shopping season across the country. And I encourage you all to go shopping more" (Bush, 2006). Shopping becoming a patriotic action to help our country. In the downturned economy, I can remember my mother half-joking with me as a teenager and echoing Bush's words as we were at a store, and she swiped her credit card, "We're just doing our civic duty." I remember seeing the importance of us buying in order to help create more jobs. I have always felt the economic downturns at home. Economic downturn, or as a child what I knew as "business being slow" or "going into a recession." These were words I feared. It meant my father being stressed and angry. Even having worked at the same company since he was a teenager, which means presently he has spent approximately fifty years there, he was still vulnerable—he has no college degree. However, he is an engineer of contact tools. The design and manufacture sector is "always first to feel" the economic downturn. My father, without a college degree and having spent his entire life with the same company, would always be nervous when these recessions would hit, and that translated into a tense home.

So, when the President said that we needed to go out and buy in order to help the economy, it helped soothe my fears, and I readily wanted to participate. It was rational. If we buy, then more things had to be manufactured and sold. However, what I also knew, but in the fear of the present didn't necessarily recognize, was that more and more of the manufacturing was being outsourced.

I can remember as a child going with my father and hearing the roar of the metal work machines. His office overlooked the factory, and he would take me down to see the machines. I would look at the reams of meatal that were at least three times my height, so shiny and ready to be cut. The workers with their earplugs in would wave to my dad and me. I just stood at the heart of this industrial machine, and I would look around amazed. There was that industrial smell, a mix of oil, grease, friction. It wasn't like a car shop; this is cleaner, more efficient. Everything is moving. Then, my father took me to a side room, where there were a couple of guys working on a machine.

"Did you get it working?" my father asked.

"We'll see. It's been a bitch." I watched the machine as the water streamed through. I wondered how it worked. As they talked, I observed the machine go, and then, WHOOSH! I jumped back, startled by the sudden spurting of water against the glass.

One man chuckled. "Should've warned you about that. It's just cooling the machine down."

They opened it up and took out the part. It just looked like a strip of metal to me, but they studied it and measured it.

"Mother ...." The voice trailed off, not hiding the intended swear.

My eyes wider. My mother never swore. But, here I was in a new culture. I watched as my father got his hand inside the machine. He was fumbling about, and then I heard his fingers slip, and I waited for the "You f—ing bastard." My father swore ... swears. I don't think I can remember my mother swearing. Then, he slammed the machine shut, and I waited, watching to see if it worked and thinking of what he had just done. My father's an engineer. I say it no longer to verify it but rather because he was, with or without college degree. As a child, it was my way of explaining his job to my peers and teachers. If I said he's a contact tool designer, nobody really understood. In addition, all my friend's dads had college degrees. My best friend's father was an engineer with a degree, and so mine was too; I just tried evade the degree question. It had come up before about where he had gone to school and how he couldn't be. I fought for that word. So, when we had that career day in fifth grade and all the dads came in—I don't remember a mother coming in, but maybe my mind fails me. The question always came up of where they went to college. I always hoped that nobody would ask me where my dad had gone. When asked what he did, I would say engineer, but I would feel a lump in my throat. My best friend's dad had a *degree.* My dad was just a worker.

My dad worked hard his whole life, but he feared when those college degreed bosses came in, "thinkin' they knew something." He knew every piece of this company. "I crawled around under these machines swallowing shit that would have OSHA in an uproar. What the f—do they know?" In such an odd way, college degrees were both a threat and security to me. My dad was a hard worker. He "busted his ass," and he was a loyal worker to his company, but, in the end, those with degrees were the ones with power. Loyalty to company and loyalty to country is not the same as company loyalty and country loyalty. John F. Kennedy (1961) said, "Ask not what your country can do for you; ask what you can do for your country." Words that many U.S. citizens know, but is this an ideology of selflessness or servitude?

The economy is constructed as a tool of liberation, but it is also conversely a tool of oppression. We buy more, but the majority of profits are going to ... not us. Yet, we still work our fingers to the bone. Being a hard worker is the pulmonary artery of the colonial mentality that helps shape the biopolitics of our lives. Quijano (2000) discusses how "[i]n America, however, for five hundred years capital has existed as the dominant axis of the total articulation of all historically known forms of control and exploitation of labor, thus configuring a historical-structurally heterogeneous model of power with discontinuous relations and conflicts among its components" (p. 571). Although his discussion is focused on Latin American and European colonization, we can see similar networks of power within the U.S. throughout its industrial history. The ritualized sayin' of "work hard and get ahead," directing our movements and thoughts. However, not much thought is given to those who get ahead but don't work as hard. I present my students with this quote and ask them if it is a true or false:

> [T]he number of people making more than $1 million increased by 20 percent over 2009. The median paycheck—half made more, half less—fell again in 2010, down 1.2 percent to $26,364. That works out to $507 a week, the lowest level, after adjusting for inflation, since 1999. (Johnston, 2011)

Interestingly the proportion of students who believe this is true has changed over the past five years. Most now believe it is true whereas originally many thought it was ludicrous. They are increasingly aware of class inequality, but it seems to be something that is hopelessly natural. Keep your head down and keep working. Be thankful for what you have. Anger in general is directed more at the lower class than upper. Most of my students and acquaintances focus on the bottom who "do nothing but sit on a couch all day ... our taxes at work." They are aware of corporate welfare, but it is social welfare that they attack—these are the despicables of society. The top, they're *working.* They may get more than their fair share, but they *are working.* You have the freedom to work; less we be reminded of so called freedom notoriously known through these words, "Arbeit macht frei." Work sets you free into what? There is danger in freedom and liberalism when it is defined by the oppressor.

In today's global society, we perhaps have more freedom than ever given the world seeming to be boundary-less in the digital age. Who governs us? Foucault (2008) describes how "government is basically no longer to be exercised over subjects and other things subjected through these subjects. Government is now to be exercised over what we would call the phenomenon of republic of interests. The fundamental question of liberalism is: What is the utility value of government and all actions of government in a society where exchange determines the true value of things?" (p. 46). Power exercised through ideas and hegemony instead of physical force. Freedom has no physical domain. It is political. Boundaries need not be drawn on a map but spoken in discourse.

The world can be huge or small depending on the power network. President George W. Bush (2006) said,

> And the message will be, that, You, Iran, are further isolated from the world. My message to the Iranian people is, You can do better than to have somebody try to rewrite history. You can do better than somebody who hasn't strengthened your economy. And you can do better than having somebody who's trying to develop a nuclear weapon that the world believes you shouldn't have. There's a better way forward.

Here is the *economy of power* that is "internally sustained … by this interplay of freedom and security" (Foucault, 2008, p. 65). Klein's (2007) conceptualization of the shock doctrine comes into play in which public consciousness is shocked by these disasters. These attacks on the psyche are also on the spirit and corpus; make the body fear and control the mind.

The freedom and security to buy, which begins with keeping our economy growing. The debt that most Americans carry around is a metaphorical ball and chain. It allows people to live beyond the present, but those cards are weapons of power. Lazzarato (2012) details how "[c]redit is a mechanism of power that bears on undetermined possibilities and whose actualization/realization is subject to a radical and not probabilistic uncertainty" (p. 68). Freedom is not stable. We live in a country of liberty, but students are censored in schools and so are teachers. Freedom of speech for whom? Freedom is produced because "[t]he new governmental reason needs freedom therefore, the new art of government consumes freedom. It consumes freedom, which means that it must produce it" (Foucault, 2008, p. 63). To produce freedom, you must produce fear—a political ritual. In his address to Congress after 9–11, Bush (2001) added,

> The course of this conflict is not known, yet its outcome is certain. Freedom and fear, justice and cruelty, have always been at war, and we know that God is not neutral between them …. Fellow citizens, we'll meet violence with patient justice, assured of the rightness of our cause and confident of the victories to come. In all that lies before us, may God grant us wisdom and may he watch over the United States of America.

The inculcation of God as the patriarchal being sanctifies the most violent of actions and makes truth an unquestioning absolute. There is the right way, and there is the wrong way. This can be seen in the Christian pastorate in which work is connected with salvation under a particular truth, making it:

> a mode of individualization by subjection (*assujettissement*) .... And finally, if Christianity, the Christian pastor, teaches the truth, if he forces men, the sheep, to accept a certain truth, the Christian pastorate is also absolutely innovative in establishing a structure, a technique of, at once, power, investigation, self-examination, and the examination of others, by which a certain secret inner truth of the hidden soul becomes the element through which the pastor's power is exercised, by which obedience is practiced, by which the relationship of complete obedience is assured, and through which, precisely, the economy of merits and faults passes. (Foucault, 2009, p. 239)

Christianity has a way of classifying people under violent regimes of truth. Violence is justified because individuals have not found salvation through legitimated truth. The construction of heathen and good Catholic is one. Foucault (2010) discusses "how the coupling of a set of practices and a regime of truth form an apparatus (*dispotif*) of knowledge-power that effectively marks out in reality that which does not exist and legitimately submits it to the division between true and false" (p. 19). This has to do with the colonialities of knowledge and power, but also being. Christianity provides a good arena to discuss these different veins of knowledge and power.

As a child with a Catholic mother and a Protestant father, I always felt stuck between these truths. I was schooled in both. *Service*—not mass—on Sunday with my father, which came with Sunday school, and then Mondays were CCD (Confraternity of Christian Doctrine), and sometimes I also had *mass* on Saturday or Sunday. For me, it was simple; they both were about love of God and Christ. You know, 10 Commandments, Hail Mary, Noah's Ark, Act of Contrition, etc. But, there were little things like Holy Spirit vs. Holy Ghost—the former is Catholic and the latter is Protestant, and in CCD we weren't told it had to do with translation, just that one was right and one was wrong.[2] I would remember to codeswitch, correcting myself on the proper word. As a young child, I was quite gregarious, and I would share with my teachers and classmates when the lessons from Sunday school would crossover from CCD. Interestingly, my Sunday school would be generally hands-on or about reading the Bible and then doing an activity, whereas my CCD classes always came with a workbook. Then one year, I had a CCD teacher who knew my father was Protestant. We were talking about faith and someone asked how could we be absolutely certain of God and heaven? I had just had this conversation with my father, so I enthusiastically stated, "My dad explained that it's okay if you aren't absolutely certain. He says that faith grows."

My CCD teacher lost it on me, telling me not to bring "Protestant teachings"—ironically, this wasn't Protestant but the ecumenical words of his *Catholic*

Portuguese grandmother—into the classroom and how I was wrong, and that basically it was heathenism to say what I just did. To be fair, her position on the inferiority of my Protestant knowledge had been foreshadowed. She had done this previously when I would say, "I just learned about this story yesterday …." She would cut me off and say that she would teach me the right way. My friend even questioned why I always had to talk about what I had learned in the Protestant church. I came out of CCD that night crying. My father was going to hell. I was stupid. The world had ended. My mother comforted me, and she told me it was completely unacceptable what the teacher did.

"I don't care! I'm never going back!"

I did go back. There was no choice in the matter, but my mother had my teacher switched to a woman who had a Protestant husband. In there, I was accepted. But, I always had my silent revolt against the Catholic faith every time I crossed myself and said the trinity, "In the name of the Father, the Son, and the Holy *Ghost*. Amen." I made sure to enunciate that penultimate word—my tongue the avenger. Although my eyes would always dart to see if I was to be scolded. Salvation was to be had but only with the right words and right knowledge. There is but one God and, more importantly, one truth ….

Biko (2002) discusses the "universal truth" of Christianity that was spread through inflicting fear and inferiorization in the indigenous despite the fact that there were similarities between the native religion and Christianity. Both had one God and saints, but there was no separation of worship from daily life, and "there was no hell in our religion" (p. 93). Christianity feeds off fear. It spouts words of love, but love is not unconditional. It comes through confession, through masses, through a "Christian-life"—Just as society currently preys on the fear of difference as well. We say that we are a country of democracy and liberty, but slowly all those rights are given away for the sake of security. The government does not need to take them away. We will readily give them up in the name of the rational, the scientific. Of course, you can search my belongings. Of course, there should be security cameras on the streets. This is the art of biopolitics.

Governance not of lands but of rationalities. It is the colonization of the mind, in which, similarly to Christianity, "[b]y some strange and twisted logic, [missionaries] argued that theirs was a scientific religion and ours was superstition" (Biko, 2002, p. 93). Foucault's words intersect with Biko's. What Biko (2002) is describing relates to Foucault's discussion of the pastoral as well as to the regime of truth. Here is where cultural invasion (Freire, 2009), the regime of truth (Foucault, 1980), de/colonizing of the mind (Thiong'o, 1994) all dance in Biko's (2002) words: "This cold and cruel religion was strange to the indigenous people and caused frequent strife between the converted and the 'pagans,' for the former, having imbibed the false values from white society, were taught to ridicule and despise those who defended the truth of their indigenous religion" (p. 93). The power in invading a culture and knowledge to create those who are within the circle of power know the truth involves colonizing the mind. Religious fervor is detrimental to the spirituality of the people because it anesthetizes the people from feelings and connection, instead blinding them in the power of a truth. Religion when dialectical can bring a sense of communion. However, religion that remains didactic and hierarchical just becomes a tool of education into oppression. Religion is seen in the rituals at church but also in rituals of standardized testing and scripted teaching. What is the difference of reading from the Bible and from reading from a Pearson textbook? Both impart knowledge on what to know and consequently how to be. Decolonization involves becoming aware of what is beyond question.

In decolonial symphony, Biko (2002) discusses the need for black consciousness, Freire (2009) describes conscientização, Nkrumah (1964) explains consciencism. Different terms with varying degrees of conceptual difference. However, they all are part of decolonization and the critical consciousness needed in order to pierce the tentacles of biopolitics; this consciousness is part of Mignolo's discussion of body-politics. In body-politics, we must unravel the mysticism and ambiguity that fuels the biopolitical regime and understand that "mysticism develops on the basis of, and in the form of, absolutely ambiguous experiences, in a sort of equivocation, since the secret of the night is that it is an illumination. The secret, the force of illumination, is precisely that it blinds. In mysticism ignorance is a knowing, and knowledge has the very form of ignorance" (Foucault, 2009, p. 212). Decolonization and body-politics must disrupt ignorance as knowing and the ambiguities and mysticism that fuel the regime of truth. Body-politics involves engaging in conscientização and consciencism.

2 Canary in the Mind

The process of decolonizing our thinking has no ending. A post-colonial world is to purport a colorblind, or rather a powerblind, ideology. The idea of coloniality being the political project of colonialism perhaps clarifies for people the difference. That is not to say the colonialism is not political, but colonialism enacts the rationalities that colonialities and imperialism construct. Imperialism is the power structure that legitimizes actions as due to national or economic pride.

Let me take the example of the canary in the mine and use it as a metaphor to explain this system. The miner and his peers are part of colonization, tearing from the native land precious ores to feed the desires of the outside. As the miner enters the mine, he carries the canary with him in the cage. That canary becomes the sacrificial subaltern. Those who, due to their vulnerable state in the economic and political power structure, are more susceptible to the poisonous gases that are present to all of us in the air. The miner toils with this canary by his side, feeling safe as long as it still breathes as long as it still sings.

> The caged bird sings with a fearful trill/of things unknown/but longed for still/and his tune is heard/on the distant hill/for the caged bird/sings of freedom. (Angelou, 1983, p. 16)

The miner works and works until his shift is over. The controlling of time, the controlling of his fate, which is no more his than the canary's. He works for the future: the future money, the future to breathe air; the present exists only to produce the future. Innerarity (2012) claims, "Human beings and their societies always live at the expense of what is awaiting them" (p. 108). Coloniality is present in the miner's willingness to enter that mine with the canary. To risk his life and the canary's under the guise of security. *If the canary dies, I will be able to know that I am in danger*—a rationalized sacrifice for his life. This sacrifice involves the colonization of memory.

For humans to keep and value a promise "means constructing a memory for him, endowing him with interiority, a conscience, which provide a bulwark against forgetting. It is within the domain of debt obligations that memory, subjectivity, and conscience begin to be produced" (Lazzarato, 2012, p. 38). This conscience and memory is what enables us to begin to allot values to our actions and to the imperious nature of profit.

Despite the imperialism of the company and its insatiable need for more coal, for more profit, this man is part of something bigger. He is building a company—a company that he is proud of. In 1938, William Sulzer, Governor of New York, declared,

> Those who decry mining are ignorant of history. If they knew anything about metals, they would know that all business, all industry and all human progress depends on mines. The wealth from mines, from the dawn of time, is the epic of human advancement, of man's heroic march along the path of progress. Show me a people without mines and I will show you a people deep in the mire of poverty and a thousand years behind the procession of civilization ... [Miners] poured the golden streams of mineral wealth into the lap of civilization, into the channels of

> trade, into the avenues of commerce and into the homes of happiness .... All honor to the miner. All hail the prospector. (Sulzer, 1998)

Mining is a source of pride, gilded oppression of imperialism. Rhetoric constructs the miner as serving civilization in a place of honor. This quote reveals several important mental colonizing aspects of mining: (a) the inculcation of national and company pride and loyalty; (b) the honor of serving; (c) mining as source not only of economic progress but moral progress; (d) dismissal of the human costs of mining due to reverence of material gains. Mining came with pride despite the deplorable and dangerous conditions. The wealth of mines did bring "progress" and "homes of happiness" for some, but at the cost of the lives of the miners as well as the homes and natural resources of the indigenous. The land is stripped of its value for the sake of progress; lives lost for the sake of humanity, nationalism, or company loyalty.

The twisting of company pride and nationalism was perhaps nowhere better delivered than in the case of Bisbee where miners tried to unite for higher pay but were in the end actually attacked by an anti-union union, the Workman's Loyalty League, which, orchestrated by a mining manager, took a pledge to "support the Constitution of the United States and the laws of the State of Arizona" (Houston, 1976, p. 44). The sheriff declared that "the strike was not in the interest of organized labor but was a direct blow at the government, financed by German capital" (p. 44) and that the Wobblies, the union strikers, were directed by the Kaiser and working with Pancho Villa (Houston, 1976, pp. 44–45). Using people's fears that were present during WWI, this rhetoric was potent. In fact, 1,200 men were rounded up, shoved into boxcars, and deported to New Mexico to the U.S. Army camp in order to be tried for treason. The Army did not go through with treason charges but had to hold the miners while the whole ordeal was sorted out (Houston, 1976, p. 47). The experiences of the miners in Bisbee reveals the multiple layers of the colonial power of the mining industry. The economics of mining demanded a psychological and sociological colonization. Bisbee should have been the public's canary in the coal mine for understanding the immense powers that can manipulate their rationalization of reality.

Canary in a coal mine. An expression so ubiquitous that it has become a cliché. But, this sayin' comes from a long history of class struggle and oppression. The origins of the canary in the coal mine dates back to John Scott Haldane, who was the first to suggest using a canary to detect the poisonous carbon monoxide after recognizing that the men didn't die from lack of oxygen in the Tylorstown explosion in 1896. After experimenting on himself, he recognized that the canaries, due to their sensitive respiratory systems, could detect these noxious gases, so canaries were used until 1987 (Prior, 2012). Interestingly, some miners were upset when the canaries were taken away and replaced with more advanced mechanical systems. The relationship between the miners and the canary was one not just of biological precaution but perhaps one of symbiotic spiritual oppression. Miners were willing to go into the mine with the canaries recognizing that they were safe as long as that canary breathed, a willing sacrifice. Figure 4.2 is a clipping that has "A Miner's Prayer." The canary was not

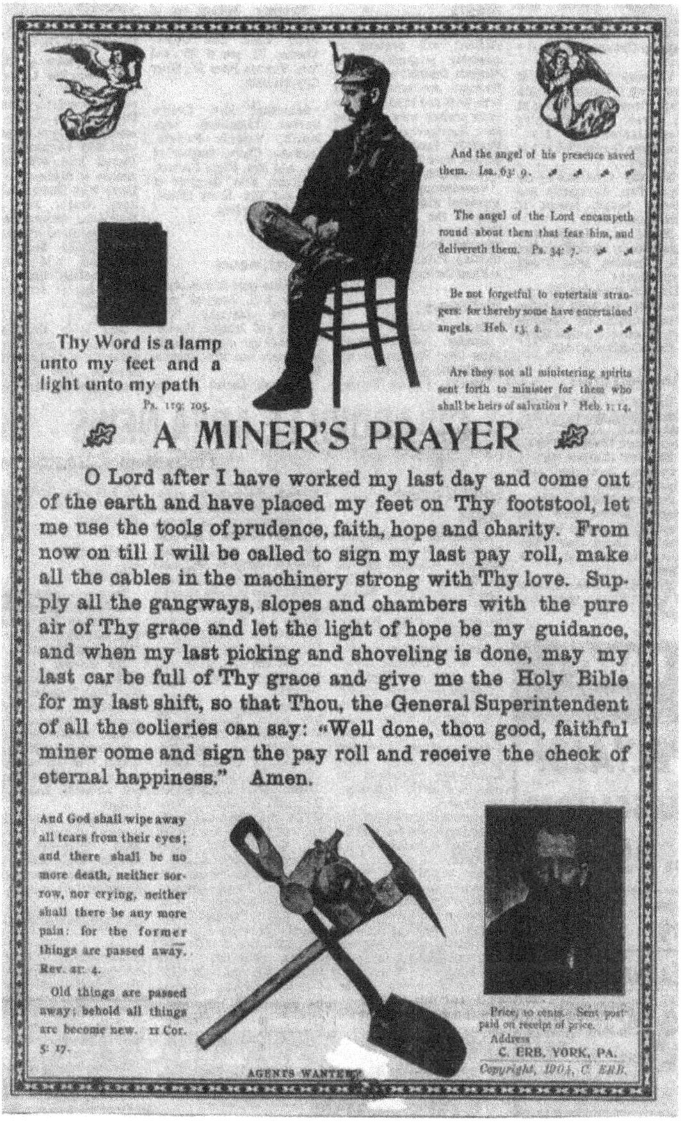

FIGURE 4.2 A Miner's Prayer (1904) (from C. Erb York, Pennsylvania)

the only one whom miners may have taken with them into the mine, and the mind. Mining actually reveals the power of religion in getting men to act even when in dangerous situations. Reading through this prayer with phrases such as "with the pure air of Thy grace and let the light of hope be my guidance," reveals the way religion can act as blindfold so that we don't acknowledge the dangers around. The miners are trusting in Him. Even their work of shoveling coal "may my last car be full of Thy grace." Their spirituality is colonized by this religious rhetoric, and they are willing to go into fire because He is by their side, similar to the canary who becomes a legitimized sacrifice. However, this analysis needs to be taken a step further.

The ritual of bringing the canary into the mine was in reality a canary in the mind. A feathery yellow spectacle to distract from the more prominent dangers. Pull up most mining fatalities, and it will reveal that carbon monoxide poisoning is not the foremost cause of death. In fact, "it will be noted that 50 per cent of all the fatal accidents and 39 per cent of all the nonfatal accidents were the result of falls of roof and coal, and that accordingly these are the most prolific source of accidents in the coal mines of the United States" (Coal Mining Institute of America, 1907, pp. 8–9). Also, further data from the late 1800s reveals that the majority of deaths were due to falls (45.5 percent from slate and roof and 20.7 percent from coal), except for in 1891 in which firedamp was the major cause (American Gas Light Journal, 1867, p. 128), so even before the canary was used the primary cause of death was not whitedamp, the term used for carbon monoxide in mines. Furthermore, the Center for Disease Control (CDC) records from 1839 to 2010 reveal that only 7 out of the 727 entries pertaining to deaths in mining accidents were due to suffocation (NIOSH, 2013). In 2014, relatively few miners died in mines: 14 out of 116,010 miners (MSHA, 2014). However, survival within a mine does not equate to survival outside of the mine.

The National Institute for Occupational Safety and Health (NIOSH) found that the occurrence of pneumoconiosis (black lung) has actually gone from being almost eradicated, with only 0.33% of active miners being infected in 1990s (Blackley, Halldin, & Laney, 2014). Now, NIOSH estimates that on average approximately 10% of all miners are being infected (Berkes, 2012). Despite the risk, many miners willingly go to work in the mines. For instance, James Marcum mined for 20 years. He even went to college for a bit, but the money that could be made in a mine in the present had an allure that a future away from the mines didn't. He found out that he had the beginnings of black lung after being hospitalized due to an explosion, but he kept going, saying, "It was good money … I had my kids to raise, and I just had to work. … I never said nothing. I just went on and done my job." His story, part of a study done by CPI and NPR, reveals that mining is one of the only job options in the area, and that fear of companies finding out that they have black lung keeps miners from getting screened. Even though MHSA passed a law in 1980 that gives miners with black lung a letter that mandates the company give them a job for the same pay away from the dust, only approximately 900 of the 3,000 letters issued have been used (Hamby, 2012). This is exemplifies colonialities of being and biopolitics.

Mining not only affects the miners, but those who live in the surroundings areas. For instance, 5.5 million pounds of explosives are used each day for mountain top mining, which sends off toxins that land on the houses, which are slick to touch containing "diesel fuel, ammonium nitrate, and silica dust," as well as flooding that infects wells with selenium (Caskey, 2012). The canary in the mine is easy to focus on and to understand. It is a concrete security. The way our thinking is colonized to focus on that which we can see instead of that which we cannot. If we think back to the vignette with Dana, Colleen, and myself, Dana in her research is beginning to conceptualize this. Do the security checks at airports really protect us or are they giving us an illusion of security at the expense of others? Does the right to carry a gun protect people from a mass shooting? We cling to these as a rationalization of security. At the same time, people ignore the dangers that are around them constantly. Jobs that impact their health. Jobs that take them from their families.

> Oh as I was young and easy in the mercy of his means, Time held me green and dying Though I sang in my chains like the sea. (Thomas, 1952, p. 226)

The canary in the mine epitomizes how colonialism and imperialism are able to construct the dangers of society as well as what needs to be caged in civilization. We need to understand that the canary in the mine is more about the mind than mine in today's geopolitics and biopolitics. Tlostanova and Mignolo (2006) discuss border thinking and the way that it is "an anti-imperial epistemic response—the difference that hegemonic discourse endowed to 'other' people, classifying them as inferior and at the same time asserting its geohistorical and body-social configurations as superior and the models to be followed. These people refuse to be geographically caged, subjectively humiliated and denigrated and epistemically disregarded" (p. 208). These models that are to be followed are built upon imperialism's fault lines. Education is used to create systems of epistemological denigration and deification.

Teachers are embroiled in biopolitics and geopolitics. We must be intercultural translators or we risk becoming masters of powerful ideologies. Not only of mainstream ideologies in which many teachers due to the constant bombardment of policy reforms that become the Newspeak of pedagogues in which teachers lose, or never gain, the language to articulate their reality as well as students. I was fortunate to go through a teacher education program that had some revolutionary professors who helped me learn this critical language. However, still one of the hardest things for me as an educator to learn was remembering to speak with students where they are at ideologically. In a school with a strong regressive conservative fervor, I have often had to deal with mindsets that are racist, sexist, Islamophobic, homophobic, xenophobic, etc. I recall emailing a former professor my first year of teaching, desperately unsure of how to challenge the racist and anti-Semitic thoughts of my students when many of my colleagues felt that it was a losing battle. Suddenly, you are no longer trying to fight out an argument with a peer but rather you have to be cognizant of your position of power and engage in a dialogue in which you caringly question more than assertively state. One must be careful not to indoctrinate or to alienate.

While having a class discussion about why the migrants or Okies would continue to work for such low pay, a student raised his hand to ask, "Miss Janson, you know how President Obama wanted to legalize all immigrants in the country?"

I looked at him, giving him my attention, so that he could proceed. The veracity of the information not necessarily as important as the question I knew he was cooking up. The grammar of knowledge is something that I feel is used as a sword of thought. The proper punctuation of knowledge with every technical detail correct prized over the logic is one way in which we cut the tongues of youth. A point that I would like us to return to later.

"Is that a good thing?" This wasn't his real question, and I knew it.

"I don't necessarily have a problem with it. What do you think?"

"That would mean that they would have to be taxed. So, well, why wouldn't Republicans and businesses want that?"

I smiled at him. I stood on the periphery of a group of students strongly engrossed in a conservative ideology. "Think about it. The answer is in your question. Why wouldn't businesses want all these immigrants to be legal? What's the benefit of having them as illegals?"

He looked at me, and, on my opposite side, Joel looked at me. Noelle and Nathan were still copying down notes. The other boys discussing the last thing we talked about, but their ears were slowly tuning back in.

In their minds, they were uncovering the biopolitics that control people's lives. I could not have led them to this place. A dialogue occurs in which they enter at different rates and at different ideological positions. Freire talks with Horton and says, "The teacher is of course an artist, but being an artist does not mean that he or she can make the profile, can shape the students. What the educator does in teaching is to make it possible for the students to become themselves" (Horton & Freire, 1990, p. 181). My job as a decolonial pedagogue is to help them dig deeper to question and analyze. In order to be a decolonial pedagogue, one could switch out pedagogue and put learner. You must continuously learn and engage in a "process of creating new problems out of our solutions to earlier problems, using strategies to build organizations and interventions that redefine political power itself" (Guinier & Torres, 2002, loc: 1829). A decolonial pedagogue cannot be alone or in isolation but be part of a theoretical network that helps analyze the contradictions and power mechanisms within our lives and beings. Furthermore, I model my own doubts and try not to be afraid to expose my vulnerabilities; I am fallible. This fallibility is part of spirituality. I may mispronounce a word or I may get a fact wrong. Please correct me. Do not fear me. In a space of colonial power, I must constantly remember that I hold in one hand a colonial truncheon and in the other my decolonial heart.

Biko (2002) claimed that "the most potent weapon in the hand of the oppressor is the mind of the oppressed" (p. 68). Many fear the tangible objects that they can lose. For my students, as soon as their cell phones disappear, a fury of panic sets in. They frantically search. Where is this object? Where is my other me? This phone is in a way their canary that alerts them to the dangers surrounding them as well as sings to them the joys of their beings. Snap chats after snap chats. Actions controlled by the beeping, ringing, vibrating, flashing lights. Our attention is drawn by it, directing what we see of the world while the world and its dangers surround us outside of that odd mixture of master and canary. Foucault (2009) describes how "[a] physics of power, or a power thought of as physical action in the element of nature, and a power thought of as regulation that can only be carried out through and by reliance on the freedom of each, is, I think, something absolutely fundamental. It is not an ideology; it is not exactly, fundamentally, or primarily an ideology. First of all and above all it is a technology of power" (Foucault, 2009, p. 71).

Like it or not, the cell phone asks for our obedience. When someone texts, we are summoned to notice. Increasingly my students and colleagues, and me, leave our cell phones on vibrate instead of silent. Instant notice and attention of the message delivered. Notifications from Facebook, Twitter, Instagram, apps, and friend. Weather alerts. Amber alerts. Constantly we are alerted and notified. Never thinking of that which is taken out of our technological stream. What knowledge do we not drink? What ideologies do we not realize we're breathing? I can remember visiting my great uncle's restaurant in Galilee and noticing a girl on her bicycle. She was texting while riding her bike.

"What is she doing?" I asked my dad, feeling the sun beat down on my face. I shielded my eyes to look at the girl.

"She's going to fall on her face," he said. No sooner did the words leave his mouth than she wiped out.

She was dismissing the world around her—the sounds of the waves, the seagulls, the *cars*—in order to respond. The urgency of the future response silences the present world. What constitutes normativity and rationality is built through these technologies. Obedience to the master without even recognizing the obedience. How many of us leave our cell phones on the dinner table? How did our grandparents survive without it forty years ago? If we forget it at home, how many of us would go back? Without it, the demands are silenced. What part of ourselves do we obey? Foucault discusses obedience through the oriental axiom: "Everything the monk does without permission of his master constitutes a theft. Here obedience is complete control of behavior by the master, not a final autonomous state. It is a sacrifice of the self, of the subject's own will. This is the new technology of the self" (pp. 44–45). A cell phone is metonymic of the social and corporate laws that govern our lives. The demands of society through race, gender, class, etc. lines dictate what we must obey and what we must not. In order to be, we must sacrifice ourselves. Refusal to do this is to commit a crime against society and make the person disposable and disloyal. This is further part of the individualization that purports autonomy.

This subjectification that classifies independent thought as disobedience feeds off colonial mechanisms. Quijano (2008) explains how "these [colonizing] turbulent processes involved a long period of the colonization of cognitive perspectives, modes of producing and giving meaning, the results of material existence, the imaginary, the universe of intersubjective relations with the world: in short colonization of culture" (p. 189). This colonization of culture dictates not only the norms of that society but also who belongs to that culture, who is excluded, and who is invisible. The colonizers are as much a part of this system of obedience as are the oppressed. Foucault (2009) discusses how "[t]here is terror when those who command tremble with fear themselves, since they know that the general system of obedience envelops them just as much as those over whom they exercise their power" (p. 267). His words speak with Freire's (2009) that "One of the basic elements of the relationship between oppressor and oppressed is *prescription.* Every prescription represents the imposition of one individual's choice upon another, transforming the consciousness of the person prescribed to into one that conforms with the prescriber's consciousness. Thus, the behavior of the oppressed is a prescribed behavior, following as it does the guidelines of the oppressor" (pp. 46–47). This transformation of consciousness educates individuals into the oppressor and oppressed as well as prescribes fear through the vulnerability of those who maintain a position of power built on a pillar of ice that is the frozen mentalities from the waters of colonialities. Any heat applied melts their power. We must stay frozen from love of other.

I was sitting at an in-service day in which we were supposed to come up with questions for students to answer about their teachers as an alternative to the DDMs (District Determined Measures). I was on the far edge of the lab table. For me, this seemed like a great opportunity to get feedback from students. I trust the majority of my students, and I don't fear that they will purposefully bash me on reviews just to be spiteful. My classroom may in some ways be too open in which I know too frequently if my children hate the novel they are reading or if they don't want to complete the assignment because it's "stupid."

"How do we know the kids are going to be honest though?"

"This can't be a part of our evaluation measurement …."

I sat head on hand, listening and watching as teachers voiced their concerns. I can't deny that their fears were starting to cause me to question my ease.

The teacher leader of the group shook his head. "No, these won't be used to measure how effective you are. They are just another component to get feedback."

"Will they even take this seriously?"

"You'll be surprised. The kids are usually great with this stuff. I've done this before, and it can be helpful. They do this in college," I said, voicing my thoughts as much to remind myself of the humanity of my students against the sea of terror I was in as to reassure my peers.

The teacher who had been typing our notes sighed. "I mean but can you trust them not to abuse this system? If I'm a hard teacher, they'll bash me."

"I think you'd be surprised. The kids want someone who will teach them. My sophomores always complain, but, in their end of the year letters, they are always appreciative."

"But, what if the kids don't like you?"

"How can they even know what good teaching is?"

"Who are they to evaluate us?"

My mind replays different comments made that day and others. The underlying element of fear. However, one phrase I remember crystal clear. I was silent after this.

"I know," said the teacher leader, nodding and agreeing—ideology of automatization. "I don't really buy into this. I'm a firm believer in the master and learner."

Master and learner. Another sayin' so clear in our minds. I should have asked, "Are we the masters? Do you decide what to teach or did someone else?

Is teaching by PowerPoint bullets teaching or rubber bullets of epistemological oppression through consumption?" The master has a master, and, in most instances, he is not his own master.

Fear coursed through this conversation as well as that panopticon of White patriarchy: 360° of obedience. The danger in individualism within a culture of surveillance is revealed. Each person nervous to move beyond what is allowed. Fanon (1963) explains how "[t]he colonialist bourgeoisie had hammered into the native's mind the idea of a society of individuals where each person shuts himself up in his own subjectivity, and whose only wealth is individual thought" (p. 47). This idea of cutting people off from each other allows for catalyzing the colonization of the mind. It is a dialectical process the more the mind colonizes, the more it is colonized. Sioui (1997) describes how certain Aboriginal Nations have continued to live despite the violence of colonialists:

> Had we, at that time, had leaders formed in patriarchal colonial institutions, as is so often the case nowadays, many of our nations would simply not have survived beyond the eighteenth century.
>
> Seeing those young captives, patricentrist leaders would have said, as they often say today about some of their own people: 'We have no use for these children: they are white, they are black, they are not Indian. They do not have a proper quantum of Indian blood.' And we and other very weakened, vulnerable nations would have soon disappeared. But as I am implying, our good fortune was that we lived within a matricentrist, circular system, where people and other species are not qualified and destroyed because of not being what they are not. (p. 56)

The patricentrist ideology that Sioui is describing is what many times is faced in school. It is an exclusionary model. Matricentrist ideology is one of nurturing and acceptance. However, this gendered division is still fueled by notions of what is masculine and what is feminine. In schools, we cannot focus on what people are not, but rather who they are. The capitalist patriarchy that administers individual violence is part of systemic violence. Furthermore, the paradox is that, although we are a society that feeds off individualization, in fact nothing changes due to an individual. Individual action, while necessary, is caught within a web of coloniality. A principal, while in a position of power and having individual accountability, does not in fact have the autonomy to choose how to act, and even if he or she did, most are not engaged in decolonial praxis to help transform public education toward social and cognitive justice. Individual power is not held; power runs through us. An individual does not hold power but rather power holds an individual. This does not mean that we should resign ourselves to a sense of fatalism. Freire (1997) explains:

> It is not enough for me to ask: "What can one do?" Technology necessarily engenders automatism, which leads to unemployment. The unemployed must change: they should seek leisure, a fundamental theme of postmodernity. No: I do not accept this form of fatalism. (p. 35)

Fatalism forces us into a notion that we live in an absolute space of liberation in which it is within an individual's power to transform his or her situation. However, this fails to address the structural and systemic power networks that work with, against, or through our actions.

After being harassed by police and almost being arrested because he fit the description of a black man given by a white woman who had been robbed, Steve Lock (2015), a MassArt professor and blogger, wrote,

> I thought about the fact my word counted for nothing, they didn't believe that I wasn't a criminal. They had to find out. My word was not enough for them. My ID was not enough for them. My handmade one-of-a-kind knit hat was an object of suspicion. My Ralph Lauren quilted blazer was only a "puffy coat." That white woman could just walk up to a cop and talk about me like I was an object for regard. I wanted to go back and spit in their faces. The cops were probably deeply satisfied with how they handled the interaction, how they didn't escalate the situation, how they were respectful and polite.
>
> I imagined sitting in the back of a police car while a white woman decides if I am a criminal or not. If I looked guilty being detained by the cops imagine how vile I become sitting in a cruiser? I knew I could not let that happen to me. I knew if that were to happen, I would be dead.
>
> Nothing I am, nothing I do, nothing I have means anything because I fit the description.

When I read this story, I started to shiver. The cliché embodied my response. His story had flashed onto my newsfeed, and I had read it, consuming it and thinking of the past day.

I was helping my students brainstorm for their children's books that they were going to write for the preschoolers. I was dealing with overly excitable seniors last period on a Friday. I had one student who had gone to the nurse and came back with tears in her eyes.

"Why don't you and Nolan work together?" I asked after explaining the assignment. She shook her head, a turtle regressing into her shell. The two were usually inseparable. I took the adamant movement as a clear sign that something was going on. Nolan's head now rested on the smartboard. His own eyes close to tears. "Okay. Separate works too." I dealt with keeping other students on task. They were creating children's books. Vince and Anne were throwing rhymes back and forth at each other. Vince loved rap and its poetic elements—he loved playing with words. I had never seen him so excited to work on a writing assignment. Anne was feeding into it. Neither a champion of spelling but both spiritually engaged as they came up with their snowman riddle. I flitted and floated, swirling to meet all twenty of their needs. Then, the door opened and Kent walked in.

"I need to go for a walk, but, then after, may I speak with you in the hallway?" His dark hair overshadowing his eyes.

"Yeah, go ahead." I let him go off, and he returned with his art teacher this time, but she left. I made my way to the door and went with him in the hallway. I had thought nothing of it when his art teacher had come to get him. I thought he had a project to work on. When he looked up at me, his eyes were swirling with pain that I still in the euphoria and energy of hyped up seniors and children's rhymes didn't recognize.

"I need to talk to you."

I started to sober. "Okay." We weren't what I would describe as close. I had tried to reach him, but we had the traditional teacher-student relationship. I cajoled him to do work. He resisted. I cajoled some more, giving him flexibility, and he did it. However, your identity is not your own. My perception of our relationship perhaps was wrong. I often forget and fail to recognize how silence does not mean distance or apathy. Silence is sometimes noisy. Your identity is not your own.

"What's up?" I fully expected him to say that he needed more time to turn the term around. I thought the adjustment counselor had spoken with him.

He took a deep breath. "Just give me a minute." And then he was off. He explained how some girls had reported that he said that he was going to shoot up the school. "I got called into Mr. Pacheco's office. I had Officer Sousa there and Mr. O'Neil. And they started asking me if I owned a gun. They asked for my driver's license. They didn't even call my parents. They were just interrogating me. I flipped out and swore."

"Well, that's not the best way to go. You should have asked for Mr. Araujo or not said anything. You don't have to be in there alone."

"I was all alone."

"Why didn't you ask for Mr. Araujo?"

"I just flipped out. I was so mad. I was being targeted for how I dress. Just because I'm the only gothic kid in the school." I nodded with a soft smile of understanding. I remembered my own friends in high school being targeted.

"I know. I had friends who dressed gothic or punk in school, and it wasn't fair. But, there were more of them. It's harder when you're the only one."

"How is it okay for them to target me?"

"It isn't. It isn't okay. Did you call your mom?"

He had called her. "They picked on me because of how I looked. I was in there alone." His words poetic in that they stood for much larger and more complex systems of power.

I wasn't sure if the "they" was for the girls or for the police officer and administration.

"You shouldn't have been alone. What happened to you isn't okay. Your mom will fix it."

I didn't know what to say. We went back inside with a minute to the bell. I kept thinking about the fear of mass shootings being paraded in the media. How would targeting certain youth make them prime for bullying? I knew what some of my friends faced in high school for the way they dressed. Was this bullying by calling him in for questioning and girls targeting him because of how he looked? Others would say that it had nothing to do with how he dressed. Maybe it didn't. But, more than likely, it did. Was his identity sacrificial? Was this violence necessary for our security? I would return to the conversation we had about Islamophobia. Who are the shooters within schools? Not necessarily the kid with the spiked collar dressed all in black. When I read Locke's story, I thought of Kent and how he had become nobody. I thought of how Rudy's words had become true. Similarly, the two boys with iced coffees had committed the same crime, but only one is targeted. You are nobody until you are somebody to dispose of. Kent's hurt. I thought of how he was alone. There was no kind stranger in a red coat, as there had been for Steve Lock, for who he could lock eyes with.

Life resumed to the normal waves of turbulence and routines, but did it for Kent? He had suffered from emotional issues and he hadn't wanted to be in school anyways. I thought that we would continue the year. But, he came to me a week or so ago with that infamous pink sheet. The sheet where I sign you off. I say you owe me no books.

"I'm dropping out and going to get my GED at BCC."

I looked at him, regretting that things couldn't have been different. I found myself trying to cheer him up. There was no use arguing in this instance. "BCC is great. You'll like the freedom."

"Yeah. But, I'll come visit."

"We'll miss you."

"I'll definitely be back and come visit." He left.

I thought about whether his questioning had anything to do with his decision. It may have or maybe it didn't. I thought of Pinocchio. Here was one boy who would not be made "real" by the system. Yet he was with the real of the system, the violence that chopped and whittled. Here was the coloniality of His power—those who fit and those who don't. Biopolitics at work.

Notes

1 This video was entitled "The Most Racist Cartoon Ever!" and it can be viewed at https://www.youtube.com/watch?v=sls5H4xVHys

2 Ghost stems from the German *geist,* and spirit is from the Latin spiritus. Even when my mother was child, mass was given in Latin, which is a whole other set of issues since the people did not understand Latin.

CHAPTER 5

The Pinocchio Effect: Biopolitics and Coloniality

> Having found the present generation composed of materials almost unmalleable, I am about transferring my efforts to the next. Men are cast-iron; but children are wax. Strength expended upon the latter may be effectual, which would make no impression upon the former.
>
> MANN (1865, p. 83)

As a critical transformative leader, I have realized the need to fight against what I frame as the "Pinocchio Effect," in which youth in U.S. public education begin as puppets who are made real through their schooling or resist and become the "jack asses" of U.S. society. During their schooling, youth function as puppets with strings that are visible through their surrounding constraints. These strings are pulled by neoliberal forces, which demand conformity through choice. However, some students pull on the strings and meet resistance from the taut hold, learning the length of their strings of "choice." Youth must conform to the hegemonic demands in order to become "real *boys*" or resist through violence and/or pleasure-seeking actions that are often committed without a critical consciousness of questioning and understanding the larger societal forces; market and consumerist ideology lures them into these behaviors. When I asked youth, what is your culture, many had no answer.

Lance had his phone out and had been texting, so I turned to him. "Lance." He looked up. "Do you identify with American culture?"

"That's not really," he said, putting down his phone. "I don't really see that as my culture."

"Is that your nationality?" I turned to Trent. "What do you think is your nationality or culture?"

"I don't know."

"What is your culture then?" I asked Lance.

"Well, my mother is Portuguese, so we have a lot of that. But, my dad is a hodgepodge, so there's …" he shrugged. "I guess American culture."

"How would you describe American culture?"

 | DOI: 10.1163/9789004416048_005

"It's like a hodgepodge."

"So we're all just mixed up. What does that include?" I turned to Nicole who was on the back wall. "What does American culture mean to you?"

"I don't know."

I decided to turn this from looking at themselves and shift the focus to the other. Perhaps, like me for many years, they didn't see their culture. "What's Mexican culture?"

"Tacos!" exclaimed Brian.

Everyone laughed, and I pushed on. "So food is culture? So what is American food?"

Alana jumped at the question, "Fast food!"

"So American culture is fast food. What else is in culture? What is in Mexican culture?"

"Music!"

"What's American music?"

"Rap. Pop music."

"Everybody knows the Beach Boys are America's band," said one student.

They all laughed, despite the intended serious response of the student.

"Not everybody knows that," said Brian.

"What else?" I asked, changing the subject.

"Fiestas!" said Nicole.

Alana touched her shirt looking for the word.

"Clothes. What are American clothes? How do you think we dress in comparison to Italians?"

"They're all fancy. We're casual," said Alana.

"So American culture is fast food, commercialized music, and casual clothes." There were chuckles. "Do you think we value different things than other cultures? Think back to the Greeks when we studied them last year." I was asking a lot at 7:45 in the morning. "How about those of you who are in honors and read *The Odyssey* this year. What did the Greeks value? Who was the goddess that protected Odysseus?"

After a long pause, finally Briana spoke, "Athena."

"Athena! What is she the goddess of?"

Mia, not in honors, raised her hand nervously from the back corner. "The h-hunt."

"Yes, but what else?"

"Wisdom."

"Yes, wisdom. What was Odysseus known for? He was a great warrior but what else? He got himself out of tricky situations due to what?"

Shawna spoke. "He was smart."

"Yes! The Greeks valued wisdom and knowledge. What do Americans value? Do we value knowledge?"

"Looks!"

"Athletics ... Strength."

"Looks, athletics/strength."

"And, money!"

"Money?"

"Yeah, money!" they said.

"So Americans value athletics/strength, money, and looks. This explains a lot," I said. "So now think about that as we continue with the book, drama. Watch Walter. In a society that values money, strength, and appearances, if you have that, then you are somebody in U.S. society. Statistically, pretty people are more likely to get hired." Athletes make a fortune. Money is life, Walter had said. "So, if you don't have money, athletic prowess, or appearance, who are you? Are you nobody? What would you be willing to do in order to be *somebody?*" I paused to let them think. "You're going to pass judgment on Walter pretty soon, but think about that before you do."

In the U.S., we live in a culture that values objects, not people, and, if people are valued, it's as objects. Darder (2015) speaks to "the destructive impact that alienations and unbridled consumerism have had on working class students and their education" (p. 25). Youth are constantly being educated but need to be given the space to analyze how their beings are used for capitalist purposes as well as how they may resist against these neoliberal forces. I frame the need for youth and educators to engage in conscientização (Freire, 2009) or consciencism (Nkrumah, 1964) in this chapter as part of body-politics (Mignolo, 2009b), which involves them understanding their governance by neoliberal mentalities that seduce people into an ideology of disposability for those who fail to make the right choices without realizing that these are often choiceless choices.

Here I would call your attention to Disney's *Pinocchio*. If you were to stop the movie when Pinocchio is on Pleasure Island and he's taking an ax to everything including a piano. Visualize that and think of what he's doing. He is chopping up what he is in fact made of... wood. Pleasure Island is where they are allowed to be *free*. Free... for what?

Earlier when Pinocchio is stopped by Honest John, who pretends to be a doctor, and Pinocchio, who is un-educated, is manipulated as Honest John tells him to close his eyes and open them, to which he says he sees spots because Honest John had put a spotted cloth in front of him. *Dr.* Honest John keeps up his use of big words to confuse Pinocchio while legitimizing what he's saying, "A palpating syncopation of the killer diller with a wicky-wacky stamping of the boy-joy." He tells him that he is allergic, and the only cure is Pleasure Island, "[t]hat happy land of carefree boys where every day's a holiday!" Pinocchio doesn't know what "allergic" means, but he is quickly ushered by Honest John to the coach where he is to be taken to Pleasure Island. Honest John did not put a gun to Pinocchio's head to tell him to get into the carriage, but he manipulated him through the use of language. For me, this is the biopolitics of language. The way we govern and colonize through mis-education or non-education.

The 2012 results of U.S. DOE's standardized test on reading revealed that U.S. youth were doing poorly on vocabulary, with most high school seniors not knowing the meaning of the word "prosper" (Resmovits, 2012). This aligns with my experiences in the classroom in which students may not know the word prejudice, ambiguous, transmit, objective, etc. On average, Americans older than 16 read at a 7th grade reading level. Furthermore, according to the National Center for Education Statistics, "Twenty-one to 23 percent—or some 40 to 44 million of the 191 million adults in this country—demonstrated skills in the lowest level of prose, document, and quantitative proficiencies (Level 1)" (Kirsch, Jungeblut, Jenkins, & Kolstad, 2002, p. xvi). When I teach journalism, I tell them to use rich language, but to remember that newspapers are written at an eighth grade reading level. Literacy is an ambiguous term, and language is a tool of the biopolitics of knowledge. Language has power. If the information the public receives is written so low, then what is said using more complex vocabulary that the public misses? Students confess that they like Trump because he's simple; he's a man of action. He's not just going to talk. Their words offer veridiction, considering Trump's speeches are written at a 4th grade reading level vs. Sander's speeches, which are at 10th grade level (Viser, 2015).

In my student's words, "Trump's the man!"

Language marauds class, race, and gender. With Trump, he encompasses all three and many more. He appeals to a *masculine* notion of action that entices people through fear that is orchestrated by White heteropatriarchal male hegemony. Epistemicides as it has been unpacked (Santos, 2007b, 2014; Paraskeva, 2011, 2016a, 2016b, 2017) traverse this terrain. How can youth understand what they don't know if they do not even have the language to learn? Or, how about when the language is stolen and reframed?

"When Floyd is accused of *talkin' red*, what does that mean?"

"Communist."

"Yes, but what does that mean?"

"He was saying Communist things."

I wave my hand in the air, asking for more.

"It means talking about worker's rights," said Amira.

"Yes, it does."

"But isn't talking communist bad?" asked Eric.

"Not necessarily. If we're going by worker's rights as communist, then I'd rather be called a communist than a capitalist." I laughed, but they looked at me questioningly. "Is asking for equality in work bad?"

"No."

"So why is demanding worker's rights bad?"

"In history, when we talked about Communism it's always to say how terrible it is."

I smiled. "Ahhh ... yes ... the 'C' word as my AP history used to say. Brilliant man. Got his PhD from Harvard ...." I trailed off, thinking back to my history classes. I had some amazing high school history teachers. "So what is communism? If worker's rights is communism, then what is democracy?"

"Communism everything is owned by the government."

"Okay. And, who owns and runs everything now?"

"Businesses."

"What is democracy?" I must have asked that question ten times this year. The lack of response was fading.

"Government by the people."

I nodded in acceptance of the answer. "So, in capitalism there is supply and demand, right?"

"Yeah. Free market."

"Right, so what happened in *Grapes of Wrath* with the oranges?" I asked.

"They dumped them, so that the price would stay high."

"As children died," added Megan.

"Yes, as children died," I repeated. "So, people work all day and still don't have enough, as the Joads did not. The rich throw away food as kids die. You are living in a country that has a quarter of its children living in poverty while the rich get richer. They control the market." I leaned back on my table. "I wouldn't call myself a communist, but I would say that I believe in social democracy, where the people, the proletariat, have power and rights. I think capitalism exploits people."

Eric nodded, not expecting such a long answer.

"Look at China where they are selling air."

"What!" exclaimed Dakota and the others.

"The air quality is so bad in China that Canadians are bottling air and selling it ... like we buy bottle water."

"That's not a joke?"

"No, it's true. The air quality is really terrible in China because of the mass amount of factories and industries." The air quality causes 14,000 deaths per year in China (Dellinger, 2015). Mass production of items for the pleasure of people, which ultimately leads to the sacrificing of lives. To return to Pinocchio, what is the cost of Pleasure Island? Here is biopolitics. Who is a necessary sacrifice? What is one willing to sacrifice of himself or herself?

Pinocchio meets another boy, Lampwick, who is ecstatic to go to Pleasure Island "Me neither, but they say it's a swell joint ... no school, no cops. You can tear the joint apart and nobody says a word .... Loaf around, plenty to eat, plenty to drink, and it's all free." They destroy property, smoke, eat candy, etc. I never noticed it until I studied the screen capture and lightened it for a second to see the graffiti on the back wall behind the piano. What were the artists saying about the milieu for "bad boy" behavior?

The Coachman cracks a whip for his henchman to close the doors, locking the boys onto Pleasure Island as he remarks, "Give a bad boy enough rope, and he'll soon make a jackass of himself." Pinocchio is seen chopping a wooden leg. Environed in this culture, he is chopping a wooden leg when *he* is in fact wood. He is becoming a "real" boy, so he doesn't think about what he is doing, just as the other character lights a cigarette on the Mona Lisa.

Gee (2005) discusses "real Indians" to help analyze how who we are and what we are needs to be situated within a discourse of interactions and representations. Although partially due to genetics, a Native American may be of mixed kinship and seen as a "real Indian," whereas someone who has no other kinship besides Native American may not be seen as a "real Indian" (p. 15). This process of being is not finite; it continues. As Gee (2005) states, "there is no being (once and for all) a 'real Indian,' rather there is only doing being-or-becoming-a-'real-Indian.' If one does not continue to 'practice' being a 'real Indian,' one ceases to be one" (p. 15). Similarly, youth are constantly in an act of becoming "good boys" or "good girls," which, in light of their value often being conflated with an output on a data chart, has less to do with being a "good citizen" with democratic values and knowledges, and more with being trained consumers and products for the market. In order to be, one must practice the market values of being; this is part of the colonialities that commodifies youth. In fact, the Blue Fairy tells Pinocchio, "and remember a boy who won't be good might as well be made of wood."

Consequently, the resisters (although they also are in some ways really the consumers and/or products that society needs) are rejected and transformed into "donkeys"/"jack asses"—mules of production and entertainment becoming symbols of immorality and replicable objects for the system and society. Again think back to Pinocchio. The boys who are led to Pleasure Island are surrounded by all the luxuries that they could want, but the result is they turn into donkeys that the Coachmen then sends to the Salt Mines to be workers, revealing the politics of disposability, the politics of the body. Today's youth are sold into various corporatized interests including prisons and poverty (cf. Wacquant, 2009) as well as consumerism. Consumerism that is violent and costs lives. A student who wanted to research the sneaker craze and its violence, read to me that 1,200 people die each year due to sneaker violence (McCall, 2013). I thought that seemed high, but regardless, there are youth who have been killed over sneakers. Furthermore, how many children have died due to the inadequate pay of the shoe industry?

I asked my student, what made sneakers so cool to kill over, and he replied, "That's ridiculous, but people love sneakers. Sneakerheads. It all started with Jordan."

"But what's the big deal? I don't get it, they're shoes. Shoes define you?"

"They're not just shoes."

"They're your identity?" They make you somebody, I thought.

Given technical skills and constrained to be the producers of the world and not the creators (Chomsky, 2012), the working class is constantly seeking to own a piece of middle class life, living in debt as the precariat (Bauman & Donskis, 2012) in order to maintain the illusion of wealth.

U.S. culture feeds off consumerism. Youth are surrounded by a culture that is about superficiality and consuming. hooks (1992) has a conversation with herself, Gloria Watkins, in which she states, "Look at what most people do with water in this country. Many people purchase special water because they consider tap water unclean and of course this purchasing is a luxury. Even our ability to see the water that comes through the tap as unclean is itself informed by an imperialist consumer perspective" (p. 149). This is even more striking with the situation in Detroit,[1] in which the luxury of running water is currently being deprived to "hundreds of thousands of people, mostly African Americans .... Families with children, the elderly and the sick, cannot bathe, flush their toilets or cook in their own homes" (Deen, 2014), reflecting the hidden third worlds of the U.S. that is classified as a first world nation. In East Porteville, California wells are privately owned, so the inhabitants who are primarily low income and Latino are left without water when the wells dry up (Lurie, 2015).

These imperialist luxuries appear to youth, not as luxuries but as commonsensical needs and/or rights. After listening to one of my colleagues speak about Kenya and seeing photographs of his childhood school, my students were amazed that he described the current state as improved and/or acceptable. To them, a classroom outside in which students sat on tree logs or a classroom with walls but no roof seemed to be categorized as a poor school. I then asked them to reflect on how if we brought in students from an affluent community, like Barrington, they would see our school as poor, yet it serves their (my students) purpose to learn. We discussed how "need" is constructed, as is "luxury." This relates to the imperial consumerist mentality.

Even though there is nothing wrong with the pair of sneakers that students have, they must buy better ones or different ones as part of the imperialist norms, a hegemony of consumerism, which feeds the neoliberal mindset. Giroux (2011) remarks how "[y]outh are now assaulted by a never-ending proliferation of marketing strategies that colonize their consciousness and daily lives. Under the tutelage of Disney and other megacorporations, children have become an audience captive not only to traditional forms of media such as film, television and print, but even more so to the new digital media made readily accessible through mobile phones, PDAs, laptop computers and the Internet." This is the neoliberal colonization of the mind into a hegemony of consumer choices and identities that negate the spiritual. Children become subject to the influence of the media and between the media's consumerist culture and the school's anesthetization and commodification of youth, what we witness is a colonial politics of spirituality against the body and mind:

> Precisely this 'sensualism' with its revolutionary potential for the dialectical empowerment of students as both individuals and social beings is systematically stripped away from the educational experience of students in public schools ... domesticating educational policies and practices that ignore the experience of the body and reinforce abstract, fragmented, and decontextualize theories of teaching and learning seldom function in the interest of the oppressed populations. More often than not, students are socialized and conditioned into passive roles that debilitate, and can eventually annul, their sense of social agency within schools. Consequently, the very real and present physical, emotional, and spiritual needs of students are generally ignored or rendered insignificant, which facilitates efforts to obtain their obedience and conformity to the dominant culture of the schooling process. (Darder, 2002, p. 97)

Students are supposed to memorize knowledge and regurgitate it back to prove their acquisition of it through standardized exams with the intention of them becoming passive recipients of knowledge. The silencing of identities, languages, and knowledges not only oppresses youth's spiritualities but also creates resistance and reproduction of cultural norms. Zero Tolerance, Common Core, and high-stakes testing policies are "domesticating educational policies" (Darder, 2002) that function within a colonial matrix of power that promotes the hegemony of neoliberalism that belies choice. Nkrumah's (1964) words describes the anesthetizing positivist culture that thrives in U.S. schools and consequently society through the colonization of youths' minds:

> With single-minded devotion, the colonial student meanders through the intricacies of the philosophical systems .... The academic treatment is the result of an attitude to philosophical systems as though there was nothing to them but statements standing in logical relation to one another.
>
> This defective approach to scholarship was suffered by different categories of colonial student. Many of them had been hand-picked and, so to say, carried certificates of worthiness with them. These were considered fit to become enlightened servants of the colonial administration. (p. 3)

Students, who accept the knowledge and practice the discourses (Gee, 1990) of the dominant class as dictated by the Common Core and enforced through standardized testing and Zero Tolerance policies, are able to progress through society, not as critical, democratic citizens but as cognizant or pseudo-/in-cognizant colonial subjects, producing a world that only strengthens inequality and amasses more wealth for the global elite. There is a plurality of students, but, for the sake of analysis, I am classifying them, so educators may understand the different discourse we see youth exhibit that we often misinterpret and/or do not know how to engage; not that educators are exempt from these classifications. In addition, there are those youth who resist, code switching and navigating the system, playing it without being played. Then, other students who resist are labelled delinquent or "at risk." As McLaren and da Silva (1993) explain "dominant forms of literacy serve as a process of colonization whereas illiteracy often signals a resistant act of refusing, as Giroux (1987, p. 13) puts it, 'to learn the specific cultural codes and competencies authorized by the dominant cultures view of literacy'" (p. 56). Having gone through the public educational system in Massachusetts during the *golden* reign of No Child Left Behind (NCLB) and MCAS and now teaching under its continued rule through Race to the Top (RTTT), I have to recognize the colonial memory and colonialities of being that are embodied within and through me. That colonial memory is based on a highly racialized system that, as I will highlight later on, is used for economic exploitation and the subjugation of black and brown youth particularly but also youth from low socioeconomic status. Their bodies suffer violence every day, which is only emblematic of the extreme violence that colonialism perpetrated historically and currently.

Colonialism is not dead. The colonialities that rationalize the violence done to subaltern youth is built on genocide, epistemicide, and linguicide. Colonialities are constantly unfolding and developing. When Florida and Virginia developed policies that would set lower goals on tests for African American youth than for Asian or Caucasian (Kuczynski-Brown, 2012), how can we not say that this neoliberal game of colonialities is unfolding within the U.S. under an extremely racialized system that incarcerates disproportionate amount of African Americans (Alexander, 2011)? The high-stakes testing culture of the U.S. is racialized and classed, penalizing subaltern youth and colonizing youth for their place in the market.

As part of the first generation of the high-stakes testing sovereignty in Massachusetts, I'm a product of this. I was made "real" by the system. Now, I work for the system, and I must constantly challenge and critique my assumptions and practices, requiring me to look at the past, present, and future, and I must analyze others' construction of my identity as a female, teacher, etc. I learned to speak and act the language of silence, a nonbeing of production. I am useful to others, and therefore I can exist. Maldonado-Torres (2007) claims that "[t]he Cartesian formulation privileges epistemology, which simultaneously hides both what could be regarded as the coloniality of knowledge (others do not think) and the coloniality of Being (others are not)" (p. 252). My future being is important to coloniality as far as what I can do that produces knowledge and power while oppressing myself and others. Perhaps that is really the twist on the Cartesian formulation: I oppress therefore I am.

In order to break free and "be what we are not," we must first know what we don't know and finally see what has always been there, concealed by the ideology and knowledge within an *educated* view. Thiong'o (1994) adds to this that "[s]ince culture does not just reflect the world in images but actually, through those very images, conditions a child to see that world in a certain way, the colonial child was made to see the world and where he stands in it as seen and defined by or reflected in the culture of the language of imposition" (p. 17). Analysis of these instances of resistance, conformity, production, and reproduction demonstrates the need for critical transformative leaders to fight for *enunciatory* and decolonial spaces where students and teachers engage and discover identities and spiritualties. Referencing Beisiegel (1982), da Silva and McLaren (1993) remark that "Freire believed that this educational alternative should be developed within the existing order—the object was to modernize it, not to revolutionize it" (p. 36). It is here that the concept of emancipatory or liberatory pedagogy needs to be reconceptualized or at least clarified. Emancipatory and/or liberatory pedagogy should be revolutionary in that it creates a world through an individual's agency in which they are striving to go beyond the hegemonic boundaries of acceptable knowledge and being, and politicizing that space by working for a present and future in which liberation isn't confined by hegemony of the present and past. However, the term "emancipation" in the contextualized origins of the European Enlightenment "proposes and presupposes changes within the system that doesn't question the logic of coloniality" (Mignolo, 2010, p. 309). When speaking of emancipation, we must decolonize the term and the process it describes because, within the current colonial matrix of power, emancipation can be seen as being written in the language of colonization, since the hegemony of colonial values still prevails in modernity. Also, we should consider Mignolo's interview with Gaztambide-Fernández (2014) in which he discusses enunciation:

> "Representation" is a keyword in the rhetoric of modernity, that is, in Western mainstream epistemology. In this regard, thinking decolonially (that is, thinking within the frame of the decolonial option) means to start from "enunciation" and not from "representation." When you start from the enunciation and think decolonially, you shall run away from representation, for representation presupposes that there is a world out there that someone is representing. This is a basic assumption of modern epistemology. There is not a world that is represented, but a world that is constantly invented in the enunciation. The enunciation is constituted by certain actors, languages, and categories of thoughts, beliefs, and sensing. The enunciation, furthermore, is never or only enacted to "represent" the world, but to confront or support previous existing enunciations. (pp. 198–199)

In light of this, we need an education in which students are challenging dominant epistemologies, an enunciatory process, and not attempting to represent the world or emancipate themselves into the existing world order.

This process would need to recognize the oppressive culture that shapes and silences students' and educators' consciousness and spiritualities. Darder (2002) explains that "[e]ducation then is no longer the key transformation of consciousness, but education is absolutely necessary for transformation. To understand the relationship of education and consciousness it is necessary to think dialectically, in terms of ongoing apparent contradictions" (p. x). In consideration of these factors, I would claim that we need to incorporate both decolonial and critical theories within the classroom as part of a revolutionary, decolonial praxis. Darder (2002) speaks to how this "revolutionary praxis turns the traditional purpose of public education on its proverbial head, unveiling its contradictions and 'false generosity.' Instead of educating our students to become simply reliable workers, complacent citizens, and avid consumers, progressive teachers engage students in a critical understanding of the world, so they can consider innovative emancipatory directions for integrating this knowledge into their daily lives" (p. 57). This revolutionary praxis would need to decolonize the present and past in order to create a hope for a liberatory future through the process of enunciation.

Educators as pedagogues must be constantly analyzing the past, present, and future, looking at what is seen and what is unseen as well as what is heard and silent as well as what is silenced. The current neoliberal colonial sovereignty is one in which educational reforms increasingly dictate both students' and teachers' thoughts and movements. As Giroux (1988) claims, "the conditions of labor under which teachers work are mutually determined by dominant interests and discourses that provide the ideological legitimation for promoting hegemonic classroom practices .... This type of discourse not only wages symbolic violence against students in that it devalues cultural capitals they possess as a significant basis for school knowledge and inquiry, it also tends to position teachers within pedagogical model that legitimate their role as 'clerks' of the empire" (p. 91).

Colonialism is a pedagogical process with a curriculum of dialectical violence. In order for colonizers to be, they must destroy who they are in order to take on their role of the colonizer, which at times goes against the humanistic values of their culture. In order to rationalize this contradiction, the violence perpetrated against others seems necessary and just, at times part of a savior complex. This repeats until it becomes ritual and nonrational. Colonization is a dialectical violence that must be nonrationalized. One must not think but do. Action without thought therefore can't be resistance.

We can see this through the Army training put into place after WWII in which men could not pull the trigger when faced with the enemy because the enemy has their face. One must either create such hatred in another that the enemy becomes faceless and/or make the action of killing a ritual that deserves no thought besides the perfunctory action of pulling a trigger. Brigadier General Samuel Lyman Atwood Marshall (1947) wrote about the soldier in WWII, "[t]he fear of aggression has been expressed to him so strongly and absorbed by him so deeply and pervadingly—practically with his mother's milk—that it is part of the normal man's emotional make-up. This is his great handicap when he enters combat. It stays his trigger finger even though he is hardly conscious that it is a restraint upon him" (p. 78). Marshall's study found that approximately 80% of the men could not pull the trigger in combat. That number has changed dramatically.

In Vietnam, only 5% did not fire (Grossman, 1996). Grossman (1996) describes how after WWII the targets were given faces and today's soldiers are conditioned by being in full military gear in dugouts and shooting human shaped targets that fall back when *successfully* shot as well as generally given a reward as part of a token economy. He further explains that "this careful rehearsal and realistic mimicry of the act of killing permit the soldier to convince himself that he has only 'engaged' another target." So, although Marshall (1947) stated, "[h]e is what his home, his religion, his schooling, and the moral code and ideals of his society have made him. The Army cannot unmake him" (p. 78), the Army apparently can. In a public education system that is increasingly militarized, the normalization and rationalization of violence is easier to analyze when one takes out "Army" and puts in "neoliberalism"; "Neoliberalism can unmake youth." War has ethics that make it rational.

Maldonado-Torres (2007) discusses the *non-ethics of war* that, through damnation allowed for exceptions to Christian ethics due to the inferiority of those colonized and consequently the naturalization and necessitation of war and slavery. The justification in Latin America was race. U.S. public schools are a warzone. Giroux (2014b) exclaimed, "Youth are under attack!" The *non-ethics of war* in schools allows students' test scores to determine whether they are put into an *inferior* academic track. People can sugar coat it any way they want, but, when you are tracking students, you are saying these students are superior to those students. This sorting for the market is part of the colonial power matrix and the segregating of society. It goes back to Quijano's (2000) discussion of the creation of race in South American for capitalist exploitation and colonial expansion. Black and brown youth are disproportionately criminalized (Rios, 2011), medicated[2] (Steven, Harman, & Keller, 2005), expelled (Advancement Project et al., 2011), pushed out of school (Fine, 1991), tracked in schools (Oakes, 2005), and segregated (Orfield & Lee, 2007). The colorblind ideology that legitimizes this racism through a discourse of Zero Tolerance, equal treatment, high standards (of standardization) parallels Maldonado-Torres' (2007) discussion of *non-ethics of war* that legitimized the racialization and inferiorization of people during colonialism. It is important to flag that low-income youth are also flagged in many of these studies as also suffering under these conditions, which helps substantiate Quijano's (2000) and Oyěwùmí's (2002) claims, respectively, that race and gender were oppressive markers created for capitalist colonial exploitation. Colonialism is a warfront of class warfare.

Under U.S. public education policy, no one is to engage in a revolutionary praxis to address how these low test scores or GPAs may be due to societal injustices, such as racial or class bias, or due to emotional distress. The RTTT policies of rigor and college and career readiness are the great equalizers that with students' and teachers' hard work will remedy all who deserve it. Through individual efforts, social responsibility is forgotten. Zero Tolerance policies make it easy to discipline kids in a *non-ethics of war*. It is equal, and it is fair. That statement is naturalized to the point that people do not see how equal and fair are not synonymous. A score is rationally more important than a student. Teachers and parents do not speak up out of fear and consume the rhetoric that this is what is best for children. Parramore (2012) compares the bondage and pain displayed in *Fifty Shades of Gray* to that within the American workplace, claiming that working class people naturalize their conditions and are oblivious to how the system benefits the elite. Furthermore, "[f]ear and frustration can even make us crave authority. We collaborate in our own oppression" (Parramore, 2012). There is a denial of alternatives in the workplace but also in education. The facts, data walls, data charts, DDMS, AYP, PPI, charts—they are all part of Césaire's (2000) equation "colonization = 'thingification'" (p. 43). In education, teachers and youth live under "a dictatorship of no alternatives" (Unger, 2005, p. 1). We must fight to find spaces for other alternatives and recover a pedagogy of hope.

Educators must work with students to fight against these forms of symbolic violence that entrench youth in an ideology of disposability (Giroux, 2009). Pedagogues and students need to be creating a curriculum within schools that is decolonial, in which it uses an enunciatory theory of curriculum that analyzes "the field of production and distribution of knowledge itself, and consequently of education, as a field of struggle and search for hegemony" (McLaren, & da Silva, 1993, p. 47), but also deconstructs the epistemologies and languages enabled by that hegemony as part of a broader colonial matrix of neoliberal power. It is within this frame that we can see the accepted *ethics* of creative destruction:

> The process of neoliberalization has, however, entailed much "creative destruction," not only of prior institutional frameworks and powers (even challenging traditional forms of state sovereignty) but also of divisions of labor, social relations, welfare provisions, technological mixes, ways of life and thought, reproductive activities, attachments to the land habits of the heart. In so far neoliberalism values market exchange as an "ethic in itself, capable of acting as a guide to all human action, and substituting for all previously held ethical beliefs," it emphasizes the significance of contractual relations in the marketplace. It holds that the social good will be maximized by maximizing the reach and frequency of market transactions, and it seeks to bring all human action into the domain of the market. This requires technologies of information creation and capacities to accumulate, store, transfer, analyse, and use massive databases to guide decisions in the global marketplace. (Harvey, 2005, p. 11)

U.S. schools are part of this neoliberalization and acceptance of creative destruction in which even students' tests scores are sold. The encroachment of privatization on public education is deemed acceptable because of the public's fear in the failure of schools and the economy (cf. Ravitch, 2010; Fabricant & Fine, 2012). Consequently, people continue to buy into the consumer culture, perhaps looking for some sense of security through owning and objects. McLaren and da Silva (1993) claim "[g]lobal capitalism's theater of terror continues to shape the social imagination of both the First and the Third Worlds with its insipid colonizing logic and its delusion-producing politics of desire" (p. 47). This shaping of the social imagination is done through globalization and the control of knowledge across nations. Ironically, globalization is often seen as a positive union of the world, but, as Darder (2002) explains, "'globalization' has become the new buzz-word for economic imperialism and its ruthless mechanisms to maximize capital accumulation" (p. 8). This liquid modernity (Bauman, 2013) has meant the "[d]ecentralization of control [which] has resulted in corporations becoming global webs, with stakeholders becoming a large diffused group, spread over the world—less visible, less accountable, and less noisy than national stakeholders" (Darder, 2002, p. 9). The U.S. is classified as a first world nation, but there is an increasing wealth gap in which approximately 23% of children in the U.S. live in poverty (UNICEF, 2012, p. 3). Yet, the U.S. is home to some of the biggest corporate economies in the world, relating to what "John Cavanaugh (1996) terms 'global economic apartheid,' for of the 100 largest economies in the world, 51 are now global corporations. The Ford Motor Company is bigger than the economy of South African and Wal-Mart is bigger than the economies of 161 countries" (Darder, 2002, p. 10). It should be incredulous to the U.S. public that practically one out of four children is living in poverty, while companies like Wal-Mart make a grotesque amount of profit.

However, this seems legitimate and commonsensical under the regime of truth (Foucault, 1980) that believes in the ethos of the meritocracy of capitalism as fueled by neoliberalism. This dominant system of knowledge appears irrefutable based on the legitimized facts. However, "[t]he geopolitical world arena, with its industrial and corporate co-efficients and the steady encroachment of multinationals, is producing just not just a monopoly on information but what could also be called empires of consciousness—regimes which structure our desires transculturally" (McLaren & da Silva, 1993, p. 48). Furthermore, this has created an "epoch permeated by global mechanisms of oppression, ever more sweeping machineries of surveillance, and increasingly brutal structures of violence which tunnel through the flesh and marrow of everyday life and into the very core of what Raymond Williams calls our 'practical consciousness,' only to burrow further to the domain of the unconsciousness, Freire continues to exhibit courage and a persistent commitment to freedom and social justice" (da Silva & McLaren, 1993, pp. 50–51). This failure to look at the individual effects and the reshaping of the consciousness is not an innocent mistake but a systemic violence as part of the colonization of the mind by neoliberalism. Giroux (2012) elaborates:

> [T]here is little or no attempt on the part of the wealthy class of educational misinformers to analyze schooling as a place where students learn about the operations of power and what it means to take risks, engage in critical dialogue, embrace the important lessons that come with shared responsibilities, or learn the knowledge, skills, and values needs to be imaginative and critically responsible citizens. Instead, we are told—not surprisingly by the hedge fund reformers and billionaire gurus—that schooling is about the production of trained workers; memorization is more important than critical thinking; standardized testing is better than teaching students to be self-reflective; and learning how to read texts critically is not as important as memorizing discrete bodies of allegedly factual knowledge. Having their desires and skills shaped in such a way, students and teachers are reduce to permanent underclass, denied the opportunities to develop the capacity and motivation to challenge the power and authority of a rich elite. Pedagogical practice in this neoliberal framework is cleansed of any emancipatory possibilities, stripped clean of its ability to teach students how to engage in thoughtful dialogue and use their imagination in the service of understanding lies and experiences of individuals and groups different from themselves. (pp. 21–22)

The failure of U.S. public education to engage in an analysis of the epistemologies and languages destroyed is part of the cult of positivism that also sees science as superior to other forms of knowing and consequently, being. Castro-Gómez (2008) details how "[o]ne of the consequences of the hubris of the zero degrees is the invisibilization of a particular place of enunciation, which is then converted into a place without a place, into a universal. The tendency to convert local history into global design run parallel to the process of establishing that particular place as a center of geopolitical power" (p. 279). As the boundaries of the world become liquid, there is an invisibilization because land no longer means a concrete reality but can rather signify the denunciation of that reality. Shiva (1993) contends that:

> Emerging from a dominating and colonising culture, modern knowledge systems are themselves colonising. The knowledge and power nexus is inherent in the dominant system because, as a conceptual framework, it is associated with a set of values based on power which emerged with the rise of commercial capitalism. It generates inequalities and domination

> by the way such knowledge is generated and structured, the way it is legitimised and alternatives are delegitimised, and by the way in which such knowledge transforms nature and society. (pp. 9–10)

Even the classification of "modern knowledge system" denotes the colonial nature in which there is a system, a power dynamic that colonizes the world for the sake of modernity; public acceptance of this reflects coloniality of being, power, and knowledge.

Modernity shines the glass slippers of coloniality, continuing the fairytale for the global elite. Mignolo (2009b) claims that "[k]nowledge-making in the modern/colonial world is at once knowledge in which the very concept of 'modernity' rests as the judge and warrantor of legitimate and sustainable knowledge. Shiva (1993) suggested 'monocultures of the mind' to describe Western imperial knowledge, its totalitarian and epistemically non-democratic implementation" (p. 18). These monocultures of the mind tunnel acceptability to one dominant culture that reflects the knowledges and beliefs that benefit the economy for the wealthy, which hides the underside of this knowledge for the subaltern. This connects to coloniality of being and ongoing colonization:

> Over and above rendering local knowledge invisible by declaring it non-existent or illegitimate, the dominant system also makes alternatives disappear by erasing and destroying the reality which they attempt to represent. The fragmented linearity of the dominant knowledge disrupts the integrations between systems. Local knowledge slips through the cracks. It is eclipsed along with the world to which it relates. Dominant scientific knowledge thus breeds a monoculture of the mind by making space local alternatives disappear. (Shiva, 1993, p. 12)

Such process of invisibilization has occurred over time, and the hegemony of the "monoculture of the mind" makes the irrational seem rational and silences the possibility of a critical, democratic future in the omissions of the past.

In the creation of a decolonial space within the classroom, pedagogues should consider:

> The future of which we dream is not inexorable. We make it, produce it, else it will not come in the form that we would more or less wish it to. True, of course, we have to make it not arbitrarily, but with the materials, with the concrete reality, of which we dispose, and more as a project, a dream, for which we struggle. While for dogmatic, mechanistic positions, the consciousness that I call critical takes shape as a kind of

> epiphenomenon, a 'spin off'—an automatic, mechanical result of structural changes—for dialectic, the importance of consciousness is in the fact that, not being the maker of reality, neither is it, at the opposite pole, a pure reflex of reality. It is precisely on this point that something of basic importance turns—the basic importance of education as an act of cognition not only of the content, but of the 'why' of economic, social, and political, ideological, and historical facts, which explain the greater or lesser degree of 'interdict of the body,' our conscious body, under which we find ourselves placed. (Freire, 2014, pp. 91–92)

The socio-political function of U.S. education within the colonial power matrix as furthered by neoliberalism engenders colonialities of being that silence and produce spiritualities; therefore, critical transformative leaders need to work with youth to decolonize the written, performed, and hidden curriculum in a process of enunciation. It is also important to understand how Itinerant Curriculum Theory (ICT) comes into play within these processes (cf. Paraskeva, 2011, 2016a).

1 Itinerant Theory as an 'Alternative to Think about Alternatives'

Paraskeva's (2011, 2014) ICT is a vivid example of what Santos (2014) calls 'alternative ways of thinking about alternatives'. He explains how ICT proposes that "new possibilities open up for a mutually enriching exchange between counter-hegemonic human rights politics and progressive political ideologies" (Paraskeva, 2016a, p. 11). In the act of teaching, it is necessary to not only consider confronting hegemonic ideologies but also the spaces within counterhegemonic rationales to further decolonize ideologies. Educators are part of this powerful network of ideologies controlled by language in which they "are responsible for teaching languages that are often unrecognized and treated as fact instead of discourses of dominance" (Janson & Motta Silva, 2017, p. 4). Schubert (2017) adds to this that "[e]ven though paradigm is associated with worldview, language seemed more embedded and embodied in lived experience, representing the ways many of us wanted to envision the scholarly work that needed to be done" (p. 5). Language is essential to consider when unraveling ideologies of dominance in school, not just language as in English and Portuguese but language as in how students, educators, parents, janitors, etc. are allowed to express themselves and conversely how they are heard or *interpreted* by others. This becomes the curriculum of our lives, and, thus, ICT becomes a way to engage with this curriculum and to analyze it. Furthermore, ICT

> pushes one to think in the light of the future as well as to question how can 'we' actually claim to really know the things that 'we' claim to know if 'we' are not ready specifically to think the unthinkable, but to go beyond the unthinkable and mastering its infinitude. ICT is to be (or not to be) radically unthinkable. ICT is a metamorphosis between what is thought and non-thought and un-thought, but fundamentally about the temerity of the colonization of the non/un/thought within the thought. ICT attempts to understand how big is infinite, the infinite of thought and action. If one challenges infinity, 'then it is chaos because one is in chaos'; that means that the question or questions (whatever they are) are inaccurately deterritorialized and fundamentally sedentary. The focus is to grasp that ICT implies an understanding of chaos as domestic, as public, as a *punctum* within the pure luxury of immanence. (p. 254)

It is important to understand that ICT works within the dialectics of teaching that is essential in a decolonial classroom. No classroom is ever the same. Teacher preparation programs are in fact counterintuitive. They prepare you for behaviors, while excluding beings. Curriculum is portrayed as an itemized or narrative entity. Add to this that teachers are:

> [t]rained (not educated) in dealing with a numerology cult; teachers and educators codify crucial approaches such as Santos', as frivolous knowledge. Philosophy has no value to them as they are crunched to work within a scientific paradigm that continuously disvalues their intellectuality. The lack of interest stems in part from the conception of theory and philosophy as a luxury of the past that within a hyper-capitalist present, catalyzed by neoliberal steroids, cannot be afforded. Educators deal with the present knowing the wrath of the future. Teaching and learning in many ways are an act of scourging. Instead of an act of discovering, education is an act of covering. (Janson & Paraskeva, 2015, p. 964)

As Moreira (2017, p. 3) argues, Paraskeva's ICT is a commitment to "deterritorialize curriculum and teacher education" which cannot be done without counteracting linguisticides or "epistemological euthanasia" (Paraskeva, 2016a, p. 238) carried out by the colonial powers in the past (but still going on in the present). ICT helps challenging the "linguisticides, a form of epistemicide exerted on indigenous languages. By targeting indigenous languages, linguisticides eradicate indigenous knowledges in a particular sociolinguistic group" (Moreira, 2017, p. 3). In this sense, Paraskeva's ICT is

> an extremely useful and relevant tool for analysing and critiquing the situation of schooling for ethnolinguistic minorities and the way language teacher education has been responding (or not) to the needs of these children. (Moreira, 2017, p. 11)

Curriculum is messy and incongruous. Curriculum is everywhere within the classroom and beyond. To try to confine it to the boundaries of a traditional lesson plan is equivalent to trying to predict the weather in New England. For those of you from beyond this anomalous region, it can have rain on one side of the street and sunshine on the other. There is no rhyme or reason to what is. Teachers rather need to develop an ideological philosophy to understand what *can* be. Teacher education must understand the chaos and help create spaces for educators to be leaders where they learn the courage to be, which is to educate. Every interaction that educators and students have is one of becoming, which is also one of educating.

Also, educators must be cognizant of the abyssal line, which ICT addresses. Jupp (2017) claims, "[w]ith disappearing knowledge traditions across the abyssal line, Western condemnation to abyssality is an enormous, tragic, and eugenic cleansing of localized geo-regions' knowledges and practices whose existence is increasingly tenuous in an age of whitening globalizing capitalism" (p. 5). Important to note is that the cleansing of localized knowledges occurs on either side of the line in which many children of the "North" have their knowledges and identities dismissed and replaced by the *W*hite, color of their ideology, knowledge to serve capitalistic purposes, while anesthetizing their spirits. It is here that the Pinocchio Effect takes place where we see the manufacturing of youth as either servants to the system or as the refuse, so easily disposed of it. Yet, it is also here where we see the need for ICT.

We must challenge teachers to decolonize their thinking and to see beyond the normative into the world of social and cognitive justice. ICT provides a theoretical framework for this decolonial pedagogy in which educators are faced with a curriculum of becoming not a curriculum of standardization that seeks to homogenize students and teachers into master and student. Teachers needs to constantly question with students not for and to see the curriculum as in the act of becoming through this relationship.

As curricularists, Price (2017, p. 6) states, "our personal stories as intersect with the political malaise associated with the history of the New Taylorism" framed by standards, high stakes testing, accountability, deskilling of teachers, heavy creed on issues such as classroom management, a pandemonium that Paraskeva's (2016a) defines as "momentism" where every moment must be accounted for. ICT, as Price (2017) argues short-circuit such New Taylorism, that needs to be seen as the re-escalation of the epistemicide through teacher preparation programs.

> [ICT] provides insight into the affairs of teacher education, providing the tools to unpack the meanings behind the official white papers regarding the imagined new teacher, or neoliberal teacher. To consider another kind of teacher is to engage in this type of deterritorialized inquiry, and this work represents an exercise that is well past due and entirely consequential to the relationship between curriculum theorizing and teacher education. If we recall, reconceptualist curriculum studies as a movement in the 1970s through the early 2000s, emerged out of a rejection of the notion that the sum total of inquiry into curriculum matters must be relegated and bound to the practice of schooling. Acknowledging, yet impatient with (now) territorialized reconceptualist curriculum discourses, Paraskeva avoids framing ICT as the new recipe for curriculum theorizing or curriculum framework. It is not a "how to" theoretical frame for theorizing or development, but it might be a guide to reimagining teaching, learning, and education. Working from outside of the (re)colonized New Taylorism of teacher training and preparation, ICT seems like a potential direction for curriculum study to decolonize itself from both curriculum development and reconceptualist curriculum studies, and—through shared labor—thrive again. (Price, 2017, p. 11)

As the new synoptic momentum (Pinar, 2013) that provides "a conceptual grammar moves along three broad dimensions emphasizing (a) the coloniality of power, knowledge, and being; (b) epistemicides, linguicides, abyssality, and the ecology of knowledges; and, (c) poststructuralist hermeneutic itinerancy" (Jupp, 2017, p. 4), ICT, as Darder (2018, p. x) insightfully argues, demands teachers as intellectuals "epistemologically fierce and deeply anchored in the sensibilities of our subalternity—the only place from which we can truly rid ourselves of the heavy yoke of Western sanctioned tyranny, which has wrought bitter histories of impoverishment, colonization, enslavement, and genocide." Such complex grammar is, "a clarion call against epistemological fascism perpetrated by the field of curriculum studies, controlled both in its form and content by belligerent battles between and within traditional and non-traditional epistemological forms within the Western Modern

Eurocentric platform." Paraskeva's (2011, 2016a) "concerns are justifiable, and irreversibly push the debate into a different terrain, a terrain in which Western Modern Eurocentric dominant and counter dominant rationales have lost their hegemonic totalitarian position" (Süssekind, 2017, p. 1). In fact, ICT challenge both "hegemonic and counter-hegemonic curriculum theory and work are historically ingrained in epistemicides" (Oliveira, 2017, p. 6). That is, Oliveira (2017, p. 6) adds. "through a lethal cult of the uniqueness and infallibility of a positivist scientificity promulgated by functionalistic, hegemonic pedagogical movements, as well as the incapability of specific counterhegemonic traditions to wipe out hegemonic perspectives and avoid falling into a sort of functionalist nightmare, curriculum has historically advanced epistemicide." This is not a minor issue and it might help progressive critical teachers addressing some challenges faced by critical pedagogies, as it has been raised by scholars such as Ellsworth (1989). It is such itinerant commitment that allows, ICtheorists, Zaho (2019, p. 175) argues, "to break the boundary between East and West, North and South," and in doing so for example, propose a historical archeological mode of inquiry as a paradigm to unpack other forms of Chinese knowledge in its historicity.

Notes

1 "This is the worst violation of the human right to water I have ever seen outside of the worst slums in the poorest countries in failed states of the global South," said Barlow, a one-time senior advisor on water to a former President of the U.N. General Assembly. Last March, the Detroit Water and Sewerage Department (DWSD) announced plans to shut off water service for 1,500 to 3,000 customers every week if their water bills were not paid. And on June 17, the City Council approved an 8.7-percent water rate increase. According to a DWSD document, more than 80,000 residential households—in a city of 680,000 people—are in arrears, with thousands of families without water, and thousands more expected to lose access at any moment" (Deen, 2014).

2 Note here that more white, working class youth are on stimulant treatment for ADHD, but the number of white, working class youth on medication is disproportionate to the number of middle and upper class.

CHAPTER 6

Colonialities and Spiritualities: Voices, Silences, and Experiences in the Classroom

> The prime function of education on the elementary level, and to a large extent on the secondary level, is to place the child in possession of his spiritual heritage,—the heritage of skill, knowledge, standard, and ideal which represents the gains that the race has made.
>
> BAGLEY (1921, p. 292)

Eurocentrism continues and has a legacy that feeds, starves, and neglects every aspect of our society. It is important to flag at this point that much of colonial and critical studies dichotomizes the world into Southern and Northern or Western and Eastern or simplifies the argument with terms, such as Eurocentric. Eurocentric, Northern, and Western must be deepened to be seen as a metonymic words for the cultural hegemony of the global elite. Drawing a geographic line blinds us from the Norths and Wests within the Souths and Easts as well as vice versa. The world is not a binary. Santos (2014) discusses an abyssal line and the need for postabyssal thinking. We need to see beyond a line into the liquid planes of modernity under neoliberalism.

The neoliberal power can still be qualified as Eurocentric but increasingly has less to do with the geography or race of "Europe" and more to do with the color of ideology and liquid capital. However, historically, the denotation of "Eurocentric" tends to occlude those who, although within the boundaries of "Europe" were also subject to oppression and produced outside of its power. Europe didn't just exploit foreigners but also youth, the working class, and women, without needing justification or causing alarm. One can look at the coal mines in which children were used because they were so small, women's persecution as witches or prostitutes, or the cotton factories in which men weren't making a living wage. These are not necessarily things of the past. Instead of being persecuted as witches, women are persecuted as bitches, and the criminalization of prostitution continues without looking at the society that created a space for this exploitation. Living wages are still being fought

 | DOI: 10.1163/9789004416048_006

for in the U.S. and in other countries. Look to how minimum waged McDonalds U.S. employees have a hotline to call, so they can get food stamps (Cohn, 2013). Children may not be used in mines, but their perceived innocence leaves them open to exploitation by drug cartels as mules (McIntyre, 2014) or couriers (Topping, 2014). Also, the marketing of unhealthy food and entertainment is just another form of exploitation; their bodies and minds consuming toxins for the profit of the elite. However, for now, let's turn to the roots of capitalist exploitation and expansion in colonialism—the shine of modernity.

Looking back to the 16th Century, "[a] new world, one that encompassed both metropolitan and colonial territories, appeared on the horizon of European imaginaries" (Moraña et al., 2008, p. 1). The division of colonial and metropolitan begins the structure of colonialism in which Europe imagined its likeness reproduced across the globe. An image of imitation as well as exploitation arises in which Europeans also painted themselves as the saviors to these barbarians. Here, we get at the heart of colonialism to which Césaire (2000) claimed is the "bridgehead in a campaign to civilize barbarism, from which there may emerge at any moment the negation of civilization, pure and simple" (p. 40). The power of the colonizer was in the ability to dehumanize individuals into Barbarians where at the same time legitimizing their humanity. Quijano (2000) in his extensive discussion of race and coloniality explains:

> The colonized peoples were inferior races and in that manner were the past vis-à-vis the Europeans. That perspective imagined modernity and rationality as exclusively European products and experiences. From this point of view, intersubjective and cultural relations between Western Europe and the rest of the world were codified in a strong play of new categories: East-West, primitive civilized, magic/mythic-scientific, irrational-rational, traditional-modern—Europe and not Europe. Even so, the only category with the honor of being recognized as the other of Europe and the West was 'Orient' .... This binary, dualist perspective on knowledge, particular to Eurocentrism, was imposed as globally hegemonic in the same course as the expansion of European colonial dominance over the world. (p. 542)

Forming within this colonization process is a single narrative that begins when Europe "found" the Americas, negating the civilizations and knowledges that existed before their "discovery." This historical monologue continues today in different currents as increasingly, knowledge production is about production and standardization, not creation or analysis. Giroux (2009) draws attention to how corporation are invading youth's culture and producing "new neoliberal subjects" (p. 50). This is done through advertisements, social media, video games, television, movies, music, etc. Knowledge and discourses are open to a transglobal, privatized assault. Globalization has created an agora in which discourses and knowledges are part of an open market for all to buy—*if* they have the capital and locality to do so. In a globalized world, the interconnections as well as breaks and silences among people remain imperative. Moraña, Dussel, and Jáuregui (2008) discuss colonial difference as "the differential timespace where a particular region becomes connect to the world-system of colonial domination" (p. 6). A differential timespace that is impacted significantly by class, race, and gender relations for market. In *Globalization and the Decolonial Option*, Mignolo (2010) demonstrates how "modernity is presented as the rhetoric of salvation, it hides coloniality, which is the logic of oppression and exploitation. Modernity, capitalism and coloniality are aspects of the same package of control of economy and authority, of gender and sexuality of knowledge and subjectivity" (p. 9). However, important to remember is that in

> the beginning colonialism was a product of a systematic repression, not only of the specific beliefs, ideas, images, symbols or knowledge that were not useful to global colonial domination, while at the same time the colonizers were expropriating from the colonized their knowledge, specially in mining, agriculture, engineering, as well as their products and work. The repression fell, above all, over the modes of knowing, of producing knowledge, of signification, over the resources, patterns, and instruments of formalized objectivized expression, intellectual, or visual. It was followed by the imposition of the use of the rulers' own patterns of expression, ad of their beliefs and images with reference to the supernatural. These beliefs and images served not only to impede the cultural production of the dominated, but also as a very efficient means of social and cultural control, when the immediate repression ceased to be constant and systematic. (Quijano, 2010, p. 23)

The production of knowledge is a process of legitimation of truths and the designation of "official knowledge" (Apple, 1993), which involves the colonization of the mind as well as subjugation of the spiritual under the seduction of inalterable truth and future certainty. Furthermore, Quijano (2010) writes, "[t]he colonizer also imposed a mystified image of their patterns of producing knowledge and meaning. At first, they placed these patterns far out of reach of the dominated. Later, they taught them in a partial and selective way in order to co-opt some of the dominated into their own power institutions. Then, European culture was made seductive: it gave access to power. After all, beyond repression, the main instrument of all power is its seduction" (p. 23).

It is this seduction of neoliberalism that is nefarious through society, especially considering that way we are bombarded with images and sound bites that are engaging constantly in a dialogue or put us before a telescreen in which we hear and are heard, being mentally shaped and altered whether conscious or not. Santos (2014) flags the imagocentric culture:

> On the internet (most dramatically Facebook), identities are doubly imagined, as flights of imagination and as sheer images. People are free to create roots at their pleasure and then reproduce their options ad infinitum. Thus, the same image can be seen as a root without options or as an option without roots. Hence, it no longer makes sense to think in terms of the root/option equation. Actually, we come to realize that the equation only makes sense in a conceptual, logocentric culture that speculates on social and territorial matrixes (space and time), subjecting them to criteria of authenticity. As we move on to an imagocentric culture, space and time are replaced by instances of velocity, matrixes are replaced by mediatrixes, and at this level the authenticity discourse becomes an incomprehensible gibberish. There is no depth but the successions of screens. (p. 86)

This is a process of the colonialities of being through education that needs to be considered in relation to Tillich's (1952) discussion of being and nonbeing as well as to Fullilove's (2002) root shock, which, "at the level of individual, is a profound emotional upheaval that destroys the working model of the world that had existed in the individual's head." Fullilove (2002) explains that "[w]hen the mazeway ['a way to run the maze of life'], the external system of protection, is damaged, the person will go into root shock .... Imagine the victim of an earthquake, a hurricane, a flood, or a terrorist attack. He suffers from root shock as he looks at the twisted remains of known universe." The discussion of roots in liquid modernity has much to do with digital roots that stem from the individual's heart, his or her mobile phone. Pieces of metal, glass, and mineral have become essential to the identities in which extreme anxiety and anger is caused by its removal. It is not an unusual occurrence for a student to engage in violence when a cell phone is taken away.

Not too long ago, I was sitting on the floor of a counselor's office with one of my students crying because her cell phone had been confiscated, and it was "her life." The older guidance counselor and myself looked at each other in a knowing recognition of what could comically be called cell phone withdrawal, but the pain and tears in her eyes stemmed from true anxiety, fear, and abandonment. Yes, abandonment. That phone is her gateway to her other selves.

Her body does not house who she is. In this light, consider how Facebook creates a space for insidious forms of construction of selves that negate authentic social interaction; body and mind are not needed, just pixels. This has been a societal transformation stemming from the late 90s with Giga pets and Nanos as well as games, like SIMS.

As a child, I had to leave my baby Nano with my mother while I went to camp, and my cousins had to come over to help save "my child." The hours spent and pride built while today's youth play Minecraft, which, when they come into the classroom bleary eyed, I teasingly refer to as *Mind*craft. Their physical wellbeing is slave to their virtual self. This is coloniality of being .... There is not only a colonization of body and mind but also of our virtual selves at the denial of our spiritual selves. Walker (2011) notes that "[t]he ethics of opacity helps to structure our ability 'to effect the deconstruction of the mechanisms by means of which we continue to make opaque to ourselves, attributing the origin of our societies to imaginary beings, whether the ancestors, the gods, God, or evolution, and natural selection, the reality of our own agency with respect to the programming and reprogramming of our desires, our behaviors, our minds, ourselves, the I and the we'" (p. 110). We must decolonize our beings and our thoughts while being cognizant of the way in which many elements are opaque to us as a part of a matrix of power, the regime of truth (Foucault, 1980). Castro-Gómez (2008) adds to this that "[t]his matrix of power did not only entail militarily subjugating the indigenous peoples and dominating them by force (colonialism); it also attempted to radically change their traditional knowledge of the world, to adopt the cognitive horizon of the dominator as their own (coloniality)" (p. 281). As a U.S. educator, I would ask that we challenge the isolation of colonialism as something that is exported with coloniality as an exotic notion. The neoliberal reign through Common Core is increasingly one of subjugation and criminalization that we must reconceptualize not as a patriotic effort for the good of the people but jingoism of the elite that cannibalizes knowledge in order to silence, occlude, and miseducate, which is done through seductive language that constantly reframes knowledge and spins individuals into a dizzying frenzy of guilty ignorance or miseducation.

This is part of the colonial process, colonialities of knowledge. Maldonado-Torres (2007) claims, "while the coloniality of power referred to the interrelation among modern forms of exploitation and domination (power), and the coloniality of knowledge had to do with impact of colonization on the different areas of knowledge production, coloniality of being would make primary reference to the lived experience of colonization and its impact on language" (p. 242). Language must, as noted previously, be seen beyond the technicalization of words and as a form of expression that is intimately connected with spirituality, knowledges, and beings that are oppressed. The rationality of *science* denounces its spiritual core in the name of the reproducible, foisting technoscientific knowledge down the throats of youth and teachers in the name of STEM and "best practice." However, "[t]he 'many forms of knowledge' are situated in this way in a conception of history that delegitimizes its spatial coexistence and organizes them according to a teleological scheme of temporal progression. The diverse forms of knowledge developed by humanity throughout the course of history would lead gradually toward the only legitimate way of knowing the world: the way that is elaborated by the technoscientific rational of modern Europe" (Castro-Gómez, 2008, p. 267). Science is perceived as irrefutable despite the fact that it is the human voice and eye which announce its inalterable truth. Césaire remarked that there is "no human contact, but relations of domination and submission which turn the colonizing man into a class-room monitor, an army sergeant, a prison guard, a slave driver, and the indigenous man into an instrument of production" (p. 42). This dehumanization and disembodiment can be seen with U.S. educators and must be challenged. It fragments knowledge and limits people's views, constructing rationality under sciencism. Haraway (1988) explains that "[s]truggles over what will count as rational accounts of the world are struggles over *how* to see. The terms of vision: the science question in colonialism, the science question in exterminism, the science question in feminism" (p. 587). As McClintock (1995) claims:

> Since the 1940s, the U.S.'s imperialism-without-colonies has taken a number of distinct forms (military, political, economic and cultural), some concealed, some half-concealed. The power of U.S. finance capital and huge multinational corporations to command the flows of capital, research, consumer goods and media information around the world can exert a coercive power as great as any colonial gunboat. It is precisely the greater subtlety, innovation and variety of these forms of imperialism that make the historical rupture implied by the term postcolonial especially unwarranted. (p. 13)

Schools bow to the religious zealousness toward STEM, which not only allows for epistemicides (Santos, 2007b, 2014; Paraskeva, 2011, 2016a, 2016b, 2017) but also limits science to the boundaries of the standards and test. From the pre-K curriculum that is engineered by the Common Core to its push for informational texts in English Language Arts, educational reform under RTTT points to the *imaginicide* that is occurring within schools, where imagination and the humanities are not just devalued but systematically killed. Giroux (2001) claims "formalistic qualities characteristic of these [dominant class's] practices are often informed by an ideology that strips them of the possibility for *conceptual literacy*; that is formalistic skills mastery (reading, writing, & speaking, etc.) exist without the benefit of sustained theoretical insight" (p. 230). Technical literacy is purported, but at the cost of what? Where are spiritualities? How can the mastery of multiple choice provide space for deeper conceptual literacy? Rising literacy rates can be a misnomer, because "language and literacy practices of the dominant class may provide the basis for functional literacy within the context of advanced industrial capitalism, but they are often simultaneously informed by modes of thoughts that represent a form of political illiteracy" (Giroux, 2001, p. 230). To contextualize this within today's testing regime, teaching kids how to "master" MCAS, PARCC, SAT, AP, etc. is a form of technical/functional literacy, which uses the language of dominant class but only functionally, not meaningfully. Youth can plug in, but they aren't allowed to create. Language and literacy becomes formulaic, a tool of STEM. This enables youth to succeed within the academic sphere but how does it silence other discourses, modes of thinking? Is this not a form of political illiteracy? This process inculcates colonialities of being. Césaire (2000) poignantly states:

> My turn to state an equation: colonization = "thingification"
>
> I hear the storm. They talk to me about progress, about "achievements," diseases cured, improved standards of living.
>
> I am talking about societies drained of their essence, cultures trampled underfoot, institutions undermined, lands confiscated, religions smashed, magnificent artistic creations destroyed, extraordinary possibilities wiped out.
>
> They throw facts at my head, statistics, mileages of roads, canals, and railroad tracks. (p. 43)

The facts, data walls, data charts, DDMS, AYP, PPI, charts—they are all part of this thingification, this colonization. In education, teachers and youth live under "a dictatorship of no alternatives" (Unger, 2005, p. 1). Yet, fear holds us back and for many teachers and youth, hegemony shapes the rising curve of data as a glimmer of hope that these reforms are pushing us toward progress. Darder (1991) explains how

> [a]t the heart of hegemonic control is political power—a power derived from control of the social structures and natural configurations that

> embody routines and practices inherent in the different social relationships resulting from both content and the manner in which knowledge is structured in society. It represents a power that is maintained through selective silence and is manifested in the fragmentation of social definitions, managements of information, and the subsequent shaping of popular attention, consent, belief, and truth (Forester, 1985). (p. 34)

Understanding hegemony helps us unravel how these colonial systems of power and education function. Education is always political. The silences of teachers and parents that do not protest the political oppression reflect both fear and consent. This is not just a localized struggle but globalized in which we must struggle against the neoliberal reign and privatization of public education.

The research is analyzed through critical theory and decolonial pedagogy and coupled with the theories of transformative educational leadership. Shields (2013) describes Freire's "conscientization" (conscientização), connecting it to transformative leadership's purpose "to critique underlying social, cultural, and economic norms, but also to offer promise—to find ways to equalize opportunities and to ensure high quality education and civil participation for all" (p. 19). In my writing, I extend the concepts of transformative leadership to students and educators through schools' rituals and curriculum, while still situating it within the analytical framework of a decolonial theory, which pulls from critical, feminist, anti-colonial, post-colonial theories, in order to reveal the spaces and silences within narratives, analyzing the objectivity and acknowledging any bias or unseen choices in memories.

Situating myself within ideological framework of decolonial theory, Freire's conscientização and Nkrumah's consciencism help me to analyze and delve beyond the positivist and functionalist paradigm that permeates schools. This means maintaining a double consciousness as a teacher of a high-stakes test subject, which traditionally functions to limit the emancipatory power of knowledge and critique within schools in transforming and understanding the world. This reveals the importance of applying Althusser's (1984) concept of the school as dominant ideological state apparatus and not a space of neutrality. Accordingly, this deepens the analysis of how truth is constructed and can disempower the identities of students, creating a "regime of truth" (Foucault, 1980). Giroux (2001) discusses the way critical theory politicizes knowledge, meaning to examine "knowledge critically, within constellations of suppressed insights (dialectical images) that point to the ways in which historically repressed cultures and struggles could be used to illuminate radical potentialities in the present" (p. 36). Through the process of writing and analyzing the narrative, I will recognize and unravel the spaces that have enabled my students, my colleagues, and myself to resist but also to produce our own meanings and knowledges in opposition to hegemony. McLaren (2001) makes an important distinction between teaching and pedagogy, explaining that:

> *Teaching* is a process of organizing and integrating knowledge for the purpose of communicating this knowledge or awareness to students through an exchange of understanding in prespecified contexts and teacher/learner environments. *Pedagogy* is distinct from teaching in that it situates the teacher/learner encounter in a wider context of historical and sociopolitical forces, in which the act of knowing recognizes and takes into account the differentiated politics of reception surrounding the object of knowledge by the students. (McLaren, 2001, pp. 121–122)

Achievements and statistics are only markers of a deeper system of coloniality that permeates the U.S. education system. I don't mean schools alone. Schools are an ideological state apparatus as Althusser (1984) noted, but let's not forget the media, which may have no box to confine individuals in like a school; it is much more *sophisticated, modernized.* The box is constructed of sound waves and pixels in which an individual creates their own box without even knowing it. As Macedo et al. (2003) wrote:

> We see our present with as little understanding as we view our past because aspects of the past which could illumine the present have been concealed from us. This concealment has been effected by a systemic process of mis-education characterized by a thoroughgoing inculcation of colonial values and attitudes—a process which could not have been so effective had we not been denied access to the truth and to part of our written history. As a consequence, we have become a people without a sense of history. We accept the present as given bereft of historicity. Because we have so little comprehension of our past, we have no appreciation of its meaningful interrelation with present. (p. 69)

Coloniality in the U.S. is not necessarily the physical force and takeover that we saw with colonialism. Coloniality is intricate. It runs on multiple planes; it can be seen in the subtle hegemonic way that it forms identities for the proletariat or precariat (Bauman & Donskis, 2012), and it can be seen in the brutal force that rules the prisons that have become commercial colonies as well as the social inequality that criminalizes the poor (cf. Wacquant, 2009), while making profits off the suppression and dehumanization of these humans as 'capital'—captives of capitalism and neoliberalism. It can be seen in the violent language of schools, which marks some as inferior and some as superior, while never even acknowledging others—the mark of invisibility. Although colonialism and imperialism are different from coloniality and coloniality is the underside to modernity, we must still examine their existence. Considering the age of liquid modernity (Bauman, 2013) and the way nations have become transnational, neoliberalism seems to be a nation that has colonial power.

CHAPTER 7

Decolonial Manifesto for Public Education

> I do not believe educators can survive the negativities of their trade without some sort of 'armed love' … without it they could not survived all the injustices or the government's contempt.
>
> FREIRE (2005, p. 74)

∵

As usual I was racing against the clock, I got to school minutes before the bell rang and jumped from my car when my cell phone vibrated …. My mother texted: "Nick needs to talk to you."

I quickly dialed the phone and held it to my ear as I cut through the parking lot.

"Nick?" I asked. Silence. "Nick?" I didn't have time for games. The weight of my school bags making it harder to race toward to the school door.

"Auntie …."

"What's up, babe? Nana said you needed to talk to me." I shifted my bag on my shoulder, squeezing my phone against my other shoulder. Balance.

"Yeah … um …. I saw the Spiderman cup, and it comes with *these* pencils, and since I was REALLY a good boy for two days in a row at school, may I *please* have the cup, AND the pencils." His words rushed out in a calculated manner.

I chuckled, thinking of how he had said he didn't care about the Spiderman cup the previous night, i.e. "That's boring [not a good present]." A child's mind can be fickle. "Yes, since you have been a good boy, but it has to be okay with Nana too."

"I can *have* them?" His voice rising on the "have," and then he rushed to add, "AND, the pencils?"

I laughed. "*And*, the pencils."

"Okay!"

I yanked open the school door, trying to think of where my keys were. "Umm …. What about … thank you, Auntie?"

He jovially sighed in only the way that a child can. "UHHHH, I always forget the thank you. I always forget that! Thank you!"

"You're welcome. Love you."

 | DOI: 10.1163/9789004416048_007

"Love you too!"

I laughed, hearing him eagerly explain the deal to my mother, and I ended the call as I raced up the stairs practically two at a time … 60 seconds to bell.

I don't start this chapter to demonstrate just the chaos of beings that teachers are entrenched in but to demonstrate my own contradictory state. Previously, I explored the colonizing of minds and oppression of spiritualities through biopolitics, which I conceptualized as the Pinocchio effect. Much of my discourse with Nick reveals this inculcation of a "good boy." When I discuss the Pinocchio effect and decolonial thinking, I do not mean to imply that we should have a world of "bad" or "good boys." I'm rather asking that we engage in an analysis of how "good boys" are made and how "bad boys" are made, as well as what the consequences are. Similarly, we could put "girl" into that question or youth to be gender fluid. Who gets to decide what is "good" and what is "bad"? In the moral development of youth, how do seductions and punishments impact how they view themselves and others?

That day, I had intended to do a Socratic seminar to discuss the schoolwide summer reading, *Zeitoun*. But, a former student had emailed me the day before about Ahmed:

> Welp, here it is, J. I don't know if you've heard about this yet but it's the culmination of a lot of different topics we often debated about in class. You've got racial profiling, police abusing authority, major problems with the system of supposed "justice," you name it. This was a 14 year old kid who built his own clock with a small pencil case and some wires and circuit boards. But, because he was of Arabic descent, he was arrested when he brought it to school. He was accused of bringing in a bomb. The police were called, we [sic: he] was questioned, and sent straight to a juvenile detention center ALL WITHOUT A LAWYER PRESENT OR EVEN BEING ABLE TO CALL HIS PARENTS.
>
> Anyway, this made me livid. If you've already read it and dissected it with your classes already I'm sorry. You're the first person I thought of after reading the article. Here's the link to the article and a YouTube video of the boy describing what happened. I know Mia's gonna love having you just as much as I did (if she doesn't already). Have a great year!
>
> Jax:)
> http://www.dallasnews.com/news/community-news/northwest-dallas-county/headlines/20150915-irving-9th-grader-arrested-after-taking-homemade-clock-to-school.ece

> https://www.youtube.com/watch?v=3mW4w0Y1OXE
>
> P.S. I saw this picture when I went back to get the URL. It's him getting arrested. His face seems to say "I told you, idiots, it's a freaking clock!" https://i.imgur.com/PMgDR7m.jpg

Imprisoned in the chaos of school, I had not heard about Ahmed. I read Jax's email as I waited to pick up Nick from 1st grade, oblivious to the spinning of the world that day. But, I was hit with report after report when I got home. As I walked into my school and thought about that email and I thought about Nick, I changed my mind about the lesson. Socratic seminar scrapped.

A student was already waiting outside my door to vent to me. I opened the door and listened as I grabbed a table and practically threw it into the center of the room. I searched in my desk for an elastic—I needed to make a bomb. Curiously, they don't teach you how to do that in teacher-ed.

I had nothing that looked like a clock bomb, so I grabbed the LA plastic water paperweight on my desk and taped a flower bookmark to it. I pulled the gavel out, grabbed some books. Then, it was show time as the bell rang.

We quickly reviewed the plot points of the book.

"I told you guys to review pages 205 to 245. What happens in those pages to Zeitoun?"

"Zeitoun was taken by the police."

"What happened to him after that?" I asked.

An orchestra of responses followed. "They put him in that prison that was a bus station." "They didn't give him medical aid." "They thought he was a terrorist!"

"Yes, yes. So, what were his rights?"

"They should have read him rights when he was arrested!"

"What are those called?" I asked.

They looked about unsure.

"Your Mir—" I began, hoping someone would finish, "—anda rights. What else did they do?"

"They didn't give him a phone call." "They didn't give him a trial." "They didn't tell him what he was charged with."

"Those are all violations of his civil rights." I fielded their continued responses. Then said, "What else? Did they violate the eighth amendment?"

Blank stares.

"Do you know what the eighth amendment is?" I paused, waiting for someone to speak, but there was nothing. "Cruel and unusual punishment."

"They used pepper spray on them and bean bag guns."

"He should have been given medical aid."

I nodded. "Yes, they did. Is that cruel and unusual punishment? What happened to the man who kept saying, 'Kiss your mother goodnight'; 'Don't do pee-pee in the bed'?"

One girl raised her hand, "Oh, isn't that the man who was mentally retarded?"

"Yes and why did they pepper spray him?"

"For touching the fence."

"Is it excessive force?" My voice seemed to keep crescendoing with each question I asked.

They nodded, waking up.

"So, I was going to talk to you about the prison-industrial complex and have you do a Socratic seminar on that, but then Wednesday happened." Befuddled looks. "What happened Wednesday?" Looks of uncertain knowledge. Fear to speak without confirmation. "Do you know who Ahmed Mohamed is?"

A couple hands shot up.

I chose a boy in the semicircle. "He was arrested for making a clock and showing it to his teacher, right?"

"I heard the clock looked a lot like a bomb."

"So, you don't call his parents? You don't confirm with a bomb squad what it is?" I asked. The look that you give when you see or hear something alien. It was a look that I was used to. "Yes. That's correct. They thought the clock was a bomb. He's a freshmen in high school. Does it seem like a normal reaction to detain somebody for making a clock?"

"No."

A girl who had been listening, perplexed by the ordeal, said, "I heard that they didn't evacuate the school. So, if they really thought it was a bomb, why didn't they evacuate?"

"That is a great question," I said.

"Then, they must have known it wasn't real."

"So, why did they do it?" I asked.

"Because he was Muslim."

"Perhaps. Who else is that similar to? Who else had their civil rights violated because of what they looked like?"

"Zeitoun."

"So, we're going to do a little acting. You guys are going to recreate what happened to Ahmed. I need four people: principal, teacher, student, and cop." A couple hands shot up, but others remained uncertain. I assigned roles quickly. "So, this is our clock bomb." They all laughed at the makeshift clock that would require every ounce of imagination as it looked more like a flower pot. "Hey, hey! Don't judge! I didn't have much time. Besides, this is exactly what a clock bomb would like. Dolphins and all," I teased as the water in the paperweight shifted, sending the dolphins flying. They weakly muffled their laughter. I handed the cop the elastic, i.e. the handcuffs. Interesting was how eager they were for the gavel. I had grabbed it, thinking maybe we would go to the courthouse. Each class fought over that gavel. That gavel emblematic of power.

They acted out the scene the way that it had been reported. Then, I asked them to act it out the way that they thought it should have gone. My principal walked in as we were acting it out. He snapped a photo for Twitter, and we were hash-tagged. We continued on. I reversed it the next few times. I gave them the scenario, "5- or 6-year-old has a temper tantrum in class." We had the same roles: teacher, principal, and cop. "How should this happen?" The teacher tried to calm the youth down.

The youth had arms folded across her chest.

"No, really act up. Be as bad as you could!" I grabbed a pile of books and put them on the desk. "Knock them over, throw the desk!" I exclaimed. The look of horror. "Be a bad five-year-old!"

"UrhhHHH! I'm not going with you," was the scream as the books went flying and then the desk, but she caught it slightly on the way down. These were my "good" well-trained level 1s, so breaking code was hard—at least for some of them. The teacher tried to calm the youth down. The principal was called. They restrained.

"Should we call the cops?" I asked.

"Yeah!" some cheered. The spectator culture was infused within the classroom even in the roleplaying of crime. Violence is seen as sport without pausing for the injustice.

"Okay. Let's try it again with the cops."

The desk got thrown with little resistance this time, but even I cringed as it fell. The cuffs went on, and the child was taken out.

"Is that excessive force? Is it necessary to cuff a five-year-old?"

"No!" was the chorus.

"But, it happened." I paused. Looks of disbelief spread across some faces. "It's happened more than once." I showed them the picture of the five-year-old in Georgia, and the seven-year-old[1] from the year before in New York.

Looks and words of "Really?"

I looked at them. "We had two," I gestured to the room to my side "beating the *S*ugar *H*oney *I*ced *T*ea out of each other last year, and I didn't use handcuffs. I didn't even have to touch them. My freshmen will remember, no?"

They remembered the day. The day when the shirtless boy came through the back doors from Colleen's classroom into mine. I detained him long enough before he stormed out, and my male colleague took over, ushering him downstairs to the office. That youth has since dropped out. Pinocchio effect.

"Let's try another one." This time we did Tamir Rice's story. "9-1-1 dispatcher gets a call. There's a boy with some kind of gun in the park. You're not sure, but you think it's a toy gun. Cops are dispatched to investigate. I need two cops and a boy. A 9-1-1 operator." Volunteers acquired, I sat on a desk. "Show me how this should go. Oh and you're," referring to the cops, "in your car." To our Tamir actor, I said, "Boy, you're circling the table with your 'gun.'" Then, I watched them role play.

The traditional, "Put your hands in the air. Drop the weapon!"

"Okay let's do this the way it happened. Cops come with me." I took the two boys into the hallway. "Okay this time—Who is the driver?" Joe raised his hand. "Good. And you're going to get out of the car before he even stops and shoot him. Got it?" Nick nodded with a look of astonishment. "OH! And, once he's down, don't check to see if he's okay, alright?" I came back inside with a side-glance at their bewildered expressions. "Okay, start circling."

Then, the door flew open with the cops speeding in, and then the cop shot the boy. He dropped to the ground. The rest of class looked at me shocked. Was this truth? The boys stood to the side, talking as the other boy was on the ground. "How about them Patriots?"

"EMT, check him out," I directed the next actor.

The EMT came. "He's dead."

There was silence. I nodded, hopping off the desk. "And that's what happened. His name was Tamir Rice. He was 12 years old, and it was an airsoft gun. Was that violence justified?"

"No."

"Why would they have acted like that?"

"But, they didn't know it wasn't a real gun!"

"Good point, so what if it was? Do we just shoot or do we try to get them to drop it?"

"They saw a black boy with a gun."

I looked at the girl who had spoken, and I smiled. "I never said he was black."

"But," she looked at me embarrassed. The others looked. Ahhh, when the veneer of political correctness cracks.

"It's okay." Her presumption was now turning the light on her. I tried to allay her shame. "You are absolutely right! He was black. How did you know?"

"I just—" I could see the panic.

"Because if it had been a little white girl with blond hair and blue eyes, would they have shot her?"

Some spoke, others sat quietly, other shook their heads. We knew the answer in silence and noise. I want to pause here though to stop and reflect. At this time, I hadn't decolonized my analysis of police. As I had students later research police brutality and began talking with some of my cop friends who were trying to unknowingly engage in what could be called *conscientização* to also understand the levels of police brutality in the media, I realized that teachers and cops are the servants of the empire. Each are trapped within public service or perhaps servitude. Police training is based on paramilitary instruction and little time is spent on how to deal with the socioemotional needs of citizens. I had a student discuss a report from the police chiefs that stated there was a lack of de-escalation strategies taught to new recruits. This coupled with Salt Lake City who gave their police officers increased training in de-escalation strategies and have interestingly not had a fatal shooting in two years.[2] We are in a way villainizing police officers for being colonized and chained to a system that they were miseducated into without recognizing their own power to be a force without using force. The colonization of the mind is not isolated to the public-school system. Miseducation contributes a great deal to the violence in U.S. society. We need to decolonize the system of power that public servants are enveloped within as well as stop creating scapegoats in humans which in fact dehumanizes them. The police officer that shot Tamir Rice was in fact a human who acted in a way that was not humane, but to villainize him is to dehumanize him, which is not emancipatory nor part of the decolonial process. With this said, we must recognize that there is a violent system of power that is based on racialized injustices that continue to blind us from seeing inequalities in many cases as could be seen from my student automatically perceiving without me saying it that Tamir was black.

Then, I showed a slide with a forum flyer and a Facebook user's response. This was a forum that youth at a local vocational school were having my administrators to discuss issues of race, gender, sexuality, and gender identity at the school. To quote the flyer,

> In light of the racial injustice occurring within GNBVT, a group of concerned students have organized a public forum. At this public forum, Mrs. Enos, Mrs. Franco, and Mr. Williams will listen to the concerns of some GNBVT students regarding the dehumanization, the harassment, and the racial profiling of students of color, females, and other protected classes within the building.[3]

I read to them the Facebook posting, "Imagine being at a school and your teacher writes this on their Facebook: 'That's what I'm saying Joe. You can't reason with thugs. Joe my 45 is loaded and ready to go. A thug walks up my driveway one bullet would be going on his direction."

"That's messed up!"

"When you hear thug, what do you think of?" I asked.

"A gangster."

"Someone who's black."

"Or brown or lower class, right?" I questioned. "Jeans hanging, oversized hoodie." They nodded. "Now imagine being a student who looks like that and your teacher says this. Would you feel safe?" I paused. "Knowing that as you walked into his classroom that if you walked up to his house, that *his 45* would be ready?"

They looked at me. "Was he fired?"

"No," I said. Eyes widened. "This was one incident. I don't know all the others yet, but I will hear this afternoon. These students united together, so that they could be heard. We acted out all these scenes today. You saw them. They are real. You all have the ability to speak up and make changes."

Crickets, crickets. Jiminy Cricket, were you sitting on their shoulders as they looked at me? They wanted that gavel of justice but failed to see how they have that gavel invisiblized in their hands too often. This was just the beginning of the journey for us this year.

I repeated this exercise throughout the day. The period before lunch. We were in the midst of acting out the 5-year-old having a temper tantrum when I saw the door open. I feared administration. Had the desk fallen one too many times? I too was a good girl, colonized. I knew the etiquette of school. I was after all a servant in my classroom; this was not my home.

My breath caught. It was a history teacher. I continued talking but felt my cheeks flush, and my nerves were on edge so much so that I remember very little of what I said. I was dialectically debriefing with them. In abbreviated form: "Were the principal and teacher justified? Should that 5-year-old have been treated as a criminal for having a temper tantrum? Can a school arrest you for doing this?"

"No, they can't!" exclaimed the boys.

"OhHHhh, but they can. Your Bill of Rights is pretty much non-existent in school. So, you can be treated like a criminal. A student got arrested for punching a locker."

The history teacher had been leaning against the wall. His arms folded across his chest. He stood up though. "She's right. There was a student arrested for writing on a desk."

I gulped as he talked to the kids about the different ways that youth were targeted.

"That's messed up," said Dane.

"Please continue," said the teacher.

"Okay, next scene!" I exclaimed. He slowly walked out. Later, he told me that he had heard the desk fall and wanted to check on me, but that he thought it was great. "They'll never forget it. They should know their rights [or lack thereof]," he told me.

At the root of decolonial thinking and research is dialogue. Colonialism enforces a monologue of being, of thinking, of knowing, silencing the plurality of knowledges and voices. The oppressor oppresses without realizing that he/she is also oppressed. Education is at the heart of colonialism and its curriculum, coloniality. Today, U.S. public education epitomizes coloniality and the ongoing colonialism. Youth and educators are under a neoliberal emperor that dictates the curriculum and pedagogy. Common Core, NCLB, RTTT and all their mercenaries surround us. The religion of capitalist ethics and standardization under the crusade of globalization is intoxicating, but we must decolonize our minds and beings from this *ethics of war* (Maldonado-Torres, 2007). There is a neoliberal violence going on in our schools and communities. Let us not forget that race and gender are deeply entrenched in a class war and exploited as part of the economic market. Neoliberalism is racialized, and it's gendered. It feeds off the subjugation of individuals that are classified as inferior through the colonialities of being. We must fight against the public pedagogy of neoliberalism with a revolutionary public pedagogy that speaks with the public and not to them. Dialogue in the classroom aids in the process of decolonization:

> In the process of teaching, dialogue is considered the self-generating praxis that emerges from the relational interaction between reflection, naming of the world, action, and the turn to reflection once more. It is a continuous, purposefully motivated, and open exchange that provides participants the space in which, together, to reflect, critique, affirm, challenge, act, and ultimately transform our collective understanding of the world. (Darder, 2002, p. 82)

Dialogue needs to be seen as more than just words. It's the body's language as well as the silence. Decolonial autoethnography creates a research space through writing to explore and understand, within U.S. public education, how the effects of colonialities of being (Mignolo, 2002) and the construction and oppression of students' and teachers' identities can be understood through the experiences that influence teachers' and students' spiritualties.

Throughout this autoethnography, I have tried to give examples of the enunciations, disruptions, violences, etc. The curriculum that students are fed is a coloniality that is a harvest of colonization. When students try to resist, they are oppressed. A group of girls, after wondering why there was a Mr. Clayton but not a Miss Clayton, approached me with their idea, but they didn't want to do a beauty pageant. They thought that it would just breed negativity as girls attacked each other.

"It would just feed into the whole culture of girls being objects …." I agreed, thinking. "So why not do a parody of beauty pageants. Do a spoof?"

"Miss J, that's awesome!" exclaimed Leandra.

"We could do like minute-to-win-it instead of a talent section," said Claire.

"Yes! And like a group dance."

"The boys from the Mr. Clayton could get on stage, and then we could mimic their talents, like lifting weights!"

I nodded. "For the Q&A, you could." I was having a hard time articulating it. "Let me find the video." I pulled up "48 Things Girls Hear in a Lifetime that Boys Don't." "You could each take one of these and then come up a comedy routine. Like Claire could be asked, 'So Claire, you're a pretty good athlete, I mean you're not bad for a girl,' and then she could challenge the judge to jumping jacks or push-ups."

"Not push-ups, I'd lose!" she laughed.

"I want the exotic one," said Leandra. She was referring to the girl who talked about how she had been told, "You're so exotic." Leandra shook her head. "I don't like that. I've gotten that before."

"You could say like the 'E-word,'" I said, leaning back in my chair.

She laughed, and waved her finger in front of her face, "Before I answer that, let me just say that the *E-word* is just so …."

All three of us laughed together.

"I like it," said Claire.

"I like it too. Let's do it. I'll share this doc with you girls. When it's time to announce the results, you could do a flash mob instead."

"I could take the envelope and rip it up!" Leandra smiled. "This'll be good."

With that we were off, outlining everything, and they enlisted girls from AP courses to auto. The goal was to make sure everyone was included and that the awards would not be based on beauty, but rather feature girls who embodied athleticism, wit, exuberance, and kindness. The narrative was sent, but it was not approved because it needed to have been planned before the school year. I was angry because other events had not been planned from the start. Amalia tried to calm me and present both sides. I was not having it.

"It was the bra straps last year, the crop tops the year before!" I exclaimed. It was the little things that girls got targeted for. Capstones that dealt with women's issues such as sexual abuse. It was the freshmen girls who didn't get new warm up athletic suits and bags, but the boys did. It's the fact that some male students in a privileged fatalism remark that gender inequity and sexualization is just human nature and racism is just there, and, by being just there, it is nonexistent.

Despite the fact that I teach in an almost completely white school, where some would claim race would not be an issue, I deal with issues of racism more often than not. I could teach in a cemetery of literature and make the themes and dialogues within the books abstracted from the reality of today. However, as we read *Raisin in the Sun*, how do I not bring up Flint, Michigan? I showed them the cartoon by Matt Wuerker entitled Segregation and Water, where there is one new water fountain that has clear water flowing with "white" above it and the other one has brown water flowing out of it and is older with "colored" above it. I had my students analyze it.

"Segregation," they called out.

"Dirty water."

"A fountain of root beer," someone joked.

"Racism."

"Okay, now look at the painting. Why is one bubbler a tower, is it a tower of white privilege? What's the other one?"

"It's like a bowl."

"It looks like a toilet bowl!" shouted someone.

I stood back and realized it did. There was a bubbling silence as we all looked at it for a moment. "What is the significance of Michigan 2016?"

Many had not heard of Flint, and we watched a small segment. We had to go over lead poisoning and why the matter couldn't just be fixed by changing the water source. They didn't know the word corrosion, even though as I explained that a battery was corrosive if broken; they understood the reality but not the language. How much of their world did they feel but could not explain because words failed them. Our conversation continued to segregation and the Youngers in *A Raisin in the Sun*. Hansberry's setting of "after WWII to present" verified through current events. The prior year I had met such firm resistance to anything that had to do with racism by a core group of boys, although there were likely girls who agreed with them, and there were definitely boys who disagreed but chose to remain silent. Yet, my failure last year was perhaps not a failure. Zac, one of my former boys who staunchly believes that racism is not an issue, came to visit me.

"Feeling better today, Miss J?" he asked.

I had been "flipping" at the end of yesterday. "Yes, I am. Thank you. I have just had it with patriarchy."

"Patriarchy? What is that?"

"It has to do with how we live in a society that is based off a male power network, but not male as in sex. A female can use that power. The construction of masculine as dominant and violent to oppress others."

"Here we go again," said Paul. "Women *have* power."

Some of my female students started to flip out. I grimaced. This was not how dialogue should occur. We needed patience, not uncontrolled passion.

"Just get out," they screamed.

"I'm trying to understand," said Zac, putting his hand to his chest as a gesture of sincerity.

"He is. Easy," I said to them. Earbuds went in to shut out the world. Some of the girls were still present.

"I just don't see the inequality. Hillary Clinton is probably going to be our next president."

"Remember, I told you patriarchy wasn't to do with sex, but gender. Hillary Clinton embodies a masculine epistemology. She will keep pulling the male party line." He stepped back and looked at me. "I'm not a feminist who promotes the advancement of women whether or not they are the best candidate. That's bad feminism."

"Now there are different sects!" exclaimed Paul.

"Of course. There are different sects of conservatives, no?"

He grumbled.

"But, she's a candidate. Women are equal today," said Zac.

"But, we're not. Women are objectified and sexualized." I explained to them how I had been touched, grabbed, verbally barraged with sexual comments, just at work as a teenager never mind beyond work, and my boss had laughed with the men, even encouraged it because it meant more business. My body for sale. My charm for sale. My gender for sale.

"I'm not saying that's right," said Zac. "But, that's just the way it is."

The girls began to lose it again. Paul chirped up, "There's always been two genders, and there's always will be. I'm not saying it's right what happened to you, but that's just how it is."

I smiled calmly about to speak when the girls started yelling again. They were trying to get Zac to leave.

"I want to understand," he said.

"He does. Leave him be. It's okay," I told them. "Fighting like that won't do anything."

"There has not always been two genders. There are cultures with three or four genders or with gender fluidity. The gender division is a capitalist mechanism. We needed the division of labor, and it still exists. Women do the majority of the unpaid labor in the U.S. still."

"You're talking about isolated cultures," said Paul.

"But it is possible to have another way. You can't say it's impossible for another way when they do exist. There are indigenous tribes in Canada that still exist only because they came from a matriarchal structure that valued acceptance instead of violence. They would have died due to genocide, but they accepted outsiders into their tribes. Whereas patriarchy thrives on violence and xenophobia."

Zac watched and listened.

"But again, they're pretty much nonexistent," said Paul. I scrunched my forehead in disapproval. "If they were really something, we would have heard of them. The indigenous are pretty much gone in Canada."

"I don't agree at all."

"Miss Janson, we haven't even heard of them. No one talks about the indigenous in Canada!" Paul exclaimed.

"You have spent two years on U.S. history. Even if you spent one year on Canada, I think you'd learn about them. You've spent two years on U.S. and guaranteed you don't even know that Dighton rock was discovered by who?"

"No, I don't know."

"A Portuguese explorer. And you're Portuguese!"

"The Portuguese discovered everything!"

"That's not true."

"It is true."

"Did you know that George Washington honored a Portuguese solider, Francisco?" He shook his head, knowledge that didn't matter. "You don't even know your own history! There are societies, places where there is a different way than exploitation." The thing was he did know *His* history; he had devoured it as had He.

"These are these communal societies. They're communist."

"No, no! Communal does not mean communist."

"Yes it does COMMUN-al, COMMUN-ist."

"So what is COMMUN-ion at Catholic mass, communist?" I exclaimed, not able to suppress a laugh.

"That's completely different."

"Exactly!" We ended up switching over to presidential candidates again, as he firmly believed despite the fact that Trump wasn't great that we need a strong conservative to balance out the "super" liberal Obama. Then, other boys joined in.

"I don't believe in corporate welfare."

"You give the money to the rich and it trickles down," said Paul.

"That never works!" exclaimed Ned.

Josh was standing on the end of one of my tables and was also shaking his head.

"Reagan," began Paul.

"Reaganomics was a disaster!" I exclaimed.

Paul disagreed and Josh agreed, and then they were off fighting again. They were debating welfare, drugs, prison, etc.

"We have a prison population that is bigger than the other first world countries combined!" I exclaimed. "Most of them are in there for drug related offenses."

"You can't have those people on the street though," said Paul.

"We waste so much money on locking people up. We should put it toward rehabilitating people."

"That doesn't work. You can't make people do what they don't want to."

"But, prison does? Portugal decriminalized and put the money into rehabilitation and saw a dramatic decrease."

The bell rang. "Dude, she has a point."

As she walked toward the door, Kara said, "You don't know about this stuff. Miss Janson does."

"No, she doesn't. She hasn't researched it," said Paul.

Kara and her group of girls stopped. "She's getting her *PhD*."

"Yeah, but that doesn't—" The word missing was "count" as he silenced himself.

I looked at him. "I have researched it. I'm getting a PhD in policy."

"I thought you were getting it in education."

"Yes, educational policy, which is social policy."

"No it's not."

"Of course it is. Education has everything to do with social policy. From poverty to drugs to national security. Education is in the National Defense Act!" He was shaking his head as he walked out the door.

Cassandra walked up to me. "I had to put my earbuds in. I just—"

"I know. When I was your age, I would probably have lost it too." It was partially a lie. I was quiet when I was her age. If someone had been attacked, I might have spoken. "But nothing will change if we argue. It has to be a dialogue."

While all this had been going on, I had a sophomore and senior working as well as looking up patriarchy and feminism shirts. They had been whispering and exchanging ideas about whether they would get in trouble for wearing them. If I pull back from that contact zone, I see my position within the symphony or cacophony of discourses. Meanwhile, my phone flashed blue an email from Leandra, "If we do the pageant outside of school, let's donate the money to Dorian, the little boy in Rhode Island who is dying from cancer." I smiled, loving that instead of surrendering she was finding another way. We could have fought power directly, but we most likely would have been crushed or won the battle to lose the war. This was her process of enunciation. I emailed her back excited. Zac came back into my room for a pass because he was supposed to have been going to the bathroom, but instead spent 25 or more minutes in my room. "Thanks, Mama J," he said.

He was proof for me that decolonial pedagogy is grounded in a critical hope and faith. We must have the faith to see and decolonize, but we also must have the faith that, even when we are being forced back, that counteractive force is feeling our resistance and feeling is part of learning. If they never have to push back, nothing will ever be learned. Decolonial engagement is not to get from point A to point B. It is not.

I thought on this point as the sun burned into my skin because my window shade had been duct taped on, but, after almost a year, it had finally let go. I saw the chaos of spiritualities, a cacophonic symphony. Was I the conductor? I don't know. But, I could hear the students typing on laptops, trying to finish their work. I could hear others scratching on notebooks doing homework. I could hear the laughter as they used their phones to look up images of shirts, sitting under a table or by my feet. I could hear the sighs, the passions, the exhortatory words, the anger .... There were others not in my class cleaning my whiteboards and rewriting my words more neatly. Then, there was Josh who had ended class standing on my table. Another had left class to interview someone to return to type his quarterly. I had emails popping up and texts. Was I a conductor, perhaps ... each instrument or agent was technically under my control, and I conducted through my dialogue and the stream of other dialogues what solos were heard. I could have yelled at Josh to get down. I could have told Enya to put her shoes on and get off the floor. I could have told the kids in study and whatever other classes to leave. But, they were here and most were engaging in the dialogue some by listening others by speaking, all performing. Is it better for them to be in here engaging with politics, or downstairs sleeping on a table or playing Madden on their phones?

Would my administrators approve of this cacophonic symphony of ideological dialectics? I don't know. I know that I always fear that door opening because my gut tells me no because I've been reprimanded for students having earbuds in or being on cell phones, etc. I run a one room school house often, but it would be seen as un-structured. Education began as one room with many classes. Now we have to compartmentalize in the name of efficiency. Efficiency for whom and for what?

The socio-political function of U.S. education within the colonial power matrix as furthered by neoliberalism engenders colonialities of being that silence and produce spiritualities; therefore, critical transformative leaders need to work with youth to decolonize the written, performed, and hidden curriculum in a process of enunciation.

These enunciations are everywhere and have to do with body-politics as well as biopolitics. To reiterate, infusing biopolitics with decolonial theory, I conceptualize biopolitics as the way in which government no longer uses laws or physical force but rather government is the mechanism by which reason or truth is generated to in/form our subjectivities that is a colonization of the mind that employs the body as its agent for the modes of production. Body-politics involves a decolonial praxis in which individuals become aware of how their bodies are of the colonial and imperial narratives—the subjectification and objectification of their mind and bodies. It means finding authentic ways of enunciating one's self and spiritualities.

On the following page is a painting that I did in order to visualize the colonialities intertwined with the body-politics and biopolitics of de/colonial pedagogy as well as the Pinocchio effect. In its small way, it is my decolonial manifesto for U.S. public education. I had thought of doing a script, but I think that much of this study could be picked up and read or acted out. For me, the painting of this piece was my conscientização, and now it serves as a dialectical piece of this study's research. I remarked earlier that I think in images more so than words, so for me to visually reveal my mind sanctuary, I picked up a pencil. As I sketched out the different elements, I was engaging in conscientização. I thought of my position and the fear that seemed to always be shrouding me. I thought of how if felt as if I was always fighting with a gag in my mouth and my hands behind my back. How do I reach these kids? Was my pedagogy shrouded in this White heteropatriarchal suit of panoptic power? This painting started off as that.

I wanted to describe the tensions of feeling as if you are pulled in a million directions. In my head, I saw Shiva with all arms reaching out and trying to help but also being pulled. I did sketch it, but it wasn't working. It was more complicated than that and it wouldn't show the depth of power that was coursing around.

The suit was emblematic of many of those forces that both my students and I were subjected to. The suit was more than just the classroom. It also flowed to the walls beyond the classroom. I did want to represent the division of self. For practical reasons, I only divided my body in half. One half in a suit, taking on the uniform of that White heteropatriarchal suit of panoptic power, but I am merely employed by it. I do not control it. There are layers that as I painted the viewer can no longer see. There are chains on my hands that now are slicked over with oil paint. I had actually folded the piece of paper over and planned

FIGURE 7.1 De/colonial education—enunciating spiritualities, identities, and violences (drawing by Elizabeth Janson)

on cutting off where the second two panes are. However, I realized that it was still missing something.

It was missing the pedagogy of hope as well as poisonous pedagogies. Before I go through the details of my analysis, I would ask that you look at it. What do you see? What do you feel? What do you hear? Let your mind interact. Body-politics and biopolitics course through it. If we have body-politics, what is the politics of the body? Here they are.

After a trying week, I put the final touches on this painting to represent how it feels to be a teacher in today's testing and standardization regime .... I feel the panoptic power of dominant ideologies that are made by suits. Suits that surround me and suits that I put on. There is a cult of surveillance that focuses on data instead of the children that we teach and their spiritualities and needs.

It often feels as if as an educator my hands are tied behind my back, while I lose children under this violence of standardization, yet other coworkers proclaim that it is master and learner in the classroom—the violent colonization of minds.

As pedagogues, we are not only teachers who live in our classrooms but our beings transcend the classroom, pulling us to the needs of our students, families, and selves. There is a pedagogy of hope, and I see it as students enunciate themselves through their voices and actions. I struggled to find a name for this piece. How could I title the different layers? In the end, I have titled it "De/Colonial Education—Enunciating Spiritualities, Identities, and Violences."

The politics of our bodies are in the spiritualities and colonialities of beings. Children left with cut marks on arms. Eyes wide with drugs. Tears that slip invisibly down dry or wet cheeks. Swears and fights solved with ostracism for groups of days. Girls told that they "flatter themselves" if they respond that a teacher checked them out. Dismissal of opinions and grievances as mere female whining. Do not question Him.

A colleague looked at me the other day and asked, "What are you scared of? Go for it. What more can be done to you?" The politics of the body in our professionalism for donning suits. How can you engage in a decolonial praxis as a critical transformative leader when you are mummified in reams of reforms and procedures. Biopolitics which govern through the hegemonic acceptance of these policies being "for the children" or to ensure "teacher accountability."

Politics of life in money for new books for AP while the lower-levels stay with books from the 1990s that are missing pages and falling to pieces. iPads to evaluate teachers. New technology must be bought for PARCC, but why not before when it could have helped them to learn?

Regiment bodies. Regiment minds. Anesthetize spiritualities. Whittle identities.

Note in the right pane that I stand on *imaginicide*, which as a teacher of English Language Arts that is chained in standardization, I can try to resist but the fact is that *imaginicide* is committed through policies that tell a child what to think. I may resist, raising my fist.

But, at my feet are not only my family obligations, depicted by the little boy clinging to my leg, but also my "children"—my students who come with so many stories. These stories can be released through imagination and dialogue about literature, exposing as much of self or as little as possible. On the other side of the book is a student acting out a scene from A Raisin in the Sun where Walter starts by mimicking African tribal warriors but then finds himself returning to the past and the roots of his identity in an authentic majesty.

Role playing helps us think beyond the chains and shrouds that we find ourselves currently, to imagine another world, another knowledge. The whiteboard has two of my kids and the image of the world is actually to represent a comment given to me in my second year of teaching after I had been teaching a lesson about racism through *Huck Finn*, "Your expectations might be too high. They're not going to go out and change the world." I now know that he's wrong. The youth depicted presented his senior project with his classmate about how

FIGURE 7.2
Within panoptic forces (drawing by Elizabeth Janson)

drama needs to be for the masses, that it is a powerful educational tool. In the auditorium, with 75 or so other students. The students spoke up about the power of drama and how for their classmates acting out scenes from *The Scarlet Letter, A Raisin in the* Sun, etc. were for them the most memorable. Their research and passions revealed to me that they were already working to change the world. At the time of my evaluator's comment, I had felt shame. I had been embarrassed, as if I was so naïve. Stupid little girl.

I think back now that the comment had more to do with the fact that the kids had been bringing up issues of racism as related to a hockey game and in their hallways. I was calling attention to the violence of the White heteropatriarchal panopticon that exists within schools under the virginal white skirts of neutrality. Schools are not innocent places, nor do I contend that the biggest danger is bomb threats or mass shootings. The violence that occurs day in and day out is far more insidious. How are spiritualities crushed? They're crushed when students try to resist the dogma or try to resist their oppression. Schools are supposed to be operating rooms of neutrality in which we fix youth, push them out as better humans. These operating rooms cut and stitch, but what do we take out from youth?

Teachers are under increasing pressure to make youth perform and there are data systems and monitoring systems to *help*. Edwin Analytics, Scantron,

TeachPoint, DDMS, etc. I have my colleague above the iPad with her hands in her hair frazzled. The pressure is there. Race to the Top and PARCC are also present, shooting out from that suit. Then, there are our cyber responsibilities through Gmail and Twitter. My phone always lights up with students' needs. I receive emails and notifications at all hours from former and current students. I get them while I'm teaching and sleeping. Nothing like looking over at your phone at 2 a.m. and seeing the blue light flash. You've only been asleep for a few hours but already there are needs waiting. Two more hours to sleep, but the call is there. The hands that are extending from the top represent in many ways those needs and wants, all the arms reaching for you.

Twitter is a medium I choose not to use frequently, but my students do and those 140 character assaults produce word eggs that hatch into wounds. The arm that sticks out from the suit's shoulder has cut marks on it that are carved from the tears of an eye above that then turn to droplets of blood that go through the Scantron stabbed by a pencil. My colleague once had a final exam turned in with a message, the words, "I suck" bubbled in. We get little messages often on assessments apologizing or explaining or complaining. Then, you have the boy asleep on the agenda.

The agenda that is supposed to be make me a better teacher and him a better learner by providing objectives. The girl against the book has the string of the red balloon floating above her. That red balloon can be the love and hope she carries with her in a letter that you've given her telling her that she is special and smart. The question is, can it lift her up ... how far can hope get you?

She is juxtaposed against the door of another classroom in which the school's mission is pasted on a podium that stands on the books, titled Epistemicide and Imperialism.

A question I remember a professor asking a group of pre-service teachers was "What would be the three qualities of the perfect student?" I remember almost all the results had at least something to do with being well-behaved and/or quiet. My ideal had to do with one who questions. That was probably in response to having been the quiet girl in the classroom when I was younger after having been the wild girl who was taught to sit on her hands in kindergarten—being be still.

I look to the classroom in beige and green; perhaps I chose those colors unconsciously for its militaristic nature. The American flag waving. The teacher's whip in the air from his position of power. The student raising her hand was beaten back. I have been that student. I have had that student who perhaps I didn't whip, but I'm sure I silenced for the sake of preparing for MCAS. In fact, one such student presented at TRED (Transformative Researchers and Educators for Democracy) on high-stakes testing and the money trail. Her

FIGURE 7.3
De/colonial pedagogies (drawing by Elizabeth Janson)

senior Capstone was on comparing the Ministry of Truth and the takeover of Hogwarts to that of U.S. educational reform policies and its similar control of knowledge. However, I never meant to silence her but rather give her another language or Discourse so that she could succeed on MCAS. My refusal to let her write in her way for a while was just as powerful as a whip. She shut down in my class until she understood that I was trying to help her navigate power, not choke on power. In this green classroom though, the students are taught not to question. They are told to listen, to take notes. The boy and girl in the back are both on their cell phones. The girl quite clearly, hiding her cell phone behind a book. But, at least, she's quiet.

If we raise our eyes up, we can see a boy falling through into the room. I am kneeling on a Scantron sheet with my hands behind my back, using all that I have left, which is my hair. For me it conjured an image of Rapunzel, but also the idea of teaching and femininity. The only power that I have left is the power of caring and armored love. Like a mama lion, I will use my teeth to pull back my children from danger even if my arms are broken or tied up. I will let down my hair in order to try to use it as a lifeline for a youth. How strong can we be, though? Do we fall in too?

Above is a scene from my classroom in which students were acting out scenes from *The Grapes of Wrath*. Normally quiet kids became so full of life. I laughed. My colleague walked in, and she laughed. Never underestimate the power of joy in the classroom. On my walls are two posters, one says "Voice the Silences" with a boy screaming. I had asked one of my students to draw what my classroom was, and the response was conflict, arguing. I gave him the corresponding words taken from TRED's logo. On the wall, there is a purple flower, drawn by another student. Unknowingly it looked like the flower drawn by Talia on almost everything she could write on. It now is on the wrist of one of my students and is forever imprinted in my mind. I always wonder what that flower meant to her. When her former freshmen classmates walked in and saw the poster, they remarked, "It feels weird to be in here without her." Eventually, we took it down and replaced it with Maya Angelou's words and a feather, "Hope is the thing with feathers/That perches in the soul,/And sings the tune without the words,/And never stops at all,/And sweetest in the gale is heard."

Decolonization cannot be a finite process, but requires a revolutionary imagination that opens the colonized mind to the worlds of the political and possible and may be a form of utopian "thinking that refuses mere compliance, that looks down roads not yet taken to the shapes of a more fulfilling social order; to more vibrant ways of being in the world. This kind of reshaping imagination may be released through many sorts of dialogue" (Greene, 1995, p. 5). We must fight against the individualism that our society inculcates for market profit and the exploitation of our bodies and minds. Consciously enunciating spiritualities is in itself a revolutionary act that can counteract the exploitation of mind, body, and spirit. Youth and educators must fight against the anesthetizing culture within schools and find ways to hear themselves speak as individuals and as collectives.

Spiritualities are not completely silenced in schools. Students resist the anesthetization and silence that is a weapon of neoliberal colonization. I see it as they present their research. I see it when they have crawled into a corner due to the enormous pressure put on them via the high-stakes culture that has erupted in U.S. schools, where as they are huddled in a ball their spirituality is crying out for a connection beyond calculation. But, I see it when another youth moves the box aside and hugs the crying girl, despite the fact that she did not get along with her. I see it when two boys fight because one called him, "Fake." I see it when a girl leaves her class because her mother texted her, and her mom has a severe medical condition that she doesn't always treat properly; the girl cries on the office phone trying to get her mom to dismiss her, so she can go take care of her. Spirituality is there as I walk around a room in my MCAS shoes, walking at the *right* pace without noise while silently moving my head side to side, and I see youth doodle on the margins, unwilling to return to class. It's there in the love, the anger, the knowledge, the language, etc.

Is it there in their $200 Nikes when they can barely afford to eat? Neoliberalism is there, so capitalist spirituality is there. How about when I grow angry that my students are not trying to succeed or they are being selfish, racist, sexist, Islamophobic, homophobic, and/or classist; they are content to live in the confectionary delights of consumerism despite their oppression, is it there? Is this colonialities of being? If so, for whom? How can we understand that our being may not be our own, when we've never known another way? Why would we imagine change when we live in a pedagogy of hopelessness? Imaginicide is not a little problem when you consider Jules de Gaultier's (1902) words, "Imagination is the only weapon in the war against reality" (p. 308).[4]

"Things won't change, Miss J."

"Aren't your expectations too high? They are not going to change the world."

Our miseducation unites us in a b(l)inding wall that hides the epistemicides (Santos, 2007b, 2014; Paraskeva, 2011, 2016a, 2016b, 2017), linguicides, imaginicides, and genocides that occur to put it up. How do we as educators, as critical transformative leaders begin to decolonize ourselves and create decolonial spaces? How can we understand spiritualities and provide youth with the understanding and education to decolonize and enunciate themselves?

These questions are in part what led me to want to write a manifesto for the "conclusion" of this research study. I wanted to write a text that could be performed for the public, to take this research and make it accessible to the public not only in appearance but in discourse. The story about "patriarchy" perhaps encompasses this manifesto; at the very least, it is its complement. The children on desks, not in desks.

With the question remaining, does it matter? If my students and I were to act out that scene, what would the public see and feel? How can the public know when it already knows? The mis-education of the public through colonial schooling becomes a wall against analysis of experience. However, as I explained my dissertation topic to my seniors,[5] Ariana raised her hand, "So basically what I have been saying all along?"

I laughed. I had had her sophomore year too, and it had been a difficult year for her between home and school issues, connected by the fight for who she wanted to be. A feminist spirituality of struggle, oppression, and fear had connected us since then. "Yes, I never said I didn't agree with you." She nodded her head side-to-side as if to say, "True." "I told you that I hated MCAS and that I didn't believe in standardization, but that it's a language that you have to master in order to get out of here. The powers that be mandate those policies, but we have to fight to change them."

She looked at me. Her brows furrowed quizzically. "How come if we are kids and we can see it, the adults can't?"

"That's a good question." I took a deep breath, wondering how far I should enter into this conversation. "Most people were made by this system. The Pinocchio effect. They became real by learning the rules, and they got their dreams or they didn't and are made into the jackasses."

"So, they can't see?" She shook her head, exasperated.

"They've been taught not to. And, then there are those who don't want to see. Think about who this system works for …."

She leaned back with her arms crossed, thinking and knowing.

Her resistance to the "stupidity" of the standardized writing and the prescribed books sophomore year had made for a tumultuous year. Her journal writing, though, revealed her spirit and demonstrated her as a critical mind, even if only a struggling to average student in school.

Her question of "Why can't they [adults with power] see?" is a good beginning, but it's also related to "What can we do?"

It can feel as if we are trapped in a curriculum of hopelessness in which we can see tragedy but must develop an un-seeing being because of the oppressive hegemony of the limitless present in order to survive. Present is past and future, with no room for citizens to construct another tomorrow or to see a different yesterday. To see what is happening is not enough, it feeds into a historical amnesia and a desensitizing consciousness. Portions of this conclusion are in my way an aesthetic manifesto that can be taken to be performed or viewed in a way of imagining a tomorrow with hope that is full of democratic voices, spirits, and actions.

This is a conclusion only in the sense that there will be no more pages afterward, but the questions and process will be ongoing, not just with me but with my students, the readers, and my colleagues. In literary analysis, we teach youth to write in the present tense because literature is always in the act of becoming. Every time you open the book, it begins, and it may end for you but begins for another. The characters are always there; the emotions are always there, and, for each reader, it's a new becoming. That is how I would like this research to be viewed; it's always in the act of becoming. So, we begin the decolonial process to break the hegemony of neoliberalism that oppresses us as we oppress ourselves and others ....

> When evil-doing comes like falling rain, no body calls out 'stop!'
> When crimes begin to pile up they become invisible. When sufferings become unendurable the cries are no longer heard.
> The cries, too, fall like rain in summer.
> (Bertolt Brecht, 1935)

Notes

1 See ABC News "Seven-Year-Old Handcuffed over Lunch Money Dispute" during January 2013.

2 https://www.huffingtonpost.com/entry/salt-lake-city-police-de-escalation_us_591c9070e4b03b485cae1129

3 As this was a public forum, I have not used pseudonyms and have left the flyer and text as is. See for more information on the forum http://www.southcoasttoday.com/article/20150914/NEWS/150919707

4 It was difficult to trace the original of this quote, but it seems to be from his work, *Le Bovarysme, essai sur le pouvoir d'imaginer*: "pouvoir de se soustraire, par l'imagination, aux atteintes de la réalité" (p. 308).

5 Note that my students "choose" levels, and that these seniors are categorized as level 2, which is a non-4-year college prep path. For the past two years, I have challenged my denotation of them as "level 2" and have erased the 2 from my door sign, agenda, and heading. In a small way, this is me trying to undo the path they have "chosen" that often comes with a lower-class status.

References

Adichie, C. N. (2012). *Purple hibiscus: A novel.* New York, NY: Algonquin Books.

Advancement Project. (2010). *Test, punish, and push out: How "zero tolerance" and high-stakes testing funnel youth into the school-to-prison pipeline.* Retrieved November 30, 2013, from http://b.3cdn.net/advancement/d05cb2181a4545db07_r2im6caqe.pdf

Althusser, L. (1984). *Essays on ideology.* London: Verso.

American Federation of Teachers (AFT). (2015, May 3). Survey shows need for national focus on workplace stress. *American Federation of Teachers.* Retrieved November 10, 2015, from http://www.aft.org/news/survey-shows-need-national-focus-workplace-stress#sthash.g2EqN62L.dpuf

Anderson, L. (2006). Analytic autoethnography. *Journal of Contemporary Ethnography, 35*(4), 373–395.

Angelou, M. (1983). *Shaker, why don't you sing?* New York, NY: Random House.

Anzaldúa, G. (2005). Speaking in tongues: A letter to third world women writers. In J. B. de Hernandez (Ed.), *Women writing resistance: Essays on Latin America and the Caribbean* (pp. 79–90). Cambridge, MA: South End Press.

Anzaldúa, G. (2007). *Borderlands: La frontera* (3rd ed.). San Francisco, CA: Hubsta Ltd.

Apple, M. (1993). The politics of official knowledge: Does a national curriculum make sense? *Discourse, 14*(1), 1–16.

Aronowitz, S. (1992). Paulo Freire's radical democratic humanism. In P. Leonard & P. McLaren (Eds.), *Paulo Freire: A critical encounter* (pp. 8–24). New York, NY: Routledge.

Aud, S., & Fox, M. A. (2011). *Status and trends in the education of racial and ethnic groups (2010).* Washington, DC: Diane Publishing.

Autio, T. (2009). Globalization, curriculum, and new belongings of subjectivity. In E. Ropo & T. Autio (Eds.), *International conversations on curriculum studies subject, society and curriculum* (pp. 1–24). Rotterdam, The Netherlands: Sense Publishers.

Bauman, Z. (1998). *Globalization: The human consequences.* Cambridge: Polity Press.

Bauman, Z. (2013). *Liquid modernity.* Malden, MA: Polity Press.

Bauman, Z., & Donskis, L. (2013). *Moral blindness: The loss of sensitivity in liquid modernity.* Malden, MA: Polity Press.

Berkes, H. (2012, July 10). *As mine protections fail, black lung cases surge.* Retrieved February 16, 2016, from http://www.npr.org/2012/07/09/155978300/as-mine-protections-fail-black-lung-cases-surge

Biko, S. (2002). *I write what I like: Selected writings.* Chicago, IL: University of Chicago Press.

Blackley, D. J., Halldin, C. N., & Laney, A. S. (2014). Resurgence of a debilitating and entirely preventable respiratory disease among working coal miners. *American Journal of Respiratory and Critical Care Medicine, 190*(6), 708–709.

Bochner, A., & Riggs, N. (2014). Practicing narrative inquiry. In P. Leavy (Ed.), *The Oxford handbook of qualitative research* (pp. 193–222). New York, NY: Oxford University Press.

Boylorn, R. M. (2013). "Sit with your legs closed!" and other sayin's from my childhood. In S. Holman Jones, T. Adams, & C. Ellis (Eds.), *Handbook of autoethnography* (pp. 173–185). Walnut Creek, CA: Left Coast Press.

Branco, D. (2015). *Zero tolerance policies: Effects on minority urban schools through teachers' voices* (Doctoral dissertation). University of Massachusetts Dartmouth, North Dartmouth, MA.

Brooke, E. (2014, April 15). The self-tanning industry is still booming. *Fashionista.* Retrieved February 15, 2016, from http://fashionista.com/2014/04/self-tanning-industry-growth

Bush, G. (2001, September 20). *President Bush's address to a joint session of congress and the nation.* Retrieved February 15, 2016, from http://www.washingtonpost.com/wp-srv/nation/specials/attacked/transcripts/bushaddress_092001.html

Bush, G. (2006, December 20). *President Bush's news conference.* Retrieved February 15, 2016, from http://www.nytimes.com/2006/12/20/washington/20text-bush.html?_r=0

Cabral, A. (1973a). Identity and dignity in the context of the national liberation struggle. *Return to the source.* New York, NY: Monthly Review.

Cabral, A. (1973b). 'Connecting the struggle: An informal talk with black americans. *A. Cabral, op. cit*, 78–79.

Cabral, A. (1979). *Unity and struggle: Speeches and writings of Amilcar.* New York, NY: Monthly Review Press.

Caskey, A. (2012, November). *Unearthly images of Appalachian Mountains that have been blown up.* Retrieved February 16, 2016, from http://www.slate.com/articles/health_and_science/coal/2012/11/mountaintop_removal_photos_antrim_caskey_award_winning_photographer_of_appalachian.html

Castro-Gómez, S. (2008). (Post)Coloniality for dummies: Latin American perspectives on modernity, coloniality, and the geopolitics of knowledge. In M. Moraña, E. Dussel, & C. Jáuregui (Eds.), *Coloniality at large: Latin America and the postcolonial debate* (pp. 259–285) Durham, NC: Duke University Press.

Césaire, A. (2000). *Discourse on colonialism.* New York, NY: Monthly Review Press.

Chang, H. (2013). Individual and collaborative autoethnography as method: A social scientist's perspective. In S. Holman Jones, T. Adams, & C. Ellis (Eds.), *Handbook of autoethnography* (pp. 107–122). New York, NY: Routledge.

Chomsky, N. (2003). *Chomsky on democracy & education* (C. P. Otero, Ed.). London: Routledge Falmer.

Chomsky, N. (2004). Chomsky on *miseducation* (D. Macedo, Ed.). Lanham, MD: Rowman & Littlefield.

Coal Mining Institute of America. (1907). *Proceedings of the Coal Mining Institute of America*. Greensburg, PA: Press of C. M. Henry & Co. Retrieved February 16, 2016, from https://books.google.com/books?id=Mws3AQAAMAAJ

Cohn, E. (2013, October 24). McDonald's tells worker she should sign up for food stamps. *Huffington Post*. Retrieved November 1, 2013, from http://www.huffingtonpost.com/2013/10/24/mcdonalds-food-stamps_n_4151647.html

Conquergood, D. (1985). Performing as a moral act: Ethical dimensions of the ethnography of performance. *Literature in Performance, 5*(2), 1–13.

Constantino, R. (1966). The mis-education of the Filipino. *Journal of Contemporary Asia, 1*(1), 20–36.

Constantino, R. (1978). *Neocolonial identity and counter-consciousness*. London: Merlin Press.

Coolidge, C. (1926, October 27). *Address before the American association of advertising agencies*. Retrieved January 12, 2016, from http://www.presidency.ucsb.edu/ws/?pid=412

Dantley, M. (2005). The power of critical spirituality to act and to reform. *Journal of School Leadership, 15*(5), 500–518.

Darder, A. (1991). *Culture and power in the classroom: A critical foundation for bicultural education*. Westport, CT: Bergin & Garvey Publishers, Inc.

Darder, A. (2002). *Reinventing Paulo Freire: A pedagogy of love*. Boulder, CO: Westview Press.

Darder, A. (2015). *Freire and education*. New York, NY: Routledge.

Darder, A. (2018). Ruthlessness and the Forging of liberatory epistemologies: An Arduous journey. In J. Paraskeva (Ed.), *Curriculum epistemicides*. New York, NY: Routledge.

da Silva, T. T., & McLaren, P. (1993). Knowledge under siege: The Brazilian debate. In P. Leonard & P. McLaren (Eds.), *Paulo Freire: A critical encounter* (pp. 36–46). New York, NY: Routledge.

Davies, W. (2011). The political economy of unhappiness. *New Left Review, 71*, 65–80.

Deen, T. (2014, June 26). Water cut-off in Detroit violates human rights, say activists. *Truth Out*. Retrieved July 1, 2014, from http://truth-out.org/news/item/24606-water-cut-off-in-us-city-violates-human-rights-say-activists

De Gaultier, J. (2006). Le *Bovarysme, essai sur le pouvoir d'imaginer*. Paris, France: Presses de L'Université Paris-Sorbonne.

Deleuze, G., & Guattari, F. (1988). *A thousand plateaus: Capitalism and schizophrenia*. London: Bloomsbury Publishing.

Dellinger, A. (2015, December 25). Bottled air from Canada is selling like crazy in China. *Salon*. Retrieved February 16, 2016, from http://www.salon.com/2015/12/25/bottled_air_from_canada_is_selling_like_crazy_in_china_partner/

Denzin, N. K. (2003). *Performance ethnography: Critical pedagogy and the politics of culture*. Thousand Oaks, CA: Sage Publications.

Denzin, N. K. (2006). Analytic autoethnography, or déjà vu all over again. *Journal of Contemporary Ethnography, 35*(4), 419–428.

Denzin, N. K. (2014). *Interpretive autoethnography* (Vol. 17). Thousand Oaks, CA. Sage Publications.

Denzin, N. K., & Lincoln, Y. S. (2011). *Part 4: Methods of collecting and analyzing data.* In N. K. Denzin & Y. S. Lincoln (Eds.), *The Sage handbook of qualitative research* (4th ed.). Thousand Oaks, CA: Sage Publications.

Dewey, J. (2004). *Democracy and education*. New York, NY: Macmillan.

DiGangi, C. (2015, September 27). Many moms go into debt to be 'perfect parent.' *USA Parent.* Retrieved February 16, 2016, from http://www.usatoday.com/story/money/personalfinance/2015/09/27/credit-dotcom-moms-debt/72629890/

Donne, J. (1839). Meditation 17. *The works of John Donne* (Vol. 3). London: John W. Parker and Son, West Strand.

Dubofsky, M. (1961). Organized labor and the immigrant in New York City, 1900–1918. *Labor History, 2*(2), 182–201.

Duranti, A. (2010). Husserl, intersubjectivity and anthropology. *Anthropological Theory, 10*(1–2), 16–35.

Dussel, E. (2005). In L. Gordon (Chair.), *Anti-Cartesian meditations: On the origin of the philosophical anti-discourse of modernity*. Translation of presentation delivered at second annual conference of the Caribbean Philosophical Association, Puerto Rico. Retrieved August 5, 2014, from http://enriquedussel.com/txt/Anti-Cartesianmeditations.pdf

Dussel, E. (2013). *Ethics of liberation: In the age of globalization and exclusion*. Durham, NC: Duke University Press.

Eggers, D., & Calegari, N. C. (2011, April 30). The high cost of low teacher salaries. *New York Times*. Retrieved February 15, 2016, from http://www.nytimes.com/2011/05/01/opinion/01eggers.html

Ellis, C. (1999). Heartful autoethnography. *Qualitative Health Research, 9*(5), 669–683.

Ellis, C. (2004). *The ethnographic I: A methodological novel about autoethnography*. Walnut Creek, CA: Altamira Press.

Ellis, C., Adams, T., & Bochner, A. (2010). Autoethnography: An overview. *Forum Qualitative Sozialforschung/Forum: Qualitative Social Research, 12*(1). Retrieved June 5, 2013, from http://www.qualitativeresearch.net/index.php/fqs/article/view/1589/3095

Ellsworth, E. (1989). Why doesn't this feel empowering? Working through the repressive myths of critical pedagogy. *Harvard Educational Review, 59*(3), 297–324.

Ewen, S. (1976). *Captains of consciousness: Advertising and the social roots of the consumer culture*. New York, NY: Basic Books.

Fabricant, M., & Fine, M. (2012). *Charter schools and the corporate makeover of public education: What's at stake?* New York, NY: Teachers College Press.

Fanon, F. (1952). *Black skin, White masks.* New York, NY: Grove Press.

Fanon, F. (1963). *The wretched of the earth.* New York, NY: Grove Press.

Federici, S. (2004). *Caliban and the witch: Women, capitalism and primitive accumulation.* New York, NY: Autonomedia.

Feinberg, L. (1996). *Transgender warriors: Making history from Joan of Arc to Dennis Rodman.* Boston, MA: Beacon Press.

Feistritzer, C. E., Griffin, S., & Linnajarvi, A. (2011). *Profile of teachers in the US, 2011* (p. 9). Washington, DC: National Center for Education Information.

Fine, M. (1991). *Framing dropouts: Notes on the politics of an urban high school.* Albany, NY: SUNY Press.

Fitzgerald, F. S. (2010). *The great Gatsby.* London: Harper Collins.

Foucault, M., Ewald, F., & Fontana, A. (2008). *The birth of biopolitics: Lectures at the Collège de France, 1978–1979* (M. Senellart, Ed.). New York, NY: Palgrave Macmillan.

Foucault, M., & Gordon, C. (1980). *Power/knowledge, selected interviews and other writings, 1972–1977* (pp. vii–261). New York, NY: Pantheon Books.

Foucault, M., Martin, L. H., Gutman, H., & Hutton, P. H. (1988). *Technologies of the self: A seminar with Michel Foucault.* Amherst, MA: University of Massachusetts Press.

Foucault, M., Senellart, M., Burchell, G., Ewald, F., & Fontana, A. (2009). *Security, territory, population: Lectures at the Collège de France 1977–1978* (Vol. 4). London: Palgrave Macmillan.

Freire, P. (1997). *Pedagogy of the heart.* New York, NY: The Continuum International Publishing Group, Inc.

Freire, P. (2005). *Teachers as cultural workers: Letters to those who dare teach.* Cambridge, MA: Westview Press.

Freire, P. (2009). *Pedagogy of the oppressed.* New York, NY: The Continuum International Publishing Group, Inc.

Freire, P. (2013). *Education for a critical consciousness.* New York, NY: Bloomsbury Academic.

Freire, P. (2014). *Pedagogy of hope: Reliving pedagogy of the oppressed.* New York, NY: Bloomsbury Academic.

Freire, P., & Macedo, D. (1992). A dialogue with Paulo Freire: Paulo Freire and Donaldo Macedo. In P. Leonard & P. McLaren (Eds.), *Paulo Freire: A critical encounter.* (pp. 169–188). New York, NY: Routledge.

Freire, P., & Macedo, D. (2013). *Literacy: Reading the word and the world.* New York, NY: Routledge.

Fullilove, M. (2004). *Root shock: How tearing up city neighborhoods hurts America, and what we can do about it.* New York, NY: Ballantine Books.

Gadamer, H. G. (1976). On the scope and function of hermeneutical reflection. In D. E. Linge (Ed.), *Philosophical hermeneutics* (pp. 18–43). Berkley, MA: University of California Press.

Gadamer, H. G. (1989). *Truth and method* (J. Weinsheimer & D. G. Marshall, Trans.). New York, NY: Continuum.

Gates, S. M., Ringel, J. S., & Santibanez, L. (2003). *Who is leading our schools?: An overview of school administrators and their careers* (No. 1679). Santa Monica, CA: Rand Corporation.

Gaztambide-Fernández, R. (2014). Decolonial options and artistic/aesthetic entanglements: An interview with Walter Mignolo. *Decolonization: Indigeneity, Education & Society, 3*(1), 196–212.

Gee, J. P. (1990). *Social linguistics and literacies: Ideology in discourse, critical perspectives on literacy and education.* New York, NY: Routledge.

Gee, J. P. (2005). *An introduction to discourse analysis: Theory and method.* London: Psychology Press.

Giroux, H. (1988). *Teachers as intellectuals: Toward a critical pedagogy of learning.* Westport, CT: Bergin & Garvey Publishers, Inc.

Giroux, H. (2001). *Theory and resistance in education: Towards a pedagogy for the opposition.* Westport, CT: Bergin & Garvey Publishers, Inc.

Giroux, H. (2009). *Youth in a suspect society.* New York, NY: Palgrave Macmillan.

Giroux, H. (2011, August 21). How Disney magic and the corporate media shape youth identity in the digital age. *Truth Out.* Retrieved June 10, 2013, from http://truth-out.org/opinion/item/2808:how-disney-magic-and-the-corporate-media-shape-youth-identity-in-the-digital-age

Giroux, H. (2012). *Education and the crisis of public values: Challenging the assault on teachers, students, & public education.* New York, NY: Peter Lang Publishing, Inc.

Giroux, H. (2014a). *The violence of organized forgetting: Thinking beyond America's disimagination machine.* San Francisco, CA: City Lights Publishers.

Giroux, H. (2014b, April). *Where is the outrage? Defending higher education in the age of casino capitalism.* Paper presented at University of Massachusetts Dartmouth Educational Leadership and Policy Spring Colloquium, North Dartmouth, MA.

Giroux, H. (2015, June 12). *Neoliberal violence in the age of Orwellian nightmares.* Lecture presented at New Bedford Whaling Museum, New Bedford, MA.

Gramsci, A. (1971). *Selections from the prison notebooks of Antonio Gramsci* (Vol. 1, Q. Hoare & G. Nowell-Smith, Eds.). London: The Electric Book Company.

Greene, M. (1995). *Releasing the imagination: Essays on education, the arts, and social change.* San Francisco, CA: Jossey-Bass.

Grosfoguel, R. (2010). The epistemic decolonial turn: Beyond the political-economy paradigms. In W. Mignolo & A. Escobar (Eds.), *Globalization and the decolonial option* (pp. 65–77). New York, NY: Routledge.

Gross, L. (1961). Preface to a metatheoretical framework for sociology. *American Journal of Sociology*, 125–143.

Grossman, D. (1996). *On killing: The psychological cost of learning to kill in war and society*. New York, NY: Little, Brown, and Company.

Guinier, L., Torres, G., & Guinier, L. (2009). *The miner's canary: Enlisting race, resisting power, transforming democracy*. Cambridge, MA: Harvard University Press.

Hamby, C. (2012, July 8). Black lung surges back in coal country. *Public Integrity*. Retrieved February 16, 2016, from http://www.publicintegrity.org/2012/07/08/9293/black-lung-surges-back-coal-country

Haraway, D. (1988). Situated knowledges: The science question in feminism and the privilege of partial perspective. *Feminist Studies, 14*, 575–599.

Harding, S., & Norberg, K. (2005). New feminist approaches to social science methodologies: An introduction. *Signs, 40*(1).

Hartnett, S. J. (2008). The annihilating public policies of the prison-industrial complex; or, crime, violence, and punishment in an age of neoliberalism. *Rhetoric & Public Affairs, 11*(3), 491–515.

Harvey, D. (2005). *A brief history of neoliberalism*. New York, NY: Oxford University Press.

Harvey, D. (2010). *The enigma of capital: And the crises of capitalism*. London: Profile Books.

Hesse-Biber, S. N. (2012). *Handbook of feminist research: Theory and praxis* (2nd ed.). Thousand Oaks, CA: Sage Publications.

Holman Jones, S. (2013). *Collecting and interpreting qualitative materials* (4th ed.). Thousand Oaks, CA: Sage Publications.

Horton, M., Freire, P., Bell, B., & Gaventa, J. (1990). *We make the road by walking: Conversations on education and social change*. Philadelphia, PA: Temple University Press.

hooks, b. (1992). bell hooks speaking about Paulo Freire: The man, his work. In P. Leonard & P. McLaren (Eds.), *Paulo Freire: A critical encounter* (pp. 146–154). New York, NY: Routledge.

hooks, b. (2000). *All about love: New visions*. New York, NY: William Morrow.

hooks, b. (2006). *Outlaw culture: Resisting representations*. New York, NY: Routledge Classics.

Ingersoll, R. M. (2001). Teacher turnover and teacher shortages: An organizational analysis. *American Educational Research Journal, 38*(3), 499–534.

Innerarity, D. (2012). *The future and its enemies: In defense of political hope*. Palo Alto, CA: Stanford University Press.

Janesick, V. (2000). The choreography of qualitative research design: Minuets, improvisations, and crystallization. *NK Denzin, 86*, 379–399.

Janson, E. E. (2015). Globalization: The loadstone rock to education. In J. M. Paraskeva & T. S. Lavallee (Eds.), *Transformative researchers and educators for democracy: Dartmouth Dialogues*. Rotterdam, The Netherlands: Sense Publishers.

Janson, E. E., & Motta Silva, C. (2017). Itinerant curriculum theory: Navigating the waters of power, identity, and praxis. *Journal of the American Association for the Advancement of Curriculum Studies (JAAACS), 12*(1).

Janson, E. E., & Paraskeva, J. M. (2015). Curriculum counter-strokes and strokes: Swimming in non-existent epistemological rivers. *Policy Futures in Education, 13*(8), 949–967.

Jerald, C. D. (2008). *Benchmarking for success: Ensuring US students receive a world-class education.* Washington, DC: National Governors Association.

Johnston, D. C. (2011, Octovber 19). First look at US pay data, it's awful. *Reuters.* Retrieved June 22, 2012, from http://blogs.reuters.com/david-cay-johnston/2011/10/19/first-look-at-us-pay-data-its-awful/

Jones, J. L. (2002). Performance ethnography: The role of embodiment in cultural authenticity. *Theatre Topics, 12*(1), 1–15.

Jones, S. H. (2005). Making the personal political. In N. K. Denzin & Y. S. Lincoln (Eds.), The Sage handbook of qualitative research *collecting and interpreting qualitative materials* (3rd ed., pp. 763–791). Thousand Oaks, CA: Sage Publications.

Jones, S. H., Adams, T., & Ellis, C. (2013). Introduction: Coming to know autoethnography as more than a method. In S. H. Jones, T. E. Adams, & C. Ellis (Eds.), *Handbook of autoethnography* (pp. 17–48). Walnut Creek, CA: Left Coast Press.

Jupp, J. C. (2013). *Becoming teachers of inner-city students.* Rotterdam, The Netherlands: Sense Publishers.

Jupp, J. C. (2017). Decolonizing and de-canonizing curriculum studies: An engaged discussion organized around João M. Paraskeva's recent books. *Journal of the American Association for the Advancement of Curriculum Studies (JAAACS), 12*(1).

Kelly, M. (2004). Racism, nationalism and biopolitics: Foucault's society must be defended. *Contretemps, 4*, 58–70.

Kennedy, J. F. (1961, January 20). *Inaugural address.* Retrieved December 7, 2015, from http://www.americanrhetoric.com/speeches/jfkinaugural.htm

Kim, C. Y., Losen, D. J., & Hewitt, D. T. (2010). *The school-to-prison pipeline: Structuring legal reform.* New York, NY: New York University Press.

Kirsch, I. S., Jungeblut, A., Jenkins, L., & Kolstad, A. (2002). *Adult literacy in America: National center for education statistics.* Washington, DC: Office of Educational Research and Improvement, US Department of Education.

Kite, L., & Kite, L. (2014, September 24). The ugly side of tanning: How that healthy glow hurts women. *Beauty redefined.* Retrieved February 15, 2016, from http://www.beautyredefined.net/ugly-side-of-tanning/

Klein, N. (2007). *The shock doctrine: The rise of disaster capitalism.* Toronto: Random House.

Kliebard, H. M. (2004). *The struggle for the American curriculum, 1893–1958* (3rd ed.). New York, NY: Routledge.

Koch, T. (1996). Implementation of a hermeneutic inquiry in nursing: philosophy, rigour and representation. *Journal of Advanced Nursing, 24*(1), 174–184.

Krieger, N., Chen, J. T., Waterman, P. D., Kiang, M. V., & Feldman, J. (2015). Police killings and police deaths are public health data and can be counted. *PLoS Medicine, 12*(12).

Kuczynski-Brown, A. (2012, October 12). Florida adopts academic achievement standards based on race, ethnicity, echoes Virginia. *Huffington Post.* Retrieved February 16, 2016, from http://www.huffingtonpost.com/2012/10/12/echoing-virginia-florida-_n_1959151.html

Langellier, K. M. (1999). Personal narrative, performance, performativity: Two or three things I know for sure. *Text and Performance Quarterly, 19*(2), 125–144.

Laverty, S. M. (2008). Hermeneutic phenomenology and phenomenology: A comparison of historical and methodological considerations. *International Journal of Qualitative Methods, 2*(3), 21–35.

Lazzarato, M. (2012). *The making of the indebted man: An essay on the neoliberal condition.* Cambridge, MA: MIT Press.

Leavy, P. (2011). *Low-fat love.* Rotterdam, The Netherlands: Sense Publishers.

Leonard, P., & McLaren, P. (Eds.). (1992). *Paulo Freire: A critical encounter.* New York, NY: Routledge.

Locke, S. (2015). I fit the description. *Art and Everything After.* Retrieved January 30, 2016, from http://artandeverythingafter.com/i-fit-the-description/

Lugones, M. (2008). Coloniality and gender. *Tabula Rasa, 9,* 73–102.

Lurie, G. (2015, December 26). The US town where the only drinking water comes in bottles—in pictures. *The Guardian.* Retrieved February 16, 2016, from http://www.theguardian.com/us-news/gallery/2015/dec/26/east-porterville-california-water-bottles-drought-gallery

Luske, H. (Director), & Sharpsteen, B. (Director). (1940). *Pinocchio* (Motion picture). Burbank, CA: Walt Disney Productions.

Macedo, D. (1994). *Literacies of power: What Americans are not allowed to know.* Boulder, CO: Westview Press.

Macedo, D. (2000). The colonialism of the English only movement. *Educational Researcher, 29*(3), 15–24.

Macedo, D. (2013, February 20). *Conscientization as an antidote to banking education.* Paper presented at University of Massachusetts Dartmouth Transformative Leadership class, Fairhaven, MA.

Macedo, D., & Bartolomé, L. (1999). *Dancing with bigotry: Beyond the politics of tolerance.* Boulder, CO: Paradigm Publishers.

Macedo, D., Dendrinos, B., & Gounari, P. (2003). *The hegemony of English.* Boulder, CO: Paradigm Publishers.

Machel, S. (2011). The Beira speech. *African Yearbook of Rhetoric: Great Speeches of Africa's Liberation, 2*(3), 67–83.

MacLaury, J. (2004). *Government regulation of workers' safety and health, 1877–1917*. Washington, DC: US Department of Labor, Office of the Assistant Secretary for Policy.

Madison, D. S. (2003). Performance, personal narratives, and the politics of possibility. *Turning points in Qualitative Research: Tying Knots in a Handkerchief, 3*, 469–486.

Maldonado-Torres, N. (2007). On the coloniality of being. *Cultural Studies, 21*(2–3), 240–270.

Mann, M. T. P. (Ed.). (1865). *Life of Horace Mann* (Vol. 1). Boston, MA: Walker, Fuller, and Company.

Marshall, S. L. A. (1947). *Men against fire: The problem of battle command*. Norman, OK: University of Oklahoma Press.

McCall, K. (2013, December 20). Mother of man killed over new Nike shoes pushes for change. *ABC News*. Retrieved February 16, 2016, from http://abc13.com/archive/9368193/

McClintock, A. (1995). *Imperial leather: Race, gender and sexuality in the colonial contest*. New York, NY: Routledge.

McIntyre, E. S. (2014, February 18). Teenage drug mules: Cartels are tapping minors to smuggle meth, coke. *Aljazeera America*. Retrieved October 6, 2015, from http://america.aljazeera.com/articles/2014/2/18/teenage-drug-mulescartelsaretappingtheyoungesttosmugglemethcoke.html

McLaren, P. (1993). Multiculturalism and the postmodern critique: Towards a pedagogy of resistance and transformation. *Cultural Studies, 7*(1), 118–146.

McLaren, P. (2001). Che Guevara, Paulo Freire, and the politics of hope: Reclaiming critical pedagogy. *Cultural Studies Critical Methodologies, 1*(1), 108–131. Retrieved July 16, 2014, from http://pages.gseis.ucla.edu/faculty/mclaren/mclaren and che.pdf

McLaren, P., & da Silva, T. T. (1993). Decentering pedagogy: Critical literacy, resistance and the politics of memory. In P. Leonard & P. McLaren (Eds.), *Paulo Freire: A critical encounter* (pp. 47–90). New York, NY: Routledge.

McLaughlin, M. (1990). The woman warrior: Gender, warfare and society in medieval Europe. *Women's studies: An Interdisciplinary Journal, 17*(3–4), 193–209.

Meiners, E. R. (2010). *Right to be hostile: Schools, prisons, and the making of public enemies*. New York, NY: Routledge.

Mignolo, W. (2002). Geopolitics of knowledge. *The South Atlantic Quarterly, 101*(1), 57–96.

Mignolo, W. (2007). Delinking: The rhetoric of modernity, the logic of coloniality, and the grammar of de-coloniality. *Cultural Studies, 21*(2), 449–514.

Mignolo, W. (2008). The geopolitics of knowledge and the colonial difference. In M. Moraña, E. Dussel, & C. Jáuregui (Eds.), *Coloniality at large: Latin American and the postcolonial debate*. Durham, NC: Duke University Press.

Mignolo, W. (2009a). Coloniality: The darker side of modernity. In S. Breitwisser (Ed.), *Modernologies. Contemporary Artists Researching Modernity and Modernism Catalog of the Exhibit at the Museum of Modern Art, Barcelona, Spain* (pp. 39–49). Barcelona: MACBA. (Catalog of the exhibit Modernologia/Modernologies/Modernology)

Mignolo, W. (2009b). Epistemic disobedience, independent thought and de-colonial freedom. *Theory, Culture & Society, 26*(7–8), 1–23.

Mignolo, W. (2010). Delinking: The rhetoric of modernity, the logic of coloniality and the grammar of de-coloniality. In W. D. Mignolo & A. Escobar (Eds.), *Globalization and the decolonial option* (pp. 303–368). New York, NY: Routledge.

Mignolo, W. (2011). Geopolitics of sensing and knowing on (de)coloniality, border thinking, and epistemic disobedience. *European Institute for Progressive Cultural Policies*. Retrieved May 13, 2012, from http://eipcp.net/transversal/0112/mignolo/en

Mignolo, W., & Escobar, A. (Eds.). (2013). *Globalization and the decolonial option.* New York, NY: Routledge.

Mine Safety and Health Administration (MSHA). (2014). *Coal mining fatality statistics: 1900–2013*. Retrieved February 16, 2016, from http://arlweb.msha.gov/stats/centurystats/coalstats.asp

Mohanty, C. T. (2014). "Under Western eyes" revisited: Feminist solidarity through anti-capitalist struggles. *Signs, 40*(1).

Moraña, M., Dussel, E. D., & Jáuregui, C. A. (2008). *Coloniality at large: Latin America and the postcolonial debate.* Durham, NC: Duke University Press.

Moreira, M. A. (2017). And the linguistic minorities suffer what they must?': A review of conflicts in curriculum theory through the lenses of language teacher education? *Journal for the American Association for the Advancement of Curriculum Studies, 12*(1), 1–17.

Moules, N. J. (2002). Nursing on paper: Therapeutic letters in nursing practice. *Nursing Inquiry, 9*(2), 104–113.

National Institute for Occupational Safety and Health (NIOSH). (2013, February 26). *All mining disasters: 1839 to present.* Retrieved February 16, 2016, from http://www.cdc.gov/niosh/mining/statistics/content/allminingdisasters.html

Ndlovu-Gatsheni, S. J. (2013). *Coloniality of power in postcolonial Africa: Myths of decolonization.* Oxford: Codesria Book Series.

Niccol, A. (Producer), & Niccol, A., Newman, E., & Abraham, M. (Directors). (2011 October 28). *In time* (Motion picture). Los Angeles, CA: Regency Enterprises.

Nkrumah, K. (1964). *Consciencism: philosophy and ideology for decolonization and development with particular reference to the African revolution.* London: Heinemann.

Noddings, N. (2011). *The challenge to care in schools: An alternative approach to education* (2nd ed.). New York, NY. Teachers College Press.

Oakes, J. (2005). *Keeping track: How schools structure inequality* (2nd ed.). New Haven, CT: Yale University.

Oaklander, M. (2014, August 26). Skin-Whitening candy is coming. *Time*. Retrieved February 15, 2016, from http://time.com/3181942/skin-whitening-candy/

Oliveira, I. B. (2017). Itinerant curriculum theory against the epistemcide. A dialogue between the thinking of Santos and Paraskeva. *Journal for the American Association for the Advancement of Curriculum Studies, 12*(1), 1–22.

Omi, M., & Winant, H. (2014). *Racial formation in the United States*. New York, NY: Routledge.

Orfield, G., & Lee, C. (2007). *Historic reversals, accelerating resegregation, and the need for new integration strategies*. Los Angeles, CA: Civil Rights Project/Proyecto Derechos Civiles.

Oyěwùmí, O. (1997). *The invention of women: Making an African sense of western gender discourses*. Minneapolis, MN: University of Minnesota Press.

Oyěwùmí, O. (2002). Conceptualizing gender: The Eurocentric foundations of feminist concepts and the challenge of African epistemologies. *Jenda: A Journal of Culture and African Woman Studies, 2*, 1.

Palmer, P. J. (1999). Evoking the spirit in public education. *Educational Leadership, 56*, 6–11.

Paraskeva, J. M. (2011). *Conflicts in curriculum theory: Challenging hegemonic epistemologies*. New York, NY: Palgrave Macmillan.

Paraskeva, J. M. (2014). *Conflicts in curriculum theory: Challenging hegemonic epistemologies*. New York, NY: Palgrave Macmillan.

Paraskeva, J. M. (2016a). *Curriculum epistemicide: Towards an itinerant curriculum theory*. New York, NY: Routledge.

Paraskeva, J. M. (2016b). *The curriculum: Whose internationalization?* New York, NY: Peter Lang.

Paraskeva, J. M. (2017). *Towards a just curriculum theory. The epistemicide*. New York, NY: Routledge.

Parramore, L. (2012, July 12). Fifty shades of capitalism: Pain and bondage in the American workplace. *Alternet*. Retrieved August 14, 2013, from http://www.alternet.org/story/156291/fifty_shades_of_capitalism:_pain_and_bondage_in_the_american_workplace

Pinar, W. (2013). *Curriculum studies in the United States: Present circumstances, intellectual histories*. New York, NY: Palgrave.

Popkewitz, T. S. (2002). How the alchemy makes inquiry, evidence, and exclusion. *Journal of Teacher Education, 53*(3), 262.

Popkewitz, T. S. (2014). Social epistemology, the reason of "reason" and the curriculum studies. *Education Policy Analysis Archives, 22*, 22.

Popkewitz, T. S. (2015, April 9). *The impracticality of practical research: OECD's pisa and teacher education.* Lecture presented in University of Massachusetts Dartmouth, Fairhaven, MA.

Postman, N. (2011). *Technopoly: The surrender of culture to technology.* New York, NY: Vintage.

Prendergast, M., Leggo, C., & Sameshima, P. (2009). Poetic inquiry. *Educational Insights, 13*(3), 743–744.

Price, T. (2017). Welcome to the New Taylorism! Teacher education meets itinerant curriculum theory. *Journal for the American Association for the Advancement of Curriculum Studies, 12*(1), 1–12.

Prior, N. (2012, January 28). How 1896 Tylorstown pit disaster prompted safety change. *BBC News.* Retrieved February 16, 2016, from http://www.bbc.com/news/uk-wales-15965188

Quantz, R. A. (2011). *Rituals and student identity in education: Ritual critique for a new pedagogy.* New York, NY: Palgrave Macmillan.

Quijano, A. (2000). Coloniality of power, Eurocentrism, and Latin America. *Nepantla: Views from South, 1*(3), 533–580.

Quijano, A. (2010). Coloniality and modernity/rationality. In W. Mignolo & A. Escobar (Eds.), *Globalization and the decolonial option* (pp. 22–32). New York, NY: Routledge.

Ravitch, D. (2010). *The death and life of the great American school system: How testing and choice are undermining education.* New York, NY: Basic Books.

Reed-Danahay, D. (1997). *Auto/ethnography.* New York, NY: Bloomsbury Academic.

Resmovits, J. (2012, December 6). Vocabulary test results show top U.S. students losing ground, others stagnate. *Huffington Post.* Retrieved February 16, 2016, from http://www.huffingtonpost.com/2012/12/06/vocabulary-test-results-us_n_2249647.html

Richardson, L. (2000a). New writing practices in qualitative research. *Sociology of Sport Journal, 17*(1), 5–20.

Richardson, L. (2000b). Writing: A method of inquiry. In N. K. Denzin & Y. S. Lincoln (Eds.), *Handbook of qualitative research collecting and interpreting qualitative materials* (2nd ed.,pp. 923–948). Thousand Oaks, CA: Sage Publications.

Rios, V. M. (2011). *Punished: Policing the lives of Black and Latino boys.* New York, NY: New York University Press.

Ritzer, G. (1991). *Metatheorizing in sociology.* Lexington, MA: Lexington Books.

Ritzer, G. (2001). *Explorations in social theory: From metatheorizing to rationalization.* Thousand Oaks, CA: Sage Publications.

Rolfes, E. (2012, August 23). Indoor tanning industry promotes sun beds' health benefits over risks. *PBS.* Retrieved February 15, 2016, from http://www.pbs.org/newshour/rundown/tanning-fairwarning/

Rosa, R., & Rosa, J. (2015). *Capitalism's educational catastrophe and the advancing end-game revolt!* New York, NY: Peter Lang Publishing.

Russell, J. E. (1921). *Education for all children, what we can learn from England.* London: Forgotten Books.

Said, E. W. (1994). *Culture and imperialism.* New York, NY: Vintage.

Saldaña, J. (2005). *Ethnodrama: An anthology of reality theatre.* Lanham, MD: Rowman Altamira.

Santos, B. S. (Ed.). (2005). *Democratizing democracy: Beyond the liberal democratic canon.* New York, NY: Verso.

Santos, B. S. (2007a). Beyond abyssal thinking: From global lines to ecologies of knowledges. *Eurozine*, 1–33. Retrieved May 10, 2013, from http://www.eurozine.com/articles/2007-06-29-santos-en.html

Santos, B. S. (2007b). *Cognitive justice in a global world: Prudent knowledges for a decent life* (pp. 1–439). Lanham, MD: Lexington Books.

Santos, B. S. (2014). *Epistemologies of the south: Justice against epistemicide.* Boulder, CO: Paradigm Publishers.

Sartre, J. P. (2004). *Critique of dialectical reason: Theory of practical ensembles* (Vol. 1). New York, NY: Verso.

Schubert, W. H. (2017). Growing Curriculum Studies: Contributions of João M. Paraskeva. *Journal of the American Association for the Advancement of Curriculum Studies (JAAACS), 12*(1).

Shakespeare, W. (1895). *Tragedy of Romeo and Juliet.* New York, NY: Harper & Brothers.

Shields, C. M. (2013). *Transformative leadership in education: Equitable change in an uncertain and complex world.* New York, NY: Routledge.

Shiva, V. (1993). *Monocultures of the mind: Perspectives on biodiversity and biotechnology.* London: Zed Books Ltd.

Sioui, G. E. (1997). Why we should have inclusively and why we cannot have it. *Ayaang-waamizin: The International Journal of Indigenous Philosophy, 1*(2), 51–62.

Sousanis, N. (2015). *Unflattening.* Cambridge, MA: Harvard University Press.

Spivak, G. C. (1988). Can the subaltern speak? *Marxism and the Interpretation of Culture*, 271–313.

Spivak, G. C. (1999). *A critique of postcolonial reason.* Boston, MA: Harvard University Press.

Spry, T. (2001). Performing autoethnography: An embodied methodological praxis. *Qualitative Inquiry, 7*(6), 706–732.

Stevens, J., Harman, J. S., & Kelleher, K. J. (2005). Race/ethnicity and insurance status as factors associated with ADHD treatment patterns. *Journal of Child & Adolescent Psychopharmacology, 15*(1), 88–96.

Sulzer, W. (1998). Commentary: The value of the prospector. *The Northern Miner, 84*(3). Retrieved January 22, 2016, from http://www.northernminer.com/news/commentary--the-value-of-the-prospector/1000162158/

Süssekind, M. L. (2017). Against epistemological fascism. The (self) critique of the criticals. A reading of Paraskeva's Itinerant curriculum theory. *Journal for the American Association for the Advancement of Curriculum Studies, 12*(1), 1–18.

Szalavitz, M., & Perry, B. D. (2010). *Born for love: Why empathy is essential–and endangered.* New York, NY: William Morrow.

Thiong'o, N. W. (1994). *Decolonising the mind: The politics of language in African literature.* Harare: Zimbabwe Publishing House.

Thiong'o, N. W. (2009). *Something torn and new: An African renaissance.* New York, NY: Perseus Book Group.

Tillich, P. (1952). *The courage to be.* New Haven, CT: Yale University Press.

Topping, A. (2014, January 5). London gangs using children as drug mules as they seek to expand markets. *The Guardian.* Retrieved April 30, 2014, from http://www.theguardian.com/society/2014/jan/05/drug-gangs-using-children-as-mules

Tslotanova, M., & Mignolo, W. (2009). Global coloniality and the decolonial option. *KULT: Epistemologies of Transformation, 6.*

Unger, R. M. (2005). *What should the left propose?* New York, NY: Verso.

Unger, R. M. (2007). *The self awakened: Pragmatism unbound.* Cambridge, MA: Harvard University Press.

United Nations Children's Fund. (2012). *Measuring child poverty new league tables of child poverty in the world's rich countries.* Retrieved March 10, 2013, from http://www.unicefirc.org/publications/pdf/rc10_eng.pdf

U.S. Department of Education, National Center for Education Statistics. (2015). *Digest of Education Statistics, 2013* (NCES 2015-011).

Valenzuela, A. (1999). *Subtractive schooling: U.S.-Mexican youth and the politics of caring.* New York, NY: SUNY Press.

Van Manen, M. (1990). *Researching lived experience: Human science for an action sensitive pedagogy.* New York, NY: SUNY Press.

Viser, M. (2015, October 20). For presidential hopefuls, simpler language resonates. *The Boston Globe.* Retrieved February 16, 2016, from https://www.bostonglobe.com/news/politics/2015/10/20/donald-trump-and-ben-carson-speak-grade-school-level-that-today-voters-can-quickly-grasp/LUCBY6uwQAxiLvvXbVTSUN/story.html

Wacquant, L. (2000). The new 'peculiar institution': On the prison as surrogate ghetto. *Theoretical Criminology, 4*(3), 377–389.

Wacquant, L. (2009). *Punishing the poor: The neoliberal government of social insecurity.* Durham, NC: Duke University Press.

Walker, C. D. B. (2011). "How does it feel to be a problem?": (Local) knowledge, human interests, and the ethics of opacity. *Transmodernity: Journal of Peripheral Cultural Production of the Luso-Hispanic world, 1*(2). Retrieved January 10, 2012, from http://escholarship.org/uc/item/0xj5402h

Walsh, C. E. (2002). The (re)articulation of political subjectivities and colonial difference in Ecuador: Reflections on capitalism and the geopolitics of knowledge. *Nepantla: Views from South, 3*(1), 61–97.

Watts, A. W. (1966). *The book: On the taboo against knowing who you are.* Toronto: Random House.

Westermann, W. L. (1955). *The slave systems of Greek and Roman antiquity* (Vol. 40). Philadelphia, PA: American Philosophical Society.

Westervelt, E. (2015, March 4). Where have all the teachers gone? *NPR.* Retrieved January 10, 2016, from http://www.npr.org/sections/ed/2015/03/03/389282733/where-have-all-the-teachers-gone

Wilde, O. (1899). *The importance of being earnest.* London: Leonard Smithers & Co.

Wynter, S. (2001). Towards the sociogenic principle: Fanon, identity, the puzzle of conscious experience, and what it is like to be "Black." In M. F. Duran-Cogan & A. Gomez-Moriana (Eds.), *National Identities and Sociopolitical Changes in Latin America* (pp. 30–66). New York, NY: Routledge.

Wynter, S. (2003). Unsettling the coloniality of being/power/truth/freedom: Towards the human, after man, its overrepresentation—An argument. *CR: The New Centennial Review, 3*(3), 257–337.

Zhao, W. (2019). *China's education. Curriculum knowledge and cultural inscriptions. Dancing with the wind.* New York, NY: Routledge.

Zinn, H. (2001). *A people's history of the United States.* New York, NY: Harper Collins.

Index

www.ingramcontent.com/pod-product-compliance
Lightning Source LLC
Chambersburg PA
CBHW070417270326
41926CB00014B/2834